FRAMING THE WEST

Robert J. Welch 1859–1936

FRAMING THE WEST

Images of Rural Ireland 1891–1920

Editor
C I A R A   B R E A T H N A C H

Foreword by CORMAC Ó GRÁDA

IRISH ACADEMIC PRESS
DUBLIN • PORTLAND, OR

First published in 2007 by
IRISH ACADEMIC PRESS
44 Northumberland Road, Dublin 4, Ireland

and in the United States of America by
IRISH ACADEMIC PRESS
ISBS, Suite 300, 920 NE 58th Avenue
Portland, Oregon 97213-3786

This edition © 2007 by Irish Academic Press
© 2007 Chapters by contributors

www.iap.ie

British Library Cataloguing in Publication Data
An entry can be found on request

ISBN 978 0 7165 2873 9 (cloth)
ISBN 978 0 7165 2874 6 (paper)

Library of Congress Cataloging-in-Publication Data
An entry can be found on request

Printed by Antony Rowe Ltd., Chippenham, Wiltshire

Contents

Contributors

Dr Vivienne Pollock read History at the University of Sussex before embarking in the 1980s on doctoral research into the history of the Irish seafisheries at the University of Ulster at Coleraine. Her first museum job was with Derry City Council's Museum Service. She worked at the Ulster-American Folk Park in Omagh as Assistant Keeper of Agriculture and Crafts before moving to the Ulster Museum's History Department in 1991 as Curator of the collections of historic photographs, maps, paintings and prints.

Sara Smyth is a Librarian in the National Library of Ireland and is currently working in the National Photographic Archive. Her publications include *Newsplan* (rev. ed. 1998) and she has contributed to the *Irish Field Day Review*.

Marie Boran is the Special Collections Librarian at the James Hardiman Library, NUI, Galway. With an MA in History she is particularly interested in nineteenth- and twentieth-century Irish history. She is currently working on a project funded by the Irish Research Council for the Humanities and Social Sciences.

Maggie Burns née Whetnall has an MA in Modern Languages froms St Hilda's College, Oxford, a GCE from the University of York and an MA in Information Studies and Librarianship from the University of Central England. After teaching in Birmingham 1978–90, she has worked as a librarian since 1991. She is now in charge of the extensive photographic collection in the Local Studies and History Subject Information Section of Birmingham Central Library.

Dr Gail Baylis is a Research Associate in the Centre For Media Research, University of Ulster, where she researches the history of Irish photography. She also contributes to the Media Studies programme, teaching photographic theory and practice, visual culture and gender studies.

Dr Justin Carville is a Lecturer in Historical & Theoretical Studies in Photography and Visual Culture at the Institute of Art, Design & Technology, Dun Laoghaire. He is a former Government of Ireland Senior Research Scholar in the Humanities and Social Sciences (2003–04) and was awarded a PhD from Dublin City University in 2005. He has contributed essays to a number of exhibition catalogues and his writings on photography have been published in Irish and international peer-reviewed journals, including *Source*, *Circa*, *Next Level*, *Artists Newsletter* and *Afterimage*.

Ciarán Walsh is Visual Arts Director of the National Folk Theatre. A graduate of the National College of Art and Design, he has worked in a number of education contexts including Triskel Arts Centre Cork and The Arts Council, An Comhairle Éalaíon, Dublin.

Niamh Connolly lives in Killybegs, a vibrant fishing community in Donegal. She always had a interest in the maritime history of the area and has an MPhil in Irish Studies, completing a thesis on 'The Congested Districts Board and the Development of Fishing in South West Donegal, 1890–1923'. She works at present in the James Hardiman Library in NUI, Galway.

Lorna Moloney is currently pursuing a PhD in History at NUI Galway. Her research interests include medieval Gaelic Ireland, pilgrimage and local histories. Her publications include contributions to *The Other Clare* and the *Slieve Aughty journals*.

Dr Ciara Breathnach is a Lecturer at the Department of History, University of Limerick. Her recent publications include *The Congested Districts Board of Ireland, 1891-1923: Poverty and Development in the West* (Dublin, 2005) and a co-edited volume with Aoife Bhreatnach, *Portraying Irish Travellers: Histories and Representations* (Cambridge Scholars Press, 2007).

Dr Jonathan Bell was Head Curator at the Ulster Folk and Transport Museum until 2006. He has published a number of books and articles on changes in Irish farming during the last three centuries.

Dr Margaret Ó hÓgartaigh is based at the Stout Centre, Victoria University of Wellington, New Zealand. She is the author of *Kathleen Lynn: Irishwoman, Patriot, Doctor* (Dublin and Portland, 2006) and has written more than thirty articles on the history of medicine, education and the 1798 rebellion. She is co-editing, with Margaret Preston, *Gender, Medicine and the State in Ireland and the United States, 1700–1950*, to be published by the Syracuse University Press, New York, in 2007.

Mary Clancy lectures in NUI, Galway. She has published on Irish women's suffrage and political history, oral history and life stories, most recently contributing to *Teaching With Memories*, edited by Andrea Peto and Berteke Waaldijk (2006).

Dr Anne O'Dowd was awarded a PhD in Irish Folklore. A Curator in the National Museum, in 2001 her vision for a folklife museum in County Mayo was realised with the opening of the National Museum of Ireland – Museum of Country Life. She has written and lectured extensively in Ireland and abroad on Irish ethnology and folklife. She is looking forward to seeing another lifetime project ('uses of organic fibres like straw, hay, rushes etc. in an Irish context') published in 2008.

Illustrations

The images bearing references with a capital W (for instance W09-04-1) are Robert J. Welch images from the extensive Ulster Museum collection. Robert J. Welch is also referred to as R.J. Welch or Robert J. Welch, and even Robert John Welch. Those prefaced with CDB or Tuke come from the National Library of Ireland collections. All the images in Chapter 3 are from the Balfour Album, also compiled by Welch and held at the Hardiman Library, NUI, Galway. Chapter 4 uses images from the Benjamin Stone Collection, Birmingham Central Library, and some of the images in Chapter 10 are from the Annual Reports of the Lady Dudley scheme, also courtesy of the National Library of Ireland.

Foreword

CORMAC Ó'GRÁDA

Rather like successive editors of France's most influential newspaper, Irish historians and social scientists have been slow to adopt the photographic image. *Le Monde's* Hubert Beuve-Méry saw pictures as an unnecessary distraction that lowered or distorted the tone of journalistic word images. Some historians might agree. Others, however, shun pictures for the same reason that they opt for blackboard and chalk over *Powerpoint*. In Ireland, there has long been a ready market for books of old photographs, but monographs on historical topics where the accompanying photographs inform rather than dominate are still relatively rare. L.M. Cullen's *Six Generations* (1970) and Joseph Lee and Gearóid Ó Tuathaigh's *The Age of de Valera* (1982) spring to mind, although both had their origins in programmes on RTÉ. The post-1830 volumes of *The New History of Ireland* also include some interesting selections of photographs, though always corralled into a section at the end of every volume. The *Oxford Illustrated History of Ireland* (1989) makes limited but effective use of photographs, some of which are accompanied by lively, provocative captions. The contributors to *Framing the West* make a strong case for the greater use of photographs by Irish historians and others.

Photographic material on Ireland before 1880 – other than the studio portraits which became common after 1860 or so – is scarce, and particularly so for the west of Ireland.[1] No photographic image of the Great Famine survives; had the technology been up to it, John Mitchel and the Young Irelanders would have surely engaged a few politically-committed photographers to expose the gruesome horrors of the late 1840s, as Sunil Janah and others did so effectively for the Great Bengali Famine in 1943–44, or as the Red Cross did for wartime Greece in 1941–43. Some of the Red Cross images are used to great effect in Violetta Hionidou's *Famine and Death in Occupied Greece* (2006). From the

1. Analysis of photographic material like that displayed here is rarer still. One striking exception is the recent study by Breandán Mac Suibhne and Amy Martin of pictures taken of Fenian prisoners taken in Mountjoy prison in the mid-1860s.

1880s on, the development of dry-plate negatives and cheaper cameras led to a huge increase in the number of photographs of the historic and the mundane, the famous and the obscure, taken by professionals and amateurs. Photographs of incidents related to the Land War are plentiful. However, rich photographic collections such those taken a century or so ago at Sentry Hill in County Antrim, which provide the main ingredient for Brian Walker's masterly *Sentry Hill*, a work of social history where the words play second fiddle, will always be the exception.

Framing the West is both about the history of photography in Ireland and about how photographs help our understanding of the social and economic past. Two themes dominate its fourteen essays and the accompanying sixty or so photographs: Belfast photographer Robert Welch and the Congested Districts Board (or CDB). As several essays suggest, Welch was probably the most successful Irish photographer of his day, and his commissioned photographs of the west of Ireland represent only a tiny fraction of his output. Carefully crafted and executed albeit often formulaic, his pictures throw considerable light both on conditions in the west early in the last century and on the programme and ideology of the CDB.

Welch was better at photographing scenery and inanimate objects than close-range images of country people. However, his seeming inability to coax a smile or a bit of movement out of his subjects like the dour county Down housewife seated in her kitchen (Figure 1.6), or the group of spinners and carders in the 'Donegal Highlands' (Figure 13.1), was also due to the technical constraints he faced. Photography indoors or in overcast weather required long exposure times –typically a minute or more – and subjects who remained still. As a result, Welch's depiction of the sisters engaged in spade-work tidy lazy beds in Glenshesk in the Glens of Antrim (Figure 7.4) is useful, but the women and their spades, motionless and stiff, garments clean and unruffled, offer little indication of the work involved.

Even allowing for the limitations imposed by technology, Welch gives the impression that he was happier photographing buildings and mollusks and friends than country people he did not know. Nor was he a campaigning photographer in the manner of, say, Dorothea Lange or Jacob Riis. Though he certainly approved of the methods and objectives of the CDB, and was a friend of its

secretary, William Lawson Micks (1858–1928), there is little evidence of much personal engagement with the poor of the west. Very different in this respect is John Millington Synge and his 'wallet of photographs', which dates from around the same time. Closer to Synge than to Welch, both
in their more spontaneous quality and their empathy with their subject matter, are the pictures taken
by Major Ruttledge-Fair in southern Connemara – some in Cois Fharraige, some further west
around Leitir Móir – in 1892. Certain features of Ruttledge-Fair's pictures in the National
Photographic Archive (discussed by Sara Smyth in Chapter 2) are striking. For example, Ruttledge-
Fair (about whom little is known) was more likely to feature women than men, and his 'snaps' very
effectively convey the drudgery and physical demands of female labour in particular (e.g. Figure
2.3). Ruttledge-Fair's pictures must be among the earliest of their kind, as far as Connemara is concerned. One senses from the curious, unselfconscious expressions in his images of south Connemara
schoolchildren (Figures 12.4 and 12.5) that few of them in the early 1890s ever had their picture
taken before.

Most of the images reproduced here will be new to the reader, although some have already been
re-cycled once or twice.[2] Many of would not have been out of place in either W.L. Micks' first history of the CDB, published soon after its dissolution, or Sir Henry Robinson's reminiscences of the
Local Government Board, published in 1923 and 1924. Both of Robinson's volumes concentrate
on the west of Ireland, and include photographs, mainly taken in the 1900s, accompanied by wry,
sometimes condescending, captions from Sir Henry. The Congested Districts Board and the Local
Government Board were casualties of the handover of power in 1921–2, though much of their work
was continued in a different guise. Their demise was upsetting for reforming unionists like Micks
and Robinson – and possibly also for Welch.

This pioneering book covers much ground—from traveling nurses to agricultural implements,
from second-hand clothes to Galways's Claddagh. Much can be learned here about the clothes people wore, the houses they lived in, and the kind of farming and fishing they practiced. There is
much more for others to work on, however. The National Photographic Archive's Lawrence
Collection dwarfs the Welch collection in size and variety, and probably in quality too. It contains

2. I used Welch's lazy-bed photograph myself for the dust-jacket
of *Ireland Before and After the
Famine* (Manchester, 1988)
while the county Down housewife re-appears on the cover of
Joanna Bourke's *Husbandry to
Housewifery* (Oxford, 1993).

over forty thousand commercial-quality negatives dating from the 1870–1914 period. The first half of the twentieth century is also well served by Father Frank Browne, S.J., best remembered for his photographs of the Titanic. He also left about forty thousand negatives behind, and it is to be hoped that they too find their way to the National Library in due course. So there is much more scope for the kind of work on display in *Framing the West*.

BIBLIOGRAPHY: Francis M. Browne and E.E. O'Donnell, *Father Browne's Titanic Album: A Passenger's Photographs and Personal Memoir* (Dublin: Wolfhound Press, 1996).

Brendán Mac Suibhne and Amy Martin, 'Fenians in the Frame: Photographing Irish Political Prisoners, 1865–68', *Field Day Review*, No. 1 2005.

Micks, W.L. *An Account of the Constitution, Administration and Dissolution of the Congested Districts Board* (Dublin: Eason, 1925).

Sir Henry Robinson, *Memories Wise and Otherwise* (London: Cassell, 1923).

Sir Henry Robinson, *Further Memories of Irish Life* (London: Herbert Jenkins, 1924).

J.M. Synge, *My Wallet of Photographs*. Ed. Lilo Stephens (Dublin: Dolmen Press, 1971).

Brian M. Walker, *Sentry Hill: An Ulster Farm and Family* (Belfast: Blackstaff Press, 1981).

Acknowledgements

CIARA BREATHNACH

I would like to thank a number of people who have been instrumental in the production of this book. The support of Aongus Ó hAongusa, Director of the National Library of Ireland, and Sara Smyth from the National Photographic Archive were instigating factors. From the outset, Dr Vivienne Pollock at the Ulster Museum, Marie Reddan, Director of the Hardiman Library, NUIG, and Marie Boran, Special Collections Librarian, NUIG provided unconditional support. Maggie Burns and Paul Hemmings at Birmingham Central Library were also most helpful and forthcoming with the Irish images in the Benjamin Stone collection. All institutions waived reproduction fees where possible to keep expenses to a minimum. A number of people were involved in the preparation of the images and their attention to detail has been gratefully appreciated. At the Ulster Museum photographers Bryan Rutledge and Michael McKeown gave their time generously, as did Pat McLean and Michelle Ashworth, who handled rights and reproduction. A special word of thanks is due to Sara Smyth and her wonderful team at the National Photographic Archive who provided images under severe time constraints (my apologies).

Lisa Hyde immediately recognised the potential of this book, her expertise has been invaluable and her patience inexhaustible. To the staff at Irish Academic Press who were helpful, encouraging and prompt with advice and support, thank you kindly, especially Mick Alabaster and Kay Hyman. All of the contributors took time from their very busy schedules to facilitate tight deadlines. I would especially like to thank Professor Cormac Ó Gráda. On behalf of all the contributors I would like to extend our gratitude to the archivists and librarians who have facilitated this work in many ways. I am deeply indebted to my nearest and dearest, especially my sisters and their children, for keeping me in touch with the real world; to my mother, Kathleen, who is an endless font of goodwill and support, and to Kevin, my patient other half.

Introduction

1. Peter Burke, *Eyewitnessing: The Uses of Images as historical Evidence*, (Ithaca: Cornell University Press, 2001), p. 10

2. Allan Sekula, 'The Traffic in Photographs', *Art Journal*, 41.1, Photography and the Scholar/Critic, (1981), pp. 15–25.

3. While two books celebrating the extent of Welch's work have emerged from the Ulster Museum, the focus of both books differ greatly from this volume. See E.E. Evans and B. Turner, *Ireland's Eye: the photographs of Robert John Welch* (Belfast: Blackstaff Press, 1977). It reproduces many images from the Welch Collection and provides a commentary on each, but contains no references. A. Maguire, *A Century in Focus: Photographs and Photographers in the North of Ireland, 1839–1939* (Belfast: Blackstaff, 2000).

Cont.

To date scholars of Ireland have been reluctant to use photographic images as historical evidence. As Peter Burke notes, 'Relatively few historians work in photographic archives, compared to the numbers who work in repositories of written and typewritten documents', and the resulting scholarship reflects that.[1] Books that focus on photographs tend to do so exclusively and they rarely provide full context to the images, whereas the Irish historiography relies mainly on documentary sources in which photographic images are used sparingly or as an adjunct. In contrast with traditional historical writings the images used in this volume are interspersed throughout the text and all fourteen chapters provide a full context for the images used. This work focuses predominantly on images of the West of Ireland from 1890 to 1920 and aims to encourage the further use of photographs in Irish historical scholarship.

Photography in the nineteenth and early twentieth centuries was most certainly a bourgeois science, pursued and consumed by the upper classes, so all contributors to this volume exercised a fair degree of caution.[2] Adopting an historiographical approach, this volume begins with an account of the photographers, and what motivated the compilation of individual albums. It then diversifies and tackles the various themes contained in the images from an interdisciplinary perspective. To this end the contributors were drawn from a wide range of professions. Most of the images used in this volume are extracted from the extensive and multi-faceted Robert J. Welch (1859–1936) collection. Welch was one of the most prolific commercial photographers of this time and his work offers rare insights into Irish social life.[3]

Allan Sekula warns that abstracting photographs from a larger collection for the purposes of a book carries the dangers of a 'loss of context'.[4] Mindful of the necessity of contextualisation,

Vivienne Pollock's chapter looks at Welch's life and how he came to live and work as a commercial photographer in Belfast. She outlines the extent of Welch's personal interests, from natural science to ethnography, and how this affected his career as a photographer. By locating his work in the history of Irish photography Pollock helps us to realise the importance of the extensive Welch collection held at the Ulster Museum. Sara Smyth examines the significance of the Tuke Album held at the National Photographic Archive in Dublin, explaining the origins of this unique collection of images. While this chapter focuses on the work of James Hack Tuke (1819–1896), who commissioned Major Ruttledge-Fair (Baseline inspector for the Congested Districts Board – CDB) to take the photographs, it provides a full context for the poor conditions illustrated in the Album. In contrast to the motivation behind commercial photography, Smyth highlights that the true value of the Tuke Album is its sincerity as it shows clearly the difficulties endured by the people of the west.

Marie Boran studies the Balfour Album, for which Welch was commissioned in 1894. The function of this Album was to honour Arthur Balfour's infrastructural efforts in the west, notably through his Light Railways Act of 1889. It was difficult to encourage venture capitalists to locate business in the west and this chapter outlines how the Welch photographs were used to great effect in tourist literature. That Welch was a photographer well respected by his contemporaries is evidenced by successful sales. A number of his images are kept in Birmingham Central Library as part of the Sir Benjamin Stone Collection. Maggie Burns' chapter accounts for the sizeable collection of Irish images in Birmingham: they were mainly taken personally by Stone but, to fill gaps in his portfolio, some were purchased from the prolific Welch. She compares the amateur style of Stone with Welch's professionalism and provides a brief analysis of the motivations behind both sets of images.

Gail Baylis, Justin Carville and Ciarán Walsh's contributions deal with the various ways in which Welch's images were used both in the historical and the contemporary context. While Baylis' chapter discusses the equipment Welch used, it does not focus exclusively on the technical, instead providing a comprehensive analysis of the relationship between the photographer and his subject from a cultural perspective. By outlining Welch's interest and his reasons for visiting the West she places him and his approach to the 'primitive other' within a wider framework. Following along the same vein Carville

Cont.
This volume devotes a section to Welch.

4. Allan Sekula, 'Reading an Archive: Photography between Labour and Capital', in J. Evans and S. Hall (eds), *Visual Culture: The Reader* (London: Sage Publications, 1999), pp. 183.

examines the ideological function of photography in the colonial context, looking particularly at Welch's work for the CDB. Furthermore he highlights the subjective nature of the images, he is sceptical about using such images purely as evidence of modernisation and warns against viewing them in isolation. Walsh assesses Welch's role as an – all but accidental – folklorist. Again Welch's treatment of his subjects comes under scrutiny as does the perception of the 'West' as a fertile ground for ethnographers and an inspiration to artists. He argues that in many respects the photographs pave the way for the nostalgic styles adopted by Paul Henry.

The second half of this book turns to aspects of social and economic life in the west as portrayed in the various images. Niamh Connolly's contribution focuses exclusively on the efforts of the CDB in creating a commercial fishery in the West. It outlines the gender division of labour in maritime communities and the various components of the industry at the close of the nineteenth century. While some of the hard labour is evident in her selection of images, Connolly is careful not to rely completely on them. Lorna Moloney's chapter traces the origins of the unique Claddagh area of Galway City. She establishes the economic structure of this fishing quarter and shows how these images are useful in the reconstruction of family and community life. As Moloney notes, this area captivated Welch and, unlike many of his staged compositions, all of these images are spontaneous. In general Irish maritime history is poorly represented and both Connolly and Moloney's chapters are welcome additions to the existing historiography.

Jonathan Bell's chapter covers the primary function of the CDB, that of agricultural improvements. Bell begins with a general overview of agricultural conditions prior to the intervention of the CDB and proceeds by outlining its methodology. The discussion at the end of this chapter provides an expert analysis of how the CDB altered the western landscape. On the same theme, that of the changing rural landscape, Breathnach's contribution highlights and explains the poor state of rural housing by the 1890s. The Tuke Album and later Welch images provide representations of the 'before and after' effect of CDB housing schemes. This chapter argues that, without the efforts of the CDB, the Lady Dudley nurses and benevolent landlords and clergy, living conditions would not have improved until a much later period.

Margaret Ó hÓgartaigh's wonderfully detailed chapter looks exclusively at female professionals based in the West, namely the Lady Dudley nurses and primary school teachers. Through an examination of how such women came to qualify as professionals, she provides an idea of what life as a professional woman would have been like in the West. Mary Clancy's work deals with women, children and paid work in County Donegal. She traces the origins of philanthropic, female-run textile industries and then deliberates on the impact of such paid work on the employees. Finally, Anne O' Dowd's chapter examines the clothes worn by the women and children in the Welch and Tuke photographs. Using the records of the Irish Folklore Commission O'Dowd presents information on the functionality of the various items of clothing and helps us to understand other latent issues such as class, status, respectability and folkloric significance.

CIARA BREATHNACH

CHAPTER ONE

'All in a Day's Work': Robert John Welch and his World

VIVIENNE POLLOCK

Few individuals have done so much during their lifetime to inform and inspire understanding and awareness of the form and character of Ireland than the great photographer and naturalist Robert John Welch. A man of boundless energy and indefatigable curiousity, blessed with a keen and discriminating eye, enormous patience and seemingly endless stamina, his career spanned more than five decades and saw the creation of some of the most memorable and probably most widely copied images of Irish events, activities and features ever produced,[1] as well as discoveries and recordings of ground-breaking significance in several fields of natural science, archaeology and anthropology.

Welch, or 'R.J.', as he is invariably known, was born in Strabane, County Tyrone, in 1859, the second son of Martha Graham, a young local girl, and David Welch, a Presbyterian from Kircudbright in Scotland, who had come to Ireland in 1857, a time of expansion in the linen industry, to work as agent for a shirt manufacturer in the town.[2] Photography was by then becoming generally established, both as a profession and as a pastime for those who had the time, means and inclination for its pursuit. David became increasingly interested and adept in this new medium and in 1863 abandoned the shirt trade to take it up as a career. His first base was in Enniskillen, County Fermanagh, where he enjoyed the patronage of the area's major landowner, James Hamilton, 2nd Marquis (and later 1st Duke) of Abercorn, whom he had met and been encouraged by when he lived in Strabane. Abercorn's appointment to Lord Lieutenant of Ireland in 1865 enabled David to advertise himself as 'photographer by appointment to the Viceroy';[3] in doing so, he displayed a professional pride (and also, presumably, the social and

1. For example, he estimated that his photograph of the launch of the *Olympic* in 1910, which was copied across the world, must have been reproduced about 700 million times. R.J. Welch, *Excursions Diary*, p. 162.
2. For a brief history of the life of David Welch, see Maguire, W.A., *A Century in Focus* (Belfast: Blackstaff Press, 2000), pp. 34–8
3. Ibid., p. 35.

commercial cachet) in his lofty connections that was never ignored and, indeed, later assumed at even higher level by his more famous son.

The Welchs remained in Enniskillen for five years before moving to Newry, County Down, in 1868. It was here, R.J. later wrote, that he undertook his 'first photo excursions … with my father … when I was about 10–11 years old, to Dunbanagher and Dromontine Houses, and a few other places in Down or Armagh'.[4] In 1872 the family moved again, this time to Leamington in Warwickshire. Their time in England, however, was short-lived and soon they were back in Ireland. R.J's early training with his father continued through these and the next few years of wandering, and it is worth quoting in full his own memories of this increasingly well-travelled apprenticeship:

> We went to Leamington in 1872 and I then assisted him on many visits for views to Warwick Castle, Kenilworth Castle, Guy's Cliffs, St. Mary's Ch. & Beauchamp Castle and Leistershire Hospital etc., Warwick, also many short trips around Leamington. After we came back to Ireland (Kingston) [later Dun Laoghaire] some excursions to Bray and Dargle. In 1874 we went to Carlow and I went with him to Castledermott Abbey, Round T[ower] and Crosses; Moone Cross; Kilkea Castle, Mageny; Kildare cathedral and R. Tower. In Carlow to Clogrenan Castle, Carlow Castle, Brown's Hill House and Cromlech (Dolmen), Duckett's Grove, Oak Park, Old Leighlin Cathedral & other antiqs. And houses. In Kilkenny several visits to photo Castle (ext.& int., St. Francis Abbey, Black Abbey etc., etc.) Coming to Bangor [Co. Down] in 1874 we photoed Greyabbey, Clandeboye House, Crawfordsburn Falls, Glen and House, Queen's College & other Belfast views, Bangor do. [also] Many Coastguard Stations in Down and Antrim for the Board of Works [and] set of Giant's Causeway & Carrick-a-Rede.[5]

As Maguire notes, this rootless existence was not unusual for professional photographers of

4. *Excursions Diary*, p. 1.
5. Ibid.

Welch Senior's generation.[6] Portrait work, the mainstay of their livelihood, was in nature short-lived and highly competitive, and that of David's which survives shows him as able as the next in this respect. More indicative of his wider competence is the album of sixty of his original prints, put together after his death by Robert Welch and held in the Welch archive at the Ulster Museum. These are largely views of great houses and mighty buildings, a number of which, like the pottery factory at Belleek, County Fermanagh, and Lough Eske Castle, County Donegal, were brand-new when he photographed them. R.J.'s *Excursions Diary* also includes some prints that he made from wet plate negatives produced by his father in the 1860s. Under one he noted that his father had taught the first manager of the Belleek pottery, a Mr Armstrong, 'photography for use in the factory, photoing china for use in booklets etc',[7] an act that perhaps betrays a certain lack of business acumen but certainly reveals a spirit of generosity similar to that amply displayed by his more famous son. Wet collodion was notoriously difficult to work with and these prints, albeit produced with the depth of tone and detail that R.J. was able to achieve with his perfected platino-type process, together with those in the album he produced himself, are testimony to David Welch's skill as an outdoor photographer.

David Welch died suddenly in 1875 and Martha moved with her six children to 46 Lonsdale Street, Belfast, where she carried on her late husband's business by continuing to issue series of his views through a number of agents. R.J. went to work for the photographic firm of E.T. Church, Donegall Street, Belfast, with which he stayed as an assistant for seven years, according to a letter of commendation that also described him as 'having a good knowledge of his business, quick, obliging and honest'.[8] He may well, however, have also spent time with another, unnamed, firm, for he notes in his diary that, until 1883, he 'was over many parts of Ulster mainly Antrim, Down & Derry photographing houses, groups etc. for 2 employers'.[9] It was during his time at Church's that Welch produced his series of images featuring the interiors of their late Victorian photographic studio; these are preserved in the Ulster Museum and provide a marvellous evocation of the design and fittings of such palaces of fantasy.

6. Maguire, A *Century in Focus*, p. 36.
7. *Excursions Diary*, p. 212.
8. Letter of commendation from E.T. Church, dated 3 November 1883, enclosed with *Excursions Diary*, frontispiece.
9. *Excursions Diary*, p. 1

Church was himself a keen naturalist and, according to the eminent geographer and anthropologist E. Estyn Evans, who knew Welch personally in his later years, 'seemed to encourage the boy'[10] in his interests in the countryside and the natural world. These had developed, in particular, before the family removed to England, during summer holidays in Bundoran, County Donegal, where the young Robert spent his time collecting wild flowers (perhaps for his mother, who had a great fondness for them) and limestone fossils,[11] and rockpooling, a passion for which was to remain with him all his days, to judge from the many late references in his diaries to days thus spent in the company of his sister Kate's children or other young friends.[12] It was also on holiday in Bundoran that he witnessed an event that obviously affected him deeply at the time and clearly stayed with him in later life. As he recalled in his diary in 1909 following a visit to the port of Mullaghmore in County Sligo, this was his:

> First visit there since I was a boy of 8 or 9 years when I saw an emigrant ship come in and take on board a lot of emigrants for U.S.A, the keening (caoire) was dreadful. It was very rough weather and sea. I do not know how the ship got in at all. I was with my mother and father …[13]

It is perhaps also worth mentioning in this context that, according to Evans, Welch 'owed much to his mother in many ways … from her he learnt much about the traditions of the west Ulster countryside. She was born in 1840 and had many a grim tale to tell about the Great Famine and its aftermath.'[14] Certainly, many of Welch's photographs of ancient monuments and past or fading traditions are embued with a feeling of tangible loss and melancholy (Figure 1.1).

R.J. had attended the Model School in Newry, where his youthful collector's eye also had turned to bird's eggs (an abiding passion) and stamps. Little is known about where he was later taught, although between 1873 and 1879 he did gain diplomas in Drawing (his diaries reveal him to be a superb draughtsman – see Figure 1.2), Geology and Physiography (geography) from

Figure 1.1
Knocknany Cairn and site, Augher, County Tyrone. W09-04-1

10. E. Estyn Evans and Brian S. Turner, *Ireland's Eye. The Photographs of Robert John Welch* (Belfast: Blackstaff Press, 1977), p. 4.
11. Ibid.
12. See, for example, R.J. Welch, *Memo Diary*, 23 July 1926.
13. *Excursions Diary*, p. 143.
14. Evans and Turner, *Ireland's Eye*, p. 5.

(Shepherd).

Slea Head, we had

food. Then on their

scene of the

Glen Head.

Blackett

n suspect.

modern dry-built, stone dairy, a true bahire
house built by a farmer near Slea Head.

this fine modern bahire-house built by a rather
at Fahan, for a dairy. I asked him why he left
& he's – & ... I found I had to lean

Figure 1.2
Drawing of a beehive hut,
Excursion Diary, p.159

15. Ibid.
16. Excursions Diary, p. 1.
17. Kenneth James, 'A Hungry
    Lens', *The Belfast Review*
    (1985) p. 10.
18. Maguire, *A Century in
    Focus*, p. 88.
19. Excursions Diary, pp. 89–90.

the Science and Art Department of the Council on Education. His involvement with the Belfast Naturalists' Field Club (BNFC) stemmed from a visit to Belfast in 1874 by the British Association for the Advancement of Science. R.J. attended some of the lectures with his father, and was much taken by some of the archaeological exhibits arranged by some Field Club members to accompany them.[15] He joined the Club himself in the 1880–1 session, beginning a life long association of commitment, purpose and deep companionship.[16]

As Kenneth James describes it, the BNFC, founded in 1863 and the first of its kind in Ireland, 'served as an unofficial academy of the natural sciences … devoted to the practical study of natural history and archaeology'.[17] One of its popular features was an annual programme of trips to areas of scientific interest, very often in remote or isolated regions, where members could examine and record the flora, fauna, and human and geological structures they discovered. Welch entered into these activities with his usual gusto and generosity, and quickly became one of the Club's leading personalities. A steadfast committee member, he rarely, according to the Minute Books, missed a meeting and was always quick to involve himself in all levels of the Club's business; in 1908 he became its Secretary (and again in 1926) and in 1910–12 its President.

The scholarly recognition Welch won for the work he pursued and nurtured through the Field Club and the academic contacts and acclaim he established thereby were perhaps especially sweet for someone who, owing to a father's early death, had been obliged to enter the world of paid work rather than go up to Queen's College, Belfast, as an undergraduate, which he had hoped to do.[18] Eventually, and to his great pleasure, in 1923 he was awarded an honorary Master of Science degree from Queen's University (as it had then become). By then, however, he had been a life member of the Royal Irish Academy for nearly twenty years, having been elected in March 1904 after nomination by a panel of five eminent scientists, including his fellow Club member and great chum, the famous Irish botanist Robert L. Praeger.[19] This election was, however, not without controversy, for Welch's nomination was bitterly opposed by the Belfast archaeologist William Gray MRIA, fellow Field Club member and founder member of the Belfast Museum, on the grounds that he was a professional photographer and (as a tradesman) ineligible.[20]

In a more positive echo of this, Praeger later published a series of biographies of Irish naturalists, in which he described his friend Welch as 'photographer and fanatical crusader in the interests of Irish natural history'.[21] R.J.'s special passion was snails – he was the first person to discover Jenkin's Spire Snail in Ireland, in 1893 at the mouth of the River Bann[22] – and his diaries reveal him to be a principal player in the Conchological Society of Britain and Ireland, which met regularly in England and in which he served first as a committee member and later as its President, 1922–3.[23] However, his interests and achievements were myriad. A remarkable talent for spotting the unusual, which he deployed to such effect in his photographic work, no doubt helped him happen upon an exceptionally rare fungus growing in the garden of Lennoxvale, a friend's house in Belfast;[24] even more exciting to him, perhaps, was his capture in County Donegal of a spider completely new to science, which was quickly named *Erigine Welchii* after him.[25]

He is also credited with a number of photographic 'firsts'. On Rathlin Island in 1889 he made what is now accepted as the first ever photographic record of a bird's nest containing eggs;[26] and in Glencolumbkille in 1890 took what was recognised as the first clearly identifiable photograph of a chambered court tomb, a prehistoric structure largely confined to the northern part of Ireland and not recognised as a separate 'class' of early grave until the 1930s.[27] R.J. was equally clever in photographing 'lasts', and his work includes a range of this type of view as impressively eclectic as his 'firsts'– from the glass kiln in Ballycastle, County Antrim, photographed in 1875 two years before it was pulled down, to the last-standing thatched houses in Belfast, photographed in 1887 in Frederick Street just before demolition, according to his note on the back of the original print, to his impressive view of Sketterick Castle on Strangford Lough, which he was able to include in a series of castles commissioned in 1888 as illustrations

20. My thanks to Martyn Anglesea, Keeper of Art, Ulster Museum, for this information.
21. Quoted in Evans and Turner, *Ireland's Eye*, p. 14.
22. James, 'A Hungry Lens', p. 20.
23. Maguire, *A Century in Focus*, p. 99
24. James, 'A Hungry Lens', p. 20.
25. Evans and Turner, *Ireland's Eye*, p. 7.
26. ibid., p. 164.
27. ibid., p. 140.

Figure 1.3
Welch's Bookplate, from
Excursion Diary frontispiece

28. *Excursions Diary*, p. 2.
29. Evans and Turner, *Ireland's
    Eye*, p. 13.
30. Ibid.
31. See *Excursion Diary*,
    pp. 112–114.
32. Evans and Turner, *Ireland's
    Eye*, p. 13.
33. Ibid. p. 20.
34. *Excursions Diary*, pp. 148–9.
35. James, 'A Hungry Lens',
    p. 20.

for Professor Armstrong's book *The Savages of the Ards*, having photographed it on a previous visit to the area with the Field Club, 'luckily', he noted, 'as it [since] fell'.[28]

Perhaps what characterised Welch above all else (except, and closely allied to, his talent for doing two or more things at once) was his dedication to helping and supporting others. In recalling the great joint triennial meetings of the four Irish Field Clubs (Dublin, Belfast, Cork and Limerick), which Praeger had initiated and Welch busily supported, his close friend A.W. (Arthur) Stelfox described how his:

> enthusiasm was at its height, collecting his beloved snails for himself, woodlice for one friend, spiders for another, and many other forms of animal life.[29]

These meetings became essentially 'co-operative ecological surveys of a chosen district'.[30] From them came first the survey of Lambay Island, with which Welch was closely involved from a collecting and recording perspective, although naturally he combined this with some photographic work;[31] and then the great Clare Island Survey, organised by the Royal Irish Academy between 1909 and 1911, which brought together Irish, British and European specialist field workers of distinction, who worked on the natural and human history of the island for short periods at a time. The Clare Island survey was the first of its kind[32] and Welch was in the thick of it as its official photographer.[33] It was during this work that he took what he considered to be his best view[34] – a superb image of the massive sea headlands at Croaghmore (Figure 5.5) which he chose as his bookplate, using a sketch based on his photograph by the talented Belfast artist J.W. Carey (Figure 1.3).

Another of Welch's endearing characteristics was his devotion to informal education, in the widest possible sense. Particularly after the death of his mother in 1908 it became his 'special delight' to encourage young peoples' interests and it is generally acknowledged that several prominent naturalists of later years owed their introduction to his painstaking help.[35] He was also instrumental in setting up the Junior Branch of the Field Club following his re-election as President 'by acclamation' in April 1911 and his encouragement of a proposal to do so by J.A. Stendall of the Belfast Museum.[36] In his later years he lectured widely on a range of subjects including heraldry, scenery, Christian and prehistoric antiquities, gardens and shells, using his own photographs and slide series as illustrations; in addition to academic and specialist audiences he talked with relish to schools and youth groups, women's groups and, perhaps most radically, prisoners.[37] In February 1925 he gave a lecture consisting of seventy-six lantern slides to the 'Deaf and Dumb' in College Square, Belfast.[38] He was much in demand as a judge of art at county and horticultural shows,[39] and sat on the Advisory Sub-Committee for the Arts 'etc.' [sic] for the Library and Technical Instruction Committee of Belfast Corporation.[40]

R.J. was a notable supporter and attender of museums and libraries. Invariably he donated sets of prints of commissioned photographs to Belfast Public Library, Belfast Museum and other learned bodies; he was equally generous with three-dimensional objects and scientific and historical specimens he had collected. As one commentator noted in respect of Welch's photograph of a prayer stick and a tally stick, 'few photographers of his time would have taken the trouble to record these evidences of "vulgar Irish superstition"'.[41] One wonders how many photographers of any time would have taken the trouble, as Welch did, to rescue the prayer stick – a thin branch of bramble or thorn festooned with strips of rags – and take it to his local museum, where it resides still within the historical collection, a significant and perhaps unique example (as its photograph certainly is) of an object now recognised of enormous cultural significance.[42]

He established warm working relationships with experts at Manchester Museum (which held many hundreds of his geological prints), the British Museum and the National Museum of Dublin, who obviously recognised his expertise and commitment, welcomed and respected his many contributions in kind and in information and appear to have given him free rein with their collections and, more significantly, their exhibitions. In turn, his dedication could verge

36. Newspaper Report, BNFC Annual Meeting; Minute Book 4, 28 April 1911.
37. *Memo Diary,* see list at end of volume.
38. Ibid., 28 July 1925.
39. See, for example, *Excursions Diary*, p. 132.
40. Ibid., p. 115.
41. Evans and Turner, *Ireland's Eye*, p. 75.
42. UM X9-2000.

on the solicitous – in one diary entry about a museum (albeit after he had developed an interest in fire-retarded wood in connection with his work with the railway companies) he confessed himself to be 'much surprised to see how little had been done to render it fireproof in view of its matchless collections, which in many cases could never be replaced if lost'.[43] At the same time, even R.J. could have too much of a good thing, as he found out during a visit to the Victoria and Albert Museum in London where he 'had my first experience of museum fatigue, a thing I had often heard of but never experienced before'.[44] And he could be scathing if disappointed. On holiday in Nottingham in 1913 he popped over to Leeds to see his sister Kate and took his niece Eileen to the local Zoological Museum, which, for reasons unsaid, he later remembered as 'an awful place. The Leeds folk who brag so much about their educational system should be ashamed of it.'[45]

He was perhaps unusual in his encouragement of other photographers, most notably W.A. Green, who joined the Committee of the Belfast Field Club in 1902 (and was awarded a prize for photographs of archaeological subjects the following year!)[46] and whom Welch noted in 1908 had accompanied him to photograph the interiors of the *Laurentic*.[47] In 1915 he went to Donaghamore in County Tyrone to give lessons 'in the open and in developing in dark room' to a young missionary who was learning photography before going to Manchuria, predeictably combining this duty with 'a good flint hunt' in the gravel pits at Pomeroy in the company of his host and his guests.[48] He was as dogged in learning himself as he was in instructing others and was constantly trying out new techniques and equipment to hone and perfect his photographic skills. Another great friend, A.W. Stelfox, remembered him 'always trying out new emulsions and developers', remarking that in the early years of his self-employment R.J. would spend most Sundays at their family home near Ormeau Park, Belfast, 'experimenting with [my] father with new shutters, developers etc., my father providing the material and Welch doing the work'.[49] In 1926 he was a founder member of the Belfast and Northern Ireland Professional Photographer Association, acting as its first Vice-President.[50]

43. *Excursions Diary*, p. 167.
44. Ibid., p. 175.
45. Ibid., p. 184.
46. BNFC Minute Book 4, 28 April 1903.
47. *Memo Diary*, 10 September 1908.
48. *Excursions Diary*, p. 201.
49. Evans and Turner, *Ireland's Eye*, p. 16.
50. *Memo Diary*, January 1926. The Belfast photographer Abernethy was the first President, Webb the first Secretary and Hogg the first Treasurer.

Dark Proof
will be much better
lighter
printed

AW

Welch left E.T. Church in 1883 to set up on his own, at first basing his new business on adding to his father's negatives, supplemented by the 'few negs' he had obtained on Field Club excursions.[51] Although he was always ready to oblige his friends (the Ulster Museum's archive collection contains copies of beautiful group photographs taken for the wedding of Helen Barbour Reilly and John Andrews, ill-fated designer of the *Titanic* (Figure 1.4), his passion for the natural world led him largely to eschew portraiture and 'big house' work for photographing out doors. For six years he concentrated on photographing the tourist and beauty spots of South Down, North Antrim and Belfast Lough. In 1885 he took a number of views of streets decorated for the visit of the Prince and Princess of Wales to Belfast: this, he acknowledged later, was his 'first real success', being a much longer series and a much handier size than those offered by other photographers, many of which were returned by stationers when his appeared.[52] He did, however, note that 'if platino or bromide had been known, [he] could have trebled it'. Platino, in which trademark medium he was later to excel, was available then but 'too dear and not too good'.[53]

In 1886 R.J. recorded the aftermath of the Belfast riots of that year for the Royal Commission of Inquiry into the disturbances; this was an early use of this type of documentary photography and his first significant foray into the evidence-based and record work for government agencies and official bodies which was to become an important and regular feature throughout his career. For example, soon after this he was brought in to work on reports for the New Belfast Water Scheme, where his photographs were used as evidence of the superiority of the Mourne over the Glenwherry scheme.[54] His diaries are full of references to bread-and-butter legal work: in August 1908, he took three views of North Street, Belfast as 'legal work for Fennell',[55] with whom he had visited Carrickfergus Castle four days earlier in the company of F.J. Bigger, another Field Club luminary; in 1910 he photographed cracks in Gt Victoria Street for two legal firms for three weeks in a row.[56]

In 1897 he was involved in an interesting dispute involving rights of way at the Giant's

51. *Excursions Diary*, p.1.
52. Ibid., p. 2.
53. Ibid.
54. Ibid., p. 3.
55. *Memo Diary*, August 1908.
56. Ibid, 16 August–6
    September 1910.

Causeway, introduced in the middle of the case when the plaintiffs' witnesses had sworn that there were no definite roads or paths in the area in question. Welch's photographs showed clearly a road capable of carrying a wagonette going down to Port-na-Bo, and also the clear delineation of a way known as the Shepherd's Path from Portnoffer to the cliff tops above. Welch had taken his views sharply focused, while the opposition's provided no detail that the judge could discern. Welch's satisfaction at being questioned in detail and complimented about his photographic work by the adjudicator personally was palpable – he noted that 'in later years I was told when any photos of mine were handed up to him on "Lights" etc. cases he was always told that they *were* mine'. Although the case was lost on another point, and those who had argued against the existence of the old paths won the rights to make their own new ones and charge for access to them, Welch was afterwards so often in the area guiding scientific parties around that the same syndicate he had fought to thwart sent him of their own volition a pass for himself and any guests accompanying him to use their facilities free of charge.[57]

Welch made his name commercially through his 'Irish Views' series, which included geological, antiquarian and ethnographic subjects as well as scenic land-, sea- and townscapes. These were published as bound albums as well as single prints, and opened doors to a variety of other money-making opportunities. His 'views' were bought in huge quantities to display in railway carriages, hotels and transatlantic liners, used to illustrate guide books and travel literature and employed by a number of local firms to emphasise their 'Irishness' in international markets. For example, c. 1888 he took a delightful picture of a fish hawker with her donkey cart in the little village of Inver, near Larne in County Antrim (Figure 1.5), of which he later wrote:

This view was a great favourite for many years and well known in the U.S.A. It was painted, a very large size, on the gable of one of the landing stage sheds of the Hudson River as an advertisement for Ross's Royal Belfast Mineral Waters. Mr. Ross got the complete U.S.A. rights from me[58]

57. *Excursions Diary*, pp. 31–33.
58. Annotation on original print.

Figure 1.5
Fish seller, Inver, County Antrim
W47-02-06

Figure 1.6
County Down Farmhouse
Kitchen W05-10-3

Of more immediate association with their sales pitch was the series of images of linen outworkers and their homes that Welch produced in 1912 for display in the linen department of Marshall Field and Co., Chicago, and which, while idealised to no little extent, extend an important visual reference of the material world of these County Down countrywomen (Figure 1.6).

The fish seller with her cart was also made into a very popular picture postcard; a huge market for these emerged in the United Kingdom from 1902, when the Post Office at last permitted senders to write their message on the same side as the address, thereby leaving the whole front of the card free for a view. In 1903, Welch noted that the Secretary of Dublin Zoological Gardens had asked him to produce cards from a number of views he had taken at the zoo over the years. He subsequently 'got' Baird Ltd, Belfast Printers, to print over 20,000 of these, a commission new to the firm as previously picture postcard print orders had invariably gone to Germany, through German agents in London. A couple of years later, Welch also got the same Belfast firm to print around 22,000 cards of views he had taken for the Belfast and County Down Railway Company. Welch's innate generosity, previously noted, extended this time to his business clients: he explained that he had taken 'a moderate commission only on each order as [the cards] were mainly for advertisement purposes, not to make money off'.[59]

An earlier diary entry, written with hindsight, carries a rare note of resentment regarding his lack of reward for the hundreds and thousands of his images that had been copied around the world. He was describing how, also in 1903, the Lancashire and Yorkshire Railway Company had published a special illustrated guide, 'Ireland, Where to Go', in which 165 of the 'blocks' used were made from his photographs. This, he noted, was the largest number of his images freatured in any book or magazine he had illustrated across the world (published in Britain, Ireland, France, the USA and Germany). He calculated that, particularly because of the wide newspaper coverage the topic attracted in America, his shipping pictures alone may have been copied hundreds of millions of times. However, as he noted:

59. *Excursions Diary*, p. 88

As no reproduction fees were payable for this type of work I did not benefit much. Even the L&YR Guide had the views at a low reproduction fee rate to please the North of Ireland Railway Companies who wanted all the advertising this big guide could give them. As the Railways and I worked together in a very friendly way, I had to oblige them in this and many similar cases.[60]

His acceptance of the reluctance of some of his larger clients to offer realistic reward for his labour is also evident in comments he made regarding a report on the use of German basalt pillars in engineering works in England that he forwarded to the Board of Works in Ireland, who accepted it with interest and 'paid for the photographs'.[61]

Despite his reservations regarding their subsequent exploitation of his work, Welch's appointment as official photographer to the great Belfast firm of shipbuilders, Harland and Wolff, was a source of constant pride to him. He started working with them in the mid-1890s, and recorded the building of their series of increasingly massive transatlantic liners from the laying of the keels to the final sea trials. His diaries are strangely reticent about his work with the *Titanic*, which is granted only a couple of lines regarding its launch and first trial, but he was hugely impressed by her sister ship, the *Olympic*, launched in 1910. As usual, R.J.'s diaries testify to his knack of noting passing detail: for example, the *Saxon*, trialled in June 1900, was 'the first big liner [where] I saw good beds placed in a decent sized bedroom rather than a berth cabin'.[62] One of most apparently enjoyable commissions with the 'Yard' was to photograph the newly electrically lit *Rotterdam* on her trip to the Harland and Wolff workshop in Southampton in June 1908. He boarded the big ship in Belfast at midnight to find her 'a blaze of light'[63] and was thus able to photograph her saloons and other interiors as well as even promenade decks in thick fog until 3.00 a.m. He later praised the ship as 'the most brilliantly lighted of the many great liners whose trials trips I was on 1896–1914'.[64] The next day he spent taking a series of views of the

60. *Excursions Diary*, p. 69.
61. Ibid, p. 73.
62. Ibid., p. 53.
63. Ibid., p. 128.
64. Ibid., p. 213.

interiors and exteriors of the Southampton Works (a presentation album of these forms part of the Welch archive at the Ulster Museum), before attending a local Agricultural Society Show, where he was much impressed by collections of wildflowers put together by schoolchildren, and the fine exhibits made by 'little engineering works in small south of England towns. The real good quality was not that of American showy but indifferent work.'[65]

The following day he was met by his friend A.W. Stelfox to go collecting in the New Forest, where it was too hot and dry for land snails (but not for adders, for which they kept a watchful and no doubt excited eye). Welch, however, managed to find in a small pool a quantity of 'very peculiar' *Limnaiea glabura* (a freshwater snail), which he sent for identification to an expert friend, who said he 'had never seen anything like it'. He stayed in London with Stelfox that evening and the next day attended the Anglo-French exhibition at White City. When he had difficulty bringing his camera into the venue, he enlisted the support of Mr Brown, in charge of the Irish Village, who had it released from the office where it had been confiscated. In return, Welch took for him a number of views of the stands at the Irish Village, after which he 'got [his] coat off and did amateur waiter for a hour or two', catering to the hungry crowd that rushed the Village after finding the food at all the other facilities in the hall had been cleared out 'as if a swarm of hungry locusts had come'. He then visited the other exhibits, 'the flip-flap, the scenic railway, etc., like any other "cheap-tripper"', before returning to the Irish Village to help to count the money taken at the turnstiles and the refreshments stalls'. Over 600,000 people had come to the exhibition as a Whit Monday day out. To Welch, who later photographed the monster rallies and demonstrations roused by the Home Rule Crisis in 1912–13, it was 'the largest crowd I ever saw in my life'.[66]

This urban crush, which Welch seems to have relished, was a far cry from the isolated landscapes he encountered in his visits to the West and North-West of Ireland. While he was familiar from childhood with the coasts of Sligo and Donegal,[67] the first time he visited the region as an adult photographer was in May 1894, when he went to Recess and the surrounding area

65. *Excursions Diary*, p. 129.
66. Ibid., pp. 131–2.
67. Ibid., p. 148.

as part of a private excursion organised by the Tatlows of Dellbrook, the Russells and the Praegers 'to botanize and photo etc.'. The weather was appallingly wet, prompting one of the companions, Rosamund Praeger, R.L. Praeger's celebrated artist and sculptor sister, to dash off a marvellously evocative sketch of Welch coping with the deluge, dryly entitled *Wait Until the Clouds Roll By* (Figure 1.7). It was on this week-long trip, Welch noted, that he 'took his first set of Connemara negs, and Cashel'.[68]

The Recess trip appears to have opened the doors to the West for Welch and over the next three years he visited the region regularly, returning to Bundoran and Sligo in August 1894: to take golf views; to discuss with hotel proprietors about contributing blocks to the journals *Irish Tourist* and *Visit Ireland;* to spend a day being driven around photographing antiquities at Deerpark and other spots; and, of course, to devote some time to collecting unusual snails.[69] Other visits included Galway and Roundstone in July 1895, photographing and visiting antiquities;[70] Roundstone again in April 1896 with the Dublin Naturalists' Field Club (DNFC) and the Royal Irish Academy (RIA), then in May 1896 to Lambay, again with the DNFC, to photograph gulls' nests.[71] In April 1897 he went to Leenane and Killary harbour 'photoing and collecting' with a private party of naturalists before continuing to Westport to meet directors of the Midland and Great Western Railway, who were visiting their soon-to-open railway hotel with other officials from the company, spent a day on Achill Island photographing the Cathedral Caves at the Cliffs of Meenaun, where he 'got some fine Geology negs … much used in after years for various purposes', and then, before they all returned to Dublin, insisted on the Railway Secretary and the Chief Engineer accompanying him to experience the magic of the Gulf of Aille 'which they had never even heard of'![72]

In April 1900 Welch travelled to West Donegal with Henry Hamilton of the White House, a large department store in Portrush, Co. Antrim, which catered to railway and overseas visitors to the north coast, to get 'a very nice series of views of Home Industries – wool carding, spinning and weaving near Ardara, Maghera and Carrick, Teelin, etc.', also visiting Mucknos

"Wait till the clouds roll by!"

a Connemara View by Rosamund Praeger.

Figure 1.7
Cartoon by Rosamund Praeger, *Excursions Diary* p.14

68. *Excursions Diary*, p. 15.
69. Ibid., p. 17.
70. Ibid., p. 21.
71. Ibid., p. 31.
72. Ibid.

market and Killybegs before returning home via Derry.[73] Welch was back in the West in May, this time as a guest of Lord and Lady Clonbrock, who had invited him several times 'to collect and photo in Clonbrock forest', a visit that had 'always been prevented at best time by some launch or other engagement in NE Ulster'.[74] Unfortunately the weather was very dry, so collecting was 'useless' but he got 'fine' tree and flower photographs and other views, was shown around the estate and grounds, including Lady Clonbrock's famous photographic studio and, despite the unfavourable conditions, was even able to contribute to the 'mollusca list' compiled by the DNFC and RIA flora and fauna committee during its survey of the estate in 1902.

However, presumably the highlight of Welch's stay at Clonbrock was the arrival, on either his first or second day there, of a Royal Warrant, appointing him Photographer at Belfast to Queen Victoria:

> Just 34 years after my father had been appointed Photographer to the Lord Lieutenant in Ireland in 1866, [at] which time Lord Clonbrock (the Hon. Gerald Dillon) was his Private Secretary. This was the Duke of Abercorn, Baron of Paisley, who was also Duke of Chatelrault in France.[75]

The events behind Welch's being so honoured are testament both to his skill as a photographer and to the regard in which his work was held by the Congested Districts Board (CDB), even before he was specifically charged to record their endeavours in 1903 and 1914. It was his views, taken in the North and West of Ireland in the five or six years prior to the Queen's visit to the country in 1900 that were selected by them to reveal to Her Majesty:

> the character of the congested districts of the Western Seaboard and the peasant life, industries and unique antiquities etc., as far as photographs could show them.[76]

73. *Excursions Diary*, p. 48.
74. Ibid., pp. 49.
75. Ibid., pp. 49–53.
76. *Northern Whig*, 11 June 1900, illustrated in Evans and Turner, *Ireland's Eye*, p. 7.

Welch's Royal Warrant was confirmed by King Edward VII on his accession in 1901 and a special permit issued with it to allow Welch to use the Royal Arms on promotional and advertisement material.[77] As Maguire notes, the only other Irish photographers awarded a Royal Warrant by Queen Victoria during her long reign were Lafayette and Chancellor (of Dublin) and Abernethy (of Belfast). This grant, bestowed just seven years after he had gone it alone professionally, was indeed 'signal recognition of Welch's standing and achievement'.[78] It may also have earned him the commission to photograph the interiors of the Vice-Regal Lodge in Dublin as decorated for the visit of Edward and Alexandra in 1904, and see his work reproduced in the London illustrated weeklies and some dailies.[79]

In October 1903 Welch revisited an old haunt, the Rosapenna Hotel in Donegal, to photograph interiors and amenities for a new booklet. One of the guests at the hotel happened to be a Mr Duthie, fishery expert with the CDB, who asked Welch to take some views of CDB fishing boats in nearby Killybegs 'for the Board'.[80] Killybegs was at that time enjoying a boom based on the export of cured herring to the Russian and Baltic markets where Downings fish were especially prized, and the CDB was working hard to secure a local presence in this international endeavour, particularly through the provision of well-equipped seagoing vessels of much greater catching and carrying capacity than the Tory currachs Welch had seen bringing in herring in 1893, when the fishery had revived.[81] As he remarked himself, Killybegs became a favoured destination for him in later years, where he got 'many fishing boat and curing negs … usually at the time the Scotch fisher-girls were there'.[82]

Welch continued to visit the west coast at fairly regular intervals, usually travelling with his scientific circle, as in his visit to Sligo in 1905 with the Irish Field Club Union (IFCU), when he 'did not photo much being too keen on collecting for the mollusca list'.[83] In 1905 he went to the Edenvale Caves near Ennis with R.J. Ussher, 'the well-known cave explorer', to take interior and exterior views for an RIA report, and made Ussher sit in his leather cave suit to give perspective and scale to his view of the entrance to the catacombs.[84] In 1907 he went to Clare

77. *Excursions Diary*, p. 53.
78. Maguire, *A Century in Focus*, p. 90.
79. *Excursions Diary*, p. 91.
80. Ibid., pp. 88–89.
81. Ibid., p. 89.
82. Ibid.
83. Ibid., p. 95.
84. Ibid.

to photograph plants for *The Tourist's Fauna*, a task for which he displayed his infinite patience, adopting in the extremely windy conditions:

> A cumulative explosure plan, even tho' the plates were rapids. Some plates took 5–15 minutes from first exposure to last – I had 7 cumulators on one plate … the plants were never at rest for me for more than 2 or 3 seconds at a time.[85]

At least these plates were used, not like the fruits of his labours in September that year at Killybegs and St John's Point 'photographing scenery, antiquities, fishing boats and carpet factory for a guide that was never published'.[86]

In 1909 Welch went to Clare Island as part of the 7th Survey team, collecting and photographing, returning as part of the same survey in June 1910. It says much for his skill in razor-sharp record photography that the views he took on these trips were used for the survey's Botanical, Zoological, Geological and General Reports.[87] He suffered twice for his success, however, first slipping on rocks and hurting his arm and then becoming so saturated during the two days he spent working in the cloud of mist which hung permanently over the cliffs that he got 'rheumatism there at once. It was very bad for some months'.[88]

It did not, however, prevent him visiting Tory Island in July as part of a wider trip to the region as part of the sixth and last triennial meeting of the IFCU. But mist again bedevilled the journey on the way out, on the island itself (although Welch remarked that he was able to take some views of 'near at hand objects') and especially on the way back, when their boat got lost in thick fog, surrounded by the sound of the horns of warships on naval manoeuvres 'who were lost like us and not far out of the tracks of the Atlantic liners taking the north route to Glasgow and Liverpool'. The party anchored in Sheephaven Bay for the night and when day broke persuaded their unwilling captain to creep slowly round the coast until they heard the sound of work on the extension to Downings pier and knew they were nearly safely home.[89]

85. *Excursions Diary*, p. 118.
86. Ibid., p. 122.
87. Ibid., p. 149.
88. Ibid.
89. Ibid., pp. 149–152.

The Tory Island escapade appears to have been Welch's last 'organised' trip to CDB regions in the West and North-West until his formal commission to visit in June 1914. He was very busy with work for Harland and Wolff in 1911 and 1912, taking record photography of the *Olympic*, launched 1910, her sister ship, the *Titanic*, launched 1911, and a number of other large (and increasingly larger) vessels. In 1914, he attended a lecture by Alec G. Wilson to the Royal Dublin Society on Belfast shipbuilding for which he had made slides:

> From negs taken of ships, launches and details of construction with some plans of yard and old records. [The lecture hall was] well filled, several judges and a party from the Vice-Regal lodge. The slides showed especially well in the R.D.S. fine electric lantern.[90]

He also spent a considerable amount of time before the First World War travelling around England collecting and catching up with old friends and colleagues, and was also kept busy by conducting and making expeditions to the North Antrim coast.

On 9th June 1914 R.J. set forth for Dublin on his way to the region around Castlebar, Tuam and Castlerea 'to take photographs of "striped" farms and new farm houses also old improved houses etc' for the CDB to display as enlargements at the Dublin Civic Exhibition.[91] He reached Castlebar the next morning, where he was met by the Board's local district chief, a Mr Gahan, and took his first set of views. The next day was spent travelling between Castlebar and Ballinrobe before going on to Tuam (where he was distracted for a time by the collecting opportunities offered by 'the largest and thickest area of shell marl [he had] ever saw or heard of);[92] there he was joined on 12 June by new guides, CDB Engineers Messrs Gamble and Ferguson. Going over some 'very interesting if rough ground' to Lectra, he visited a corn mill driven by an underground stream taken from a lake three miles distant. Its construction had been supervised by Engineer Ferguson, who turned out to be from Belfast and conveyed Welch on to

90. *Excursions Diary*, p. 187.
91. Ibid., p. 188; see also *Memo Diary*, 9–15 June 1914.
92. Ibid.

Cappagh where he saw 'some dreadful rundale holdings [joint occupation of land, in strips] with great stone dykes on a hillside'.[93] The following day he caught up with Mr Gahan, who took him to take views of an improved village near Castlerea. Welch's description of the process of improvement is worth repeating in full. The old village, he wrote:

> Was originally 24 houses, these twenty-four tenancies had 700 separate patches [of ground] in rundale. 6 tenants were "migrated", their land was "striped" between those remaining. 8 new houses built [and] land now held in about 42 plots. Each tenant has 3 of different quality.[94]

The plates Welch took on this trip were delivered by him to Mr Micks at CDB headquarters in Dublin on 15 June and the pair spent the following day at Palmerstone House; then Welch went on to Drogheda to spend the evening with yet another CDB contact, the textile manufacturer Mr Walker.[95]

This commission and the connections he established through it may have inspired his return four weeks later 'on a run to Connemara and the West'[96] with Mr and Mrs Kempster, Mrs Kempster's sister, Miss Jones, and the two Kempster children, Margaret and Sheila. Mr Kempster took his own large motor and also hired a taxi for their luggage. They travelled first through the Boyne Valley and its antiquities before calling in to see Mr Walker in Drogheda, who commandeered Welch's itinerary for the western part of their run and, 'much improving it', insisted that they visit South-West Connemara and Garumna and that their long-bodied car was well able to manage the 'high little culverts' that acted as bridges if care were taken in crossing them. As R.J. later conceded, 'he was right but [we] had some narrow shaves one night on our way home from Cashel to Recess'.[97]

In his description of this trip Welch is instructive about the potential cosiness of the relationships between industry and the CDB, and between business and business. Mr Walker, who

93. *Excursions Diary*, p. 189.
94. Ibid.
95. *Memo Diary*, 15 June 1914.
96. *Excursions Diary*, p. 189. J.W. Kemster, DL, was Chairman of the Belfast Board of Directors, Harland and Wolff, and became a firm friend of Welch's.
97. ibid., p. 193.

had spurred them to visit the lace depots he had established in Connemara for the CDB, where they saw very fine curtains and purchased some pieces, was involved with the Drogheda Weaving Company.[98] It is also interesting to read that Mrs Allingham, wife of Hugh Allingham, MRIA, Manager of the Provincial Bank in Ballyshannon, was now herself burning in her beautiful flower painting on bone china, having formerly had this done at the pottery in Belleek![99]

Welch obviously approved of the work that the CDB was doing at Garumna, 'exemplified in new or improved housing, schools, lace class schools etc.'[100] Before they 'took it in hand', he remarked, 'it was pretty much what Gweedore, N.W. Donegal, was like 80 years ago, before Lord George Hill bought the estate and altered the condition of things'.[101] The Kempsters, too, were much intrigued by this 'awful bare rocky and stony area' and 'the changes that were taking place for the benefit of the people'.[102] On their way home the party called in at CDB headquarters in Castlebar, where officials showed them 'much that interested them of the methods of work in the west adopted by the Board for the purchase, re-arrangement and resale of lands in congested districts'.[103]

Welch was well pleased with this trip. They had fair weather all the time, except when it did not matter, and very few punctures. The Kempsters got a good idea of the condition of the west of Ireland and the activities there of both the CDB and the Department of Agriculture. They had covered eight hundred miles in eight days and, by getting early on the road and late off it, had missed very little worth seeing. Indeed, as he wrote, many other similar runs had been planned 'but the great war put an end to them'.[104]

It was not only trips to the West that the outbreak of war terminated. Wartime restrictions meant that R.J. was unable to do much work outdoors, and he was warned to stay away from the coast he loved; this, he wrote, 'killed the only chance of sales [he] had to tourists and book illustrations'.[105] The war also saw the suspension of the few investments he had left; worse, it saw the shutdown of 'all building work and almost all shipbuilding work, except for a few Admiralty commissions in 1915'.[106] His sister Sarah, who had taken over the business side of

98. *Excursions Diary*, p. 194.
99. Ibid., p. 195.
100. Ibid., p. 193.
101. Ibid., p. 194.
102. Ibid.
103. Ibid.
104. Ibid., p. 195.
105. Evans and Turner, *Ireland's Eye*, p. 6.
106. Maguire, *A Century in Focus*, p. 100.

his work following the death of his mother in 1908, died herself in 1915, compounding his financial disarray. Civil conflict and the Partition of Ireland in 1922 also badly affected his business prospects: in April 1922 he wrote that he had done 'more business in the last ten days than in all the four years ending 1921'.[107] Although work did pick up thereafter, Welch was never again to prosper as he had during his pre-war heydey, and in 1927 his friends and colleagues successfully petitioned the new government of Northern Ireland to grant him a Civil List pension of £100 per year.[108]

His final years were spent in a whirl of lecturing, collecting, visiting and photographing. Often, these activities were combined: for example, his commission from the Ormeau Bakery to photograph the Barnett wedding cake was shortly followed by an invitation to lecture to staff, workmen and friends in the bakery canteen.[109] In July 1935 he was in Warrenpoint taking views of the Promenade for a new visitor guide; in Dundalk at the GNR Locomotive Works to photograph new carriages; and at the Giant's Causeway with visiting South African bowlers, helping to take a party of ninety around the site before giving a talk on its formation.[110] He was then seventy-six years old. An inveterate monarchist to the end, his last diary entry, dated 20 January 1936, recorded the death of George V, at Sandringham at 11.55 p.m.[111] Welch himself died eight months later, on 28 September.

In his will, dated October 1931, Welch left his property to a relation by marriage, James Wilson of Newcastle, Co. Down, and to three Field Club friends, A.W. Stelfox, A.A. Campbell and J. A. Stendall (who became Curator of Belfast Museum and Art Gallery in 1942). The latter were instructed to dispose of his negatives of botanical, zoological, geological and ethnographic subjects. Negatives of scenery and antiquities were to be sold to benefit his married sister's children. As it happened, all the negatives in his possession on death (with the exception of those reserved for the LMS Railway Company) were purchased in 1939 by a sub-committee of the BNFC, convened 'with a view to providing a fitting memorial to the late R.J. Welch, MSC.'[112]

107. Quoted Maguire, ibid.
108. Ibid.
109. *Memo Diary,* January 1935.
110. ibid., July 1935.
111. ibid., January 1936.
112. Evans and Turner, *Ireland's Eye,* p. 2.

The collection of about 5,500 plates was offered to the Belfast Museum in 1940 under certain conditions,[113] one of which was the compilation of a catalogue to be offered to the public at a nominal fee. For a variety of reasons – administrative, financial, academic and methodological – this was never done. Attempts were made to comply with the provision that prints required from the negatives by students and others should be made available and that no copyright fee be charged if prints were requested for scientific purposes, but access to the collection was for years severely restricted. The establishment of the Ulster Museum in 1961 saw great improvements in resources, allowing contact prints and copy negatives to be made, which enabled the precious original glass plates to be put into protective storage. And the establishment of a Department of Technology and Local History in 1973 saw the historic collection finally gain a proper museum home. A topographic system of cataloguing these plates was finally developed, and classified catalogues for this collection, and for the collection of scientific plates (which were cared for by Natural Sciences) were soon published.

Today the historic Welch collection has been added to substantially: all original prints and lantern slides held by the History Department, many of which bear his annotations, have been catalogued; many more prints and negatives held in private and commercial hands have been archived and several volumes of original prints and published views, along with quantities of individual photographs, have been acquired. In addition to photographs, the History Department also holds Welch's field and work diaries, photographic record books, his very interesting book of autographs and many of his annotated maps. Welch's scientific views are held within the Ulster Museum's Geology Department, which also holds an important collection of photographic albums compiled by the British Association for the Advancement of Science in 1888, in which his work features prominently. Welch's close connection with the museum in its formative years has left a further legacy in the shape of various donations by him of objects, specimens and documents. The acquisition of the Harland and Wolff photographic collection by the Ulster Folk and Transport Museum, now, like the Ulster Museum, part of

113. ibid.

National Museums Northern Ireland, has ensured the survival of over two thousand of the negatives produced during his time as the firm's official photographer; like most of the other images he made under contract, for example those produced for railway companies, hotels, government departments, surveys and Commissions of Enquiry, they had remained with the purchasers.

Welch's instinct for the unusual, his passion for clarity, his devotion to documentary detail and his shunning of artifice underpin the huge significance of the photographic record he created. But his photographs also reveal the range of his interests, and his firm belief in the value of the visual to inform and educate. He was an energetic champion of informal learning, and a staunch supporter of the role of museums as places of public knowledge and popular inspiration. He is often described as a great traditionalist, with an inbuilt antipathy toward modern art, motor cars and new-fangled techniques. Yet he was also a modernist – a groundbreaker, an experimentalist and a man of tremendous foresight with regard to the significance of the ordinary and everyday. Our knowledge of the world in which he moved would be so much the weaker had he not striven so tirelessly to record it for us in all its aspects.

CHAPTER TWO

Tuke's Connemara Album

SARA SMYTH

Tuke's Connemara Album was donated to the National Library of Ireland in 2004. Encased in a green cloth binding with gold-embossed title, it might be expected to be another album of tourist snapshots but its content is in fact completely different. It is an important source for the study of the socio-economic history of the West of Ireland at the end of the nineteenth century. The photographs were taken by Major Robert Ruttledge-Fair for Mr James Hack Tuke in 1892, at a time when both men were deeply involved in poverty relief work in that region. It is a photographic record of some significance in detailing the way of life of ordinary peasant families in Connemara, but it also needs to be seen in the context of decades of work by Tuke to improve the lot of people living in the West of Ireland.

There are forty-six photographs in the album. Most of them have been captioned on the reverse but is not clear if the captions were written by the photographer or added at a later date by another hand. Either way they form an interesting postscript to the images. The locality is mentioned on only a few of the photographs, those of coastal views near Spiddal in South Connemara. Tuke's interest extended along the western seaboard and perhaps albums were created of other areas too, but maybe he had a special fondness for Connemara, which he described as 'Today basking in the full sunshine, how lovely, in its first touch of spring, is the scenery around.'[1] Major Robert Ruttledge-Fair, a native of Mayo, was closely involved in Tuke's work in the West over many years. He was a local government inspector and worked for the Congested Districts Board (CDB). Although his contribution was not as prominent as Tuke's, he was centrally involved in the work, and in addition through this

1. J.H. Tuke, Reports and papers relating to the proceedings of the Committee of 'Mr. Tuke's Fund' for assisting emigration from Ireland during 1882, 1883 and 1884 (Collected privately for use of the committee), p. 66. NLI IR3252, reprinted from *Nineteenth Century*, July, 1882.

album he has created a fascinating record of the difficulties experienced by the poor of the western regions.

James Hack Tuke was born into a Quaker family in Yorkshire on 13 September 1819. On leaving school he began work in his father's counting house. Tuke first visited Ireland during the Great Famine, touring the country to assess the situation in order to find suitable channels for the distribution of relief being planned by the Society of Friends in both England and Ireland. In his letter back to the Central Relief Committee of the Society of Friends in 1847 he described the people of Connaught as 'by far the poorest and most destitute in Ireland'.[2] This letter was published the following year and helped to raise some awareness of the severity of the Famine but even at this stage Tuke realised that fundamental changes needed to be made if Ireland were to survive. There was a belief that England had a responsibility towards Ireland to provide support during the current disaster, but also to plan to improve conditions so that such a devastating famine would never occur again. Tuke was of the opinion that native manufactures should be encouraged, along with the fisheries; indeed, he comments how Mayo and Galway are especially suited to the fishing industry but that there is a lack of equipment and skills. This visit made a huge impression on Tuke and he returned to Ireland again in 1849 when the Famine had worsened. Over the decades that followed, he never lost his interest in the country, particularly in the fate of the population of the western seaboard.

Tuke's opinions on the economic condition of the western counties of Ireland were extremely perceptive and ultimately many of them came to fruition through the CDB, established in 1891. He recognised that a uniform economic policy for the island as a whole would not be successful: a policy that worked for the more prosperous eastern side of the country with indigenous industry and tracts of arable land could not benefit the smallholding tenant farmers that made up the majority of the population of Connaught and the surrounding counties. Most areas in the West had less arable land, and the main natural resources of turf, fisheries and seaweed industries were underdeveloped. There was also the problem of remoteness due a lack of transport infrastructure,

2. J.H. Tuke, A visit to Connaught in the autumn of 1847: a letter addressed to the Central Relief Committee of the Society of Friends (London: Charles Gilpin, 1847), p. 3.

leaving many regions inaccessible to markets. Tuke stated that Ireland had to be considered in separate parts and that Donegal, Leitrim, Roscommon, Sligo, Mayo, Galway and large parts of Clare, Limerick, Kerry and Cork would need special attention, particularly the former counties. He doubted that there were the interest or resources to implement the provisions of the Poor Law amongst the Poor Law Guardians in these areas. This opinion was formed during his first visit and he retained this outlook.[3]

When Tuke visited Ireland again in 1880 it was clear to him that the circumstances of the poor of the West had not noticeably improved, and critically that the slightest dip in the economy or a poor harvest would be enough to tip the balance into famine conditions. He spent six weeks travelling around Donegal and Connaught to assess the conditions and level of relief required to assist the population. As with his writings during the Famine, the report he prepared for the Society of Friends was published.[4] He wrote extensively on the Irish situation and contributed greatly to the acceptance both in Ireland and in England that peasants in the West of Ireland were permanently living on the verge of starvation. In a letter to *The Times* he talks of the 'stealthy tread of hunger' among the stone and turf hovels and points out that 72,000 out of a population of 218,000 needed daily food relief. The tenants were dependent on the earnings from the hiring out of their children in Scotland or the Lagan,[5] and the seasonal migration of the adults for harvesting in England and Scotland. The poor harvests had affected these areas too and cut the cash income that people depended upon heavily to pay rent and settle the shopkeeper account. Tuke argued that non-payment of rent or granting of ownership could not improve conditions as most of the holdings were well below the minimum of 20 acres he believed necessary to support a family.[6] For those with reasonable holdings who wished to improve their lands huge difficulties were faced because, if a tenant improved his land or house, or if he reclaimed land that the landlord was not using, he was invariably rewarded by an increase in rent. This removed the motivation for improvement and Tuke stated that the tenants needed more certainty of terms to encourage development.[7]

3. Ibid., pp. 1–5.
4. *The Times*, 27 May 1880, p. 11.
5. The term Lagan referred to an area east of the Muckish Mountains to Antrim.
6. *The Times*, 27 March 1880, p. 4.

English politicians, and some of the population at large, were sceptical of reports of distress that came from the Irish clergy or the nationalist politicians, which they viewed as propaganda for their political aspirations. George M.W. Hill, writing in a letter to *The Times* later in 1880, described the local population of the West as 'consummate actors and imposters' and said that he knew of houses that were stripped of possessions and potatoes hidden so that they could deceive well-meaning people such as Mr Tuke and newspaper correspondents.[8] It does seem, however, that the reports of philanthropists such as Mr Tuke, and of committees such as the Duchess of Marlborough Relief Committee set up by the Lord Lieutenant's wife, and the Mansion House Committee set up by Edward Dyer Grey, editor of *The Freeman's Journal*, were generally accepted as true, indicating a genuine need for charity for the people of the West of Ireland.

Tuke did not believe that the poor relief offered by the British government through the Poor Law Unions would ever achieve anything constructive towards permanently improving the lot of the peasants with smallholdings, and he felt that 'employment is that great want of these western districts'.[9] To Tuke neither did the 1881 Land Act offer any solution as he did not believe that the Act would lead to adequate consolidation of small farms. The bad harvests of 1882 and 1883 caused widespread hardship and starvation, creating another crisis point. The problem was compounded by evictions on several estates, particularly around Clifden. While these events were occurring, Tuke had been working on a plan to assist the people. Central to this scheme was the issue of assisted emigration, which he saw as the best means of improving the situation. Following a visit to North America in 1845 Tuke developed an interest in the advantages of emigration. He saw a twofold benefit in assisting emigration from Ireland, by offering a new life to those who emigrated and relieving the plight of those who stayed behind, as the emigrants' plots could be consolidated to enlarge holdings and assist others to earn a living. He had very fixed ideas on how the process should be organised in order to maximise what could be achieved. Tuke had visited North America and Canada in 1880 to investigate the

8. *The Times*, 25 December 1880.
7. *The Times*, 27 May 1880, p. 11.
9. J.H Tuke, *Irish Distress and its remedies; The land question; A visit to Donegal and Connaught in the spring of 1880* (London: W. Ridgeway, 1880), p. 68.

potential of sending over Irish emigrants to new lands: he identified areas that had a demand for labour or where land was available and established contacts that were willing to help set up such a scheme.

Tuke published his emigration proposals in an article entitled 'Emigration from Ireland' in the periodical *The Nineteenth Century* in February 1881.[10] In March 1882 a group of like-minded men met at the Duke of Bedford's house to discuss the proposals. The result was the establishment of a subscription fund to finance an assisted emigration scheme to send the poor of the West of Ireland to North America and Canada. It had to be carefully organised and assisted, and in this he laid out his views in the 'Emigration from Ireland' article and again the following year in 'Ought emigration from Ireland be assisted?'[11] The principles of his scheme were adopted by the Committee of what became known as 'Mr Tuke's Fund' to promote 'assistance to emigrants under careful and systematic supervision'. On 4 April 1882 Tuke left England to travel to the west of Ireland to begin the process of selecting the emigrants.

Strict guidelines were drawn up and were personally overseen by Tuke. Firstly only those who wished to emigrate should be assisted and, while individuals were not strictly excluded, family units were actively encouraged. Problematically, it often happened that the most able members emigrated, which worsened the outlook for those left behind as the weaker members of the family were less likely to be able to improve their situation. Tuke's rationale was that if families emigrated together then they could look after each other on arrival at the new destination, and possibly their holdings could be consolidated by their neighbours at home. It was also essential that at least one member of the family spoke English to improve the chance of employment. All candidates were interviewed to gauge their suitability, some by Tuke himself.

On 28 April 1882 the first emigrants left Galway for Philadelphia. By June almost 1,300 people had sailed from Ireland for a new life.[12] There was a huge demand for the opportunity to leave but there were problems. In April the Clifden Poor Law Union withdrew its support over differences on how the scheme should operate. It was cheaper simply to send out emi-

10. *Nineteenth Century*, February 1881, p. 707.
11. J.H. Tuke, *Ought emigration from Ireland be assisted* (London: Strahan, 1882).
12. J.H Tuke, 'Mr. Tuke's Fund', p. 15.

grants paying only for their passage; however, Tuke believed that the emigrants should be selected according to his rules, and that it was necessary to provide assistance for additional transport costs on each side of the Atlantic and for appropriate clothing, both of which made the scheme more costly. In April, before the first emigrants left, the Union had withdrawn, along with its funding, which was essential for Tuke's plans. The Committee realised that there was a huge desire to take up the option of assisted emigration but also that a private body could not extensively subsidise such a scheme. A memo sent to government requesting state assistance instigated parliamentary debate in July and resulted in the 1882 Arrears of Rent Act granting £100,000 to help assist migration from 42 Unions. The funding supplied £5 per head with the voluntary Committee subscriptions making up the shortfall. Moran suggests that the British government realised that Tuke's approach was working and that it had long-term benefits, unlike the relief of distress option.[13]

The emigrants were moved on immediately from the ports of arrival to specific destinations. It was felt to be impractical to set up employment for them in the new country but destination areas and towns were chosen based on research establishing which areas needed labour, preferably where a support network of Irish emigrants already existed. The Roman Catholic clergy in the new areas reported back to Tuke and the Committee on the progress of the new arrivals, with almost universally positive reports, it was necessary however, for Major Ruttledge-Fair to visit Canada in 1883 following negative comments about the welfare of emigrants from an Irish priest in Toronto. He found that all the Tuke emigrants, as they were known, were in good health and living conditions. There were emigrants living in the Conway Street area of Toronto in great poverty, but they had all been sent out by the Poor Law Unions of Galway, Mayo and Kerry.[14]

Mr Tuke's Fund for emigration was not universally popular. At local level the Committee had received considerable assistance from the clergy, but this diminished greatly when the Irish bishops formally opposed the scheme in July 1883. They feared that the emigrants going

13. G.P. Moran, *Sending out Ireland's Poor: Assisted Emigration to North America in the Nineteenth Century* (Dublin: Four Courts Press, 2004) p. 175.
14. Ibid., p. 205.

to North America and Canada would be lost to the Catholic Church as many gave up religion completely or joined the church of the majority of the host population in an attempt to assimilate into the local community. The Catholic hierarchy disregarded the fact that under Tuke's scheme priests were encouraged to travel out and settle with the migrants. There was a certain paradox in this, and one that was surely not lost on members of the clergy who, day by day, could see the plight of the people but felt pressurised by their superiors to officially withdraw their support. Many priests continued to privately petition the Committee on behalf of their parishioners. The problem was compounded in October 1883 when Bishop John Lynch of Toronto stated that he would no longer support emigration from Irish Poor Law Unions as the country did not need this type of emigrant.[15]

The governments of Canada and North America also made objections, with some reason, as a number of the Poor Law Unions saw these schemes as a means of getting rid of paupers and criminals from Ireland, and the governments were worried that the incoming paupers would become a burden on the state.[16] In March 1884 the Canadian Government decided to refuse entry to Irish emigrants, mainly due to concerns about the type of emigrant arriving combined with a downturn in the Canadian economy. Assisted emigration was allowed to recommence the following year but only in close liaison with Canadian officials. There was also some opposition from the local Canadian population as they feared the influx of unskilled workers affecting their employment opportunities and wage rates, and they resented the assistance that some of the emigrants received. There was little differentiation in Canada between Tuke's emigrants and those of the Poor Law Unions. The latter were not selected on the same careful criteria nor assisted in the same manner on arrival but they all became tarred with the same brush.[17] Some Irish migrants had created a very negative impression elsewhere and indeed at various stages some Irish were unwelcome in New Zealand.[18]

Throughout 1883 and 1884 Tuke wrote letters published in *The Times* to defend his scheme

15. Ibid., p. 182–3.
16. Ibid., p. 212.
17. Ibid., p. 215.
18. Lyndon Fraser, 'Irish Migration to the West Coast, 1864–1900', in L. Fraser (ed.), *A Distant Shore: Irish Migration and New Zealand Settlement*, (Dunedin: University of Otago Press, 2000), pp. 86–105.

and to counteract criticism of assisted emigration.[19] This correspondence also included extracts from letters received from emigrants who were pleased with their new life and sending home remittances. On 12 January a letter to the editor was published which, among other extracts, included an account from the Relieving Officer at Letterfrack, County Galway: 'All the people emigrated from this district are doing well, and sent home money before Christmas, and numbers of people here are most anxious to be assisted to emigrate this year.' But some were not convinced. In response to this letter Edward W. O'Brien, late assistant Commissioner under the Land Act, stated that he accepted the generous motives of Tuke and his Committee but, while their actions greatly benefited individuals, 'we must look facts firmly in the face. Emigration cannot, in our time at least, solve the western difficulty'. The issues of poor land and how to make it productive, coupled with the necessity to amalgamate holdings, needed to be addressed.[20] He did have a point as there was little evidence to show that the smallholdings left by the emigrants were consolidated into better farms for those staying behind. Although every effort was taken to ensure that the land vacated should go to a neighbour, it did not always happen and the influence that the Committee could bring to bear was limited, as it had no powers other than persuasion. For example, in Mayo 750 families had emigrated but 38 per cent of their land was taken over by the landlord or allowed to go to waste.[21]

Some nationalist leaders protested that Tuke's scheme amounted to forced emigration and that ultimately the unfair landholding system was at the root of the problem. They encouraged people to remain and retain their holdings. Parnell strongly criticised Tuke's scheme in December 1883 at the Parnell Banquet at the Rotunda hospital in Dublin. He said that it was useless for Tuke to present carefully selected accounts of the few emigrants that were successful because he had 'full and irresistible proof' that three out of four of the emigrants ended up in poverty in the big cities. He continued to say that, whatever Mr Tuke's personal motives were, 'the committee stand exposed as an indecent attempt to assist the government to get rid of the Irish difficulty by getting rid of the Irish people and shield that government from the

19. For example, *The Times*, 12 January; 29 January; 24 December 1883.
20. *The Times*, 5 February 1883.
21. G.P. Moran, *Sending out Ireland's Poor*, p. 187.

responsibility which rightly belongs to it of providing for the inhabitants of this country as long as it insists on the right to govern us'.[22]

Neither did the support and provision of funds by the British government help public opinion, providing as it did an easy target for the nationalist politicians,who described it as expulsion. In 1884 the Irish Parliamentary Party insisted that the official funds be divided between assisted emigration and migration within Ireland. Tuke's Committee did not feel that this would be of any real assistance to the families, and it reduced funding for their real scheme, which had worked quite successfully. He continued to publish letters from emigrants who praised the scheme and their new position in Canada. A major factor in the scheme's success was that the people of the West were receiving testimonials from their family and friends who had taken advantage of it extolling the opportunities, and encouraging others to go. They also sent home remittances, which were important in augmenting income for those that remained in Ireland. This did not prevent condemnation of the scheme in different quarters: it was due to the combined criticism in Ireland, Canada and North America that Tuke ended the emigration scheme in May 1884. His interest in Ireland did not end with this setback; in fact, over the following years he helped small numbers of people to emigrate but did not solicit government funding in any of the schemes.[23]

During the next agrarian crisis in 1886 the government decided against assisted emigration and instead undertook a policy of distributing seed potatoes. Tuke was asked to administer the scheme, which he agreed to but was very frustrated as he believed that a large proportion of the money was squandered by the Poor Law Guardians. The report on the 1886 relief measures found that in some Unions the number on relief in one district actually exceeded the population and that individuals who did not qualify for aid received it, thereby diminishing the benefits of the scheme.[24] Tuke maintained that no local board or authority could be trusted to handle relief funds fairly. While the scheme did assist the starving population, the change in policy was a disappointment to him.

22. From the *The Times*,11 December 1883 p. 6.
23. G.P. Moran, *Sending out Ireland's Poor*, pp. 186–7.
24. C. Breathnach, *The Congested Districts Board of Ireland 1891–1923: Poverty and Development in the West of Ireland* (Dublin: Four Courts, 2005) p. 23.

Figure 2.1
A young woman holding her baby, man in foreground, Tuke12

25. Ruttledge-Fair, in James Morrissey (ed.), *On the Verge of Want: A Unique Insight into the Living Conditions along Ireland's Western Seaboard in the Late Nineteenth Century* (Dublin: Cránnog Books, 2001) p. 103.
26. *The Times*, 1 October 1890 p. 3.
27. *The Times*, 27 March 1880 p. 4.

In 1892 Ruttledge-Fair reported that conditions had improved for the population of Belmullet following the emigration of 250 families under Tuke's scheme.[25] Approximately 9,000, or 17 per cent of the population, emigrated from Belmullet, Oughterard, Newport and Clifden between 1882 and1884.[26] As an abstract figure this was significant but it was not enough for the land to support the remaining population as it did not depopulate the congested areas sufficiently to vastly improve the quality of life. If the scheme had been able to continue for longer it may have had much more positive results for the communities remaining in Ireland, who were still farming very small plots of poor land. Tuke's description of farms in Donegal could equally be applied to the smallholdings and tenants in Mayo and Galway: 'little farms, wrung from the bog or from land covered with granite boulders, all testify to their willingness to work under the most adverse conditions of climate or soil'.[27]

The photographs in the Connemara Album illustrate the reality of trying to extract a living from a rocky, barren landscape. While the subjects are undoubtedly aware of the camera, the photographs differ from the idealised images of the peasant lifestyle that were produced by other pictures of the period. There was a huge amount of daily hard labour involved in trying to make a livelihood from the few natural resources available, for example cutting and carrying turf, drawing dung for fuel, collecting seaweed to fertilise the land so that some crops could be grown for sustenance, or collecting a small amount of fish. It is obvious from the photographs that they had very little in the way of tools or equipment, or many household animals, to assist their work. The caption on the reverse of Figure 2.2 states that they had twelve carts between four hundred families. The Album contains many illustrations of women carrying heavy loads of dung, turf or seaweed in creels on their back. The captions describe these as 'unnatural burdens', contrasting with Figure 2.1, an image of a mother carrying a child, captioned 'mother with her natural burden'. These images suggest that the majority of the hard labour involved in transporting the few natural resources available was undertaken by women. The few males featured are leading the carts or working the land alongside women.

Figure 2.2
Carting turf, Tuke20

Figure 2.3
Women carrying baskets of seaweed, Tuke43

The struggle against the limitations of the land and the labour undertaken by the women is emphasised in a comment by Tuke in 1882. He describes a scene where huts on small plots are scattered across the stony landscape and the cultivation is only possible through the fertilisation or dressing of the land with seaweed '… and just as far as the hard working Connemara woman can carry her heavy creel of seaweed, or the ass or small horse can find its way among the bog and stones. So far and no further has the cultivation gone.'[28] This is illustrated in Figure 2.3, a photograph of women carrying baskets of seaweed. Its annotation describes the scene: 'It is drawing weed they are. The baskets weigh 2 [cwt?] each and must be carried distances from the sea varying from fifty yards to half a mile.'

The poverty of the people can be clearly seen in the photographs in the Connemara Album: they could not provide part funding for emigration, or indeed in most cases even afford the

28. Tuke, 'MrTuke's Fund' p. 69

Figure 2.4 Galway Bay from Spiddal (Tuke32)

Figure 2.5 People gathered at stone wall (Tuke7)

cost of the transport to the port in Galway or to purchase the necessary clothes for the journey. Figure 2.4, entitled 'Galway Bay from Spiddal', is captioned 'the Big Steamer on her way
to Galway to take in emigrants'. The process of migration is also captured in Figure 2.5, 'captioned' 'the Emigration Shawl', which depicts a group of people, including a young girl wearing what appears to be a new shawl acquired in advance of her departure. Even though the
assisted scheme had stopped, emigration to North America and Canada continued to take
place, with the help of remittances and income from seasonal earnings.

The coastal location of Connemara meant that the sea was an obvious source of employment
and sustenance, but it was underutilised. A woman collecting fish by the shore is illustrated in
Figure 2.6, which suggests that equipment was quite basic. There are several photographs of
men in currachs but the boats seem to be used for transport rather than fishing. A major imped-
iment was the lack of safe harbours so the CDB fostered the fishing industry through the construction of harbours and teaching of the necessary skills.

Despite disappointments Tuke retained his interest in the economic reform of the West of

Figure 2.6 A woman collecting fish (Tuke4)   **Figure 2.7** Galway mail car (Tuke21)

Ireland. The period from 1887 to August 1891 saw him in close contact with Arthur Balfour, Lord Lieutenant of Ireland, who during this period drew up the legislation that came to shape the CDB. Tuke expressed his views through letters to *The Times* to raise awareness and encourage support for the new legislation.[29] Balfour was not popular amongst the Irish nationalists, who perhaps regarded the new legislation with scepticism, seeing it as part of constructive unionism attempting to kill nationalism with kindness. Balfour was of the opinion that, if the economic welfare of the tenants improved, then interest might be lost in the nationalist cause as organisations such as the Land League and the Irish Parliamentary Party drew on the discontent surrounding the land question and poverty to gain support. He may also have felt forced into action as several distinguished persons, including Tuke, were writing and publishing on the

29. For example, *The Times*, 20, 27 May; 29 June 1889.

Figure 2.8
Laying the foundations for a new pier (Tuke28)

terrible conditions and suffering experienced in the West of Ireland. It is likely that Balfour saw the success of the emigration scheme and thought that something more constructive and economical than poor relief could be implemented; in this he was probably influenced by Tuke's opinions.

In 1889 Balfour requested that Tuke and Ruttledge-Fair carry out a detailed study of suitable lines for a light railway system in the West of Ireland. They were selected to prepare the report as their long involvement with the communities indicated they could obtain information locally that other officials could not. For Tuke such a railway infrastructure was a necessary precursor to the development of industries, including fisheries. There was no point in producing goods that could not be transported efficiently out of the regions with the additional benefit that the construction and operation of the railway would provide employment. He applauded this development, even going so far as to describe the passing of the Act to Facilitate the Construction of Light Railways in Ireland as 'a red letter day'.[30] Railways were only part of the required infrastructure.

30. Sir Edward Fry, *James Hack Tuke: A Memoir* (London: Macmillan,1899) p. 265.

New roads and bridges were necessary too, and updated modes of transport: for example, Figure 2.7 is entitled 'Galway mail car', with a note on the reverse stating 'the mail car from Galway – quite a modern institution – 1892'; and Figure 2.8 shows the building of the central pier of a bridge.

The close relationship between Tuke and successive governments may have damaged the nationalists' opinion of him to some degree. In an article entitled 'Remedies for Irish Distress' Michael Davitt described him as the mouthpiece for Her Majesty's Government. He was writing in response to a letter by Tuke published in *The Times* on 15 October 1890. Davitt objected to Tuke's assisted emigration schemes, stating that plans to emigrate families would be met with 'bitterness and opposition'.[31] He criticised Tuke's comment that the abject poverty in Ireland was an evil that no political measure could remedy and that it would occur under British or Irish rule.[32]

The Congested Districts Board was established as part of the Purchase of Land (Ireland) Act 1891, also known as the Balfour Act.[33] The CDB had powers to amalgamate holdings, fund migration and emigration from the congested districts, encourage agriculture, fisheries and local industry, and improve housing and sanitation. The term congested meant overpopulated, but not in the usual sense of high population density. Rather it indicated that the population was too high for the productivity of the area, that there was a lack of arable land, resources and industry to support the inhabitants, and that the rateable value was less than 30s. per person. The Act constituted an economic development plan for the poor western regions, aimed at creating self-sufficiency and reducing the threat of famine. It covered districts in nine counties. Although the committee members were appointed by the Lord Lieutenant the CDB was somewhat unusual in having quite a degree of autonomy from Westminster, Dublin Castle and from the local Poor Law Union Guardians. It was deliberately set up in this manner by Balfour to ensure that this independent status would encourage indigenous acceptance of the board. One of the first actions of the board was to have baseline reports drawn up to establish the economic

31. *Contemporary Review*, vol. 57, 1890, p. 631.
32. *The Times*, 1 October 1890, p. 3.
33. 54 & 55 Vict. c.48 [5 Aug 1891].

condition of each of the eighty-four districts in the West designated as congested. The questions, or headings of enquiry, used to compile the baseline reports were drafted by Tuke and Ruttledge-Fair.[34]

The provisions of the Act clearly reflected Tuke's long held aims and beliefs regarding what was necessary to improve the situation in the west of Ireland. Along with William Micks, a local government inspector, Tuke provided a range of economic data to help shape the legislation. He was overjoyed with the provisions of the Act, describing them as 'most remarkable and important measures for the congested districts'.[35] On 29 October 1892 Balfour requested that Tuke accept appointment as a Commissioner of the CDB. The committee members were selected from a divergent political and social background and because of their familiarity with Irish social and economic issues.[36] Tuke became a member of three out of the four committees set up under the new Board, the industries, fisheries and land committees. As Tuke died in 1896 he was not involved in the CDB for very long, but it must have given him great satisfaction to see his ideas for economic reform put into practice by the government and the committees.

Interestingly, in 1891 Horace Plunkett prepared a report for the CDB on the usefulness of assisted emigration; although he recommended that it be adopted, it was not pursued. The old prejudices were still apparent and, given the rising levels of sectarianism following the Parnellite split, such a project would never gain support. The CBD facilitated a degree of migration within Ireland, whereby people were moved to a new locality and provided with new concrete-built houses with slate roofs.

The CDB operated until 1923, when it was replaced by the Land Commission. In some ways it was ahead of its time in assisting the development of regions that had poor agricultural land and little industry to support their population. The CDB improved harbour safety, transport links and housing, while creating new industry in areas that had very little economic support. Some projects were successful and it was generally popular in the regions where it carried out work. It has been criticised by some historians because most of the industry was subsidised and

34. Breathnach, *The Congested Districts Board*, p. 36.
35. Sir Edward Fry, *James Hack Tuke*, p. 267.
36. Breathnach, *The Congested Districts Board*, p. 31.

could not survive competitively. Lee, for example, is very critical of the CDB's approach, describing the work as a waste of effort and money. He suggests that, if the funds had been used to develop industry in more suitable locations on the east coast, then the migration out of the congested districts would have happened naturally.[37] Further, it was not until the Land Act of 1903 that a large proportion of landlords sold the land to their tenants and essentially created an owner-occupier system of land ownership to replace the traditional system of tenurial holdings. If Balfour's aim in setting up the CDB was indeed to kill nationalism with kindness then he failed because it did not stop support for the nationalist cause. Balfour had seen first hand the dreadful poverty and living conditions during a tour of Galway and Donegal in 1890, in his capacity as Lord Lieutenant. Though it is entirely possible that Balfour created the CDB mainly for political reasons, there can be few doubts about the sincerity of feeling that Tuke had for Ireland and his belief that the encouragement of industry and the improvement of transport links could benefit the economic situation.

The Balfour Album[38] (see Chapter 3) is a collection of photographs of Connemara compiled for Balfour by grateful locals after the passing of the Light Railways Act; the content differs greatly from that of the Tuke Album. It contains mainly scenic tourist views and does not focus on the hardship of daily life but there are a few photographs of the local population, including some of the men at work constructing the railway built under the Act. The pictures were taken by Robert Welch, who was formally commissioned by the CDB in June 1914 to photograph the congested districts.[39] The photographs are an interesting companion piece to the Tuke Album images as they illustrate the improvements that had been made in terms of housing, the fishing industry and its ancillary businesses, and the availability of healthcare through visiting nurses. They do not have the same human element as the Tuke images, which possibly reflect his specific interest in the welfare of the people of the West.

It is interesting that the CDB images were specially commissioned, as it seems strange that Tuke did not use photographs as a tool during his campaign to heighten awareness of the terrible

37. J. Lee, *Modernisation of Irish Society 1848–1918* (Dublin: Gill & Macmillan, 1989), p.p. 124–5.
38. Balfour Album, NUI, Galway, James Hardiman Library Special Collections.
39. National Photographic Archive.

conditions in the West of Ireland. An interesting comparison is the Report of the Mansion House Committee published in 1898,[40] which is illustrated by photographs of destitute people in squalid cabins and involved in relief work. The pictures are very pathetic in tone and were obviously intended to arouse sympathy and support. However they have a contrived feel to them and are not as engaging as those in the Tuke Album, which seem more realistic and create the impression that the people of Connemara were hardworking and not simply seeking handouts.

The fact that the photographs in Tuke's Connemara Album were never published would suggest that Ruttledge-Fair created it as a personal memento for Tuke and not as part of his more official duties as a local government inspector. He worked for the CDB writing the baseline reports for Mayo, among other areas, and was in the West compiling these reports in the districts of Achill, Belmullet, Carna, Clifden, Letterfrack and other areas in the spring and summer of 1892. It is likely that the photographs were taken during the time when Ruttledge-Fair was compiling the reports, perhaps during one of Tuke's two visits to the West in that year.

W.L. Micks, Secretary to the CDB, described Tuke as generous and self-sacrificing, and said that given his long involvement in Ireland his opinion was sought by governments of all political views:

> Mr Tuke's published writings show that, for the improvement of the congested districts, he relied upon the extension of railways and other communications, and upon the development of the industrial and natural resources of the country. His name became widely known in connection with an emigration project about the year 1883, ... But he assisted people to leave Ireland in search of employment in foreign countries only because at that time no employment existed at home, ...[41]

Tuke invested much time and energy in the cause of improving life for the poor in the West

40. Daniel Tallon, *Distress in the West and South of Ireland 1898: Report on the Work of the Mansion House Committee* (Dublin, 1898).

41. W.L. Micks, *An account of the constitution, administration and dissolution of the Congested Districts Board for Ireland 1891–1923* (Dublin: Eason & Son, 1925), p. 174.

of Ireland, and despite the criticism he received it would be difficult to fault his dedication. There can be little doubt of the sincerity of feeling that he had for Ireland and of his belief that the encouragement of industry and the improvement of transport infrastructure could improve economic conditions. The degree of poverty that Tuke witnessed in Ireland affected him greatly: 'when once really seen and realised [it] can never, as it seems to me, be effaced from the mind or be banished until some step has been taken to attempt to relieve or diminish this mess of human degradation'.[42] He succeeded in bringing the situation to a wide audience in Ireland and Great Britain through his publishing, canvassing, fundraising and his emigration scheme. Through many of these efforts he was ably assisted by Major Ruttledge-Fair. The end of Tuke's assisted emigration scheme in 1884, despite his hard work countering the criticism levelled against it, must have come as a great disappointment; the creation of the Congested Districts Board, which embodied so many of his ideas, and his short involvement in the organisation must have brought him some satisfaction.

42. *The Times*, 12 January 1883.

CHAPTER THREE

Tools of the Tourist Trade: The Photography of R.J. Welch in the Tourist Literature of Late-Nineteenth and Early-Twentieth Century Connemara and the West

MARIE BORAN

1. Some examples of Welch's work have been chosen to illustrate this contribution. All but one are featured in the Balfour Album, although all are also to be found in other collections of Welch's photographs, most notably that in the Ulster Museum.

2. Kevin O'Connor (ed., *Ironing the land: The Coming of the Railways to Ireland* (Dublin: Gill and Macmillan, 1999), p. 78.

It will be clear from the essays and illustrations thoughout this volume that R.J. Welch's photographic subject range was extensive. One of the applications with which he is most closely associated is the illustration of tourist literature. The peak of his career as a photographer coincided with an expansion in visitors' opportunities to travel to all parts of Ireland but especially the hitherto relatively remote areas of the western seaboard. A perusal of illustrated tourist guides published for these areas between 1899 and 1920 shows that they frequently include photographs taken by Welch. Copies of his photographs were also available from commercial agents and from his own business in Belfast. They were often used to create presentation albums such as the Balfour Album, to be discussed later, which also provides us with an insight into his work. This contribution will examine the role of these publications and the employment of Welch's illustrative photography, principally in marketing the West of Ireland as a tourist destination.[1]

The Midland and Great Western Railway Company had concentrated its efforts from the mid-1840s on developing a rail line to Galway. The line was extended to Athlone and, following the construction of the major bridge over the Shannon, finally reached Galway. The rail link between the east and west of Ireland opened on 1 August 1851.[2] The coming of the railway had a major impact on tourism in the West. Within a few years several guidebooks had been published outlining the glories that visitors could enjoy by travelling to Galway on the new rail link

Figure 3.1
Construction of the Galway-Clifden railway at Recess, 1894 (*Balfour Album*, James Hardiman Library Special Collections, NUI, Galway)

and then using a variety of conveyances to bring them through Connemara. A notable variation on road transport is that mentioned in Black's *Guide to Galway and Connemara*, published in 1877, which suggests taking a steamer from Galway to Oughterard or Cong.[3] The extension of the railway to Westport in 1866 and Ballina in 1873 created further scope for round trips, allowing visitors to arrive at Galway, be conveyed through Connemara to Westport and onwards to North Mayo, from where they could return to Dublin by train.

Further major development in the transportation of tourists in Connemara occurred in 1890 with the decision finally to build a railway line to Clifden. This idea had been mooted earlier and major planning had taken place in the late 1870s and early 1880s but lack of investment capital had prevented the project going ahead.[4] Its construction was one of the causes championed by Arthur Balfour in his role as Chief Secretary for Ireland and funding

3. Black's *Guide to Galway, Connemara, the Shannon and Lough Erne* (Edinburgh, Black, 1877), p. 277.
4. See *Galway, Oughterard & Clifden Tramway and Light Railway Company Ltd Papers*, James Hardiman Library Archives, Galway.

5. Kathleen Villiers-Tuthill, *Beyond the Twelve Bens: A History of Clifden and District, 1860–1923*. (Clifden: Published by the author, 1990). pp. 93–4.

6. Ibid., pp. 96–8.

7. Ulster Museum, Belfast. R.J. Welch collection, Diaries, 1894.

8. Balfour Album, James Hardiman Library Special Collections, NUI, Galway. The Album, as well as a set of copies of the plates, may be viewed by prior arrangement with the Special Collections staff. For a more detailed account of the Balfour Album, see Marie Boran, 'The Ireland That We Made: A Galway Tribute to Arthur J. Balfour', *Journal of the Galway Archaeological & Historical Society*, LIV (2002), pp. 168–174.

9. See Roger Dixon, *Marcus Ward & Co, Belfast* (Belfast: Belfast Education and Library Board, 2004).

10. Balfour Album.

11. For further information on his involvement in the IFCU, see Chapters 1 and 6.

became available as a result. Balfour had made an extensive tour of Connemara in 1889, which convinced him that this was a necessary project.[5] Work commenced in 1893 and, at its peak, 1,500 men were employed on the Clifden line.[6] The building of the railway would have been underway when R.J. Welch made his first visit to Connemara in 1894 and it is likely that he took photographs, including that of the construction work at Recess, on that occasion[7]. The photograph in Figure 3.1 later appears as Plate 8 in the album of Welch's work that has become known to us as the Balfour Album, held in the Special Collections of the James Hardiman Library, NUI, Galway.[8] The Album was acquired by the Library in 1987 from the descendants of Arthur Balfour, who felt that it more appropriately belonged in the West of Ireland. Though representing the earlier phase of R.J. Welch's career, it is a significant example of his work, containing as it does elements of the various types of photography in which he excelled.

The Album contains fifty plates of Welch's work with their captions in calligraphy. Its superb binding is by the renowned Belfast firm of Marcus Ward, one of the leading decorative bookbinding companies in the United Kingdom at that time.[9] The Album was presented to Arthur Balfour in June 1896 as a tribute from people in Connemara for their railway. Those who contributed to the Album are listed in the illuminated address to Balfour, the fine artwork of which can probably be attributed to John Vinycombe, the Artistic Director at Marcus Ward. Prominent among the contributors are members of the local landed gentry, Poor Law Guardians and local clergy of various denominations.[10] It seems likely that Welch's work, as depicted in the Album, comes from both his earlier trip in 1894 and a later trip, in July 1895, which he took with other members of the Irish Field Club Union (IFCU).[11] These annual meetings were meticulously planned and organised beforehand, principally by the leading Irish botanist of the day, Robert L. Praeger.[12] Evidence elsewhere indicates that Praeger and F.J. Biggar was also in this group.[13] Some of the photographs that were later used to illustrate the beauties of Connemara and the activities it had to offer were probably taken at this time or during the IFCU excursion the following year. Notable in this regard are the series of photographs of Ben Lettery and the section of the Twelve Bens known today as the Glen Coaghan horseshoe. There is a particularly fine depiction of a party of ladies and gentlemen ascending Ben an Saighdiúr. The account of the IFCU excursion certainly indicates that some of the party visited this area. Mountain walking was becoming a popular pastime among the middle and upper classes in all parts of Europe, including Ireland, during this period.[14] We know from other accounts that hill and mountain walking were widely enjoyed in Connemara at this time. Indeed, shortly afterwards, in 1905, a Scottish lady is alleged to have fallen to her death from a spot in the Maamturk mountains, an event commemorated in the place name, Áille na Lady.[15]

A number of the photographs in the Balfour Album also appear in the revised edition of the Midland and Great Western Railway Company's *Handbook to Connemara, Galway, Achill and the West of Ireland*, published in 1900 and sold for 6d.[16] The *Handbook* contains forty-two photographic plates, twenty-eight of which are by Welch. Most of the remaining plates are by the Lawrence Studio, Dublin, with one by the Roche Studio, Dublin. The subject matter of Welch's photographs in the *Handbook* is unsurprising when taken in the context of his output in general. While a number, such as Lough Shindilla or the Twelve Bens, are landscapes, many are more specific in their focus. All of the photographs of archaeological remains are the work of Welch. As the *Handbook* also includes descriptions of places to visit while travelling to and from the West the archaeological photographs include plates of Sligo Abbey and the castles at Trim, County Meath, and Cloghoughter, County Cavan. The *Handbook* includes a chapter on Galway with recommendations for trips to the Aran Islands and a voyage on Lough Corrib. There are no photographic plates illustrating this chapter, which is surprising since evidence

12. For examples of Praeger's interest in visiting all parts of Ireland, see R.L. Praeger, *The Way that I Went*. (Dublin: Hodges, Figgis & Co, 1937) and *Official Guide to County Down and the Mourne Mountains* (Belfast: Marcus Ward, 1898). See also Timothy Collins, 'Praeger in the West: Naturalists and Antiquarians in Connemara and the Islands, 1894–1914', *Journal of the Galway Archaeological & Historical Society*, XLV (1993), pp. 124–54.

13. Collins, 'Praeger in the West', p. 127.

14. See for example Fergus Fleming, *Killing Dragons: The Conquest of the Alps* (London: Granta Books, 2000) and Ronald Clark, *Men, Myths and Mountains* (London: Weidenfeld & Nicholson, 1976).

15. Tim Robinson, *Connemara: Map and Gazetteer* (Galway: Folding Landscapes, 1990), p. 104

16. Midland and Great Western Railway Company, *Ireland from Sea to Sea: A Practical Handbook to Galway, Connemara, Achill and the* Cont.

Cont.
   West of Ireland, new rev.
   ed. (Dublin: Browne &
   Nolan, 1900) [hereafter
   MGWR Handbook]. There
   were no Welch plates in
   the first edition, which had
   appeared in 1896. The
   revised edition is slightly
   bigger, at 135 pages with
   additional advertisements,
   but has many more plates.
17. Boran, 'Ireland That We
   Made'.
18. E.OE Somerville and
   Martin Ross, *Through
   Connemara in a Governess
   Cart* (London: W.H. Allen,
   1893).
19. Somerville and Ross,
   Through Connemara, p.
   41–2.

from the Balfour Album indicates that Welch had splendid photographs from all three locations.[17] In particular, the photographs he took of the archaeological remains on the island of Inchagoill, in Lough Corrib, are among the first photographic representations of them.

Guidebooks, like tourist guides today, concentrated on the travel and accommodation arrangements available to the visitor as well as the noteworthy sights that each locality offered. Earlier visitors to Connemara had left descriptions of this kind after holidaying there. Even the semi-fictitious account of a holiday in Connemara that has come down to us in the writings of Edith Somerville and Violet Martin cannot altogether be dismissed. Written as it was just before the arrival of the railway, it gives us some insight into the experiences that contemporary travellers to the area were likely to enjoy, or the reverse![18]

> Our only information as to the hotels of Connemara had been gathered from a gentleman whose experience dated some thirty years back … As to the bedrooms, our friend had been most discouraging … [asserting that on requesting bed and breakfast] the door opened and a feather bed bulged though the narrow doorway into the room, and was spread on the floor by the table …[19]

Thankfully the ladies were to discover that matters had much improved in the intervening period and the greatest inconvenience they were called upon to endure were the endless conversations on fishing among their fellow guests at the Royal Hotel in Recess.

The strategic inclusion of Welch's photographs in tourist handbooks, to entice visitors to avail themselves of new and improved accommodation was a clever marketing policy on the part of hoteliers and rail companies; as time went on details of entertainment were incorporated into the literature. For example, the handbooks show photographs of hotels that were either owned by the railway company or with which they had formed strategic partnerships. Leenane, for instance, is thus described in the *Handbook to Connemara*:

Figure 3.2
The Corrib Railway Bridge 1895 (Balfour Album, James
Hardiman Library Special Collections, NUI, Galway)

Leenane, as far as the tourist is concerned, is the Leenane Hotel, connected with which is
a useful general shop, which is also the Post and Telegraph Office … the prudent traveller
should bespeak [book ahead] accommodation, since the most enterprising of landlords is
often at his wit's end when the coaches bring their loads of would-be guests unannounced.[20]

Biographers of R.J. Welch have indicated his interest in using his photographs to promote
the interests of tourism in Ireland to the extent that he designed his own tourist brochures,
illustrated by his photographs and containing annotations on local sights in his own hand.[21]
Photographs such as 'A Connemara long car' (Figure 3.3) fulfil many of Welch's objectives since
they illustrate the magnificence of the landscape, its natural features and the activities that the
tourist could hope to enjoy while visiting the area. The promotion of Connemara and other
areas also featured in Welch's publicity and advertising material.[22]

20. MGWR *Handbook*, p. 78.
21. E. Estyn Evans and Brian
Turner, *Ireland's Eye: The
Photographs of Robert John
Welch* (Belfast: Blackstaff
Press, 1977).
22. Evans, and Turner *Ireland's
Eye.* p. 5.

The plate 'Construction of the Galway–Clifden railway at Recess' (Figure 3.1) perhaps best illustrates the Balfour Album's purpose. This image shows approximately fifteen men working on the section of the line close to Recess station. We can deduce from the timescale and evidence from Welch's diaries that the photograph must have been taken during his first visit to Connemara in 1894 since, by the time he returned in 1895, the line had opened to rail traffic. Other photographs in the Balfour Album portraying the railway are views of the magnificent metal bridge constructed to carry the railway across the Corrib at Woodquay in Galway (Figure 3.2) Plates 3, 4 and 50 depict this bridge from various angles, including from inside the bridge itself.

In view of the fact that the Album was a gift to Arthur Balfour it is somewhat surprising that these photographs are the only depictions of the railway line that are featured in the Album. Other collections of Welch's photographs held in various repositories, however, appear to include other photographs of the line. Six stations were constructed during the building of the line: at Moycullen, Ross, Oughterard, Recess, Ballyinahinch and Clifden. All of the buildings, with the exception of Maam Cross station which is derelict, still survive, being used either as private dwellings or business premises. The illuminated address at the beginning of the Balfour Album gives us some idea of the expectations of people in Galway and Connemara regarding the economic improvements the railway would produce. It states:

> 'Differ as we may among ourselves as to political creeds we all cordially unite in offering to you our best thanks for the great service that you have done for us. You have put this country on the high road to prosperity and contentment, if its people will devote their best energies to practical industry and the development of its natural resources which have too long laid waste'.[23]

The service which operated for only forty years never produced the economic success so confidently predicted by the Balfour Album's sponsors: the railway was unable to compete with the

23. Balfour Album.

Figure 3.3
A Connemara Long Car (*Balfour Album*, James Hardiman Library
Special Collections, NUI, Galway)

coming of motorised road traffic. Nonetheless, while it existed it was a major benefit to the people of North Connemara, who could now trade more readily with and travel to Galway and from there to anywhere else in Ireland by rail. At peak service three trains a day travelled on the line in each direction. The first left Galway at 7.20 a.m., while a train departed from Clifden at 7.45 a.m. Initially some of the trains took up to three hours to arrive at their destination but this improved as time went on.[24]

Plate 7 of the Balfour Album 'A Connemara long car' (Figure 3.3) is a fine example of Welch's sense of context, a depiction of the means of transport as well as the spectacular scenery through which it travelled. The 'long car' was a ubiquitous vehicle in the West of Ireland until the advent of motor transport. A regular service operated between Galway and Clifden before the coming of the railway.[25] The entry in the 1856 edition of Slater's *Commercial Directory* indicates that Bianconi's car travelled to Galway every day except Sunday, starting from Carr's Hotel in Clifden at 9 a.m. A car also went in the opposite direction, departing Galway at 9.30 a.m. A mail

24. I am grateful to Mr Timothy Moriarty, Hon. Librarian, Irish Railway Record Society, for providing me with this information from the extensive collection of timetables in the Society's Library at Heuston Station, Dublin.

25. See *Slater's Commercial Directory*, 1846, 1856 and 1895.

car left Galway at 1.30 a.m. every morning, while one went to Oughterard from Clifden every afternoon at 4 p.m. Somerville and Ross, in their account of travelling in Connemara, published in 1893, describe their journey from Galway to Oughterard on a mail car:

> We had been assured, on reliable authority, that Oughterard, fourteen Irish miles from Galway, was the place we would find what we wanted, and with a dubious faith we climbed the steep side of the mail car, and wedged ourselves between a stout priest and an English tourist. Above us towered the mail baskets, and a miscellaneous pile of luggage … [the mail car] is large enough to hold six people on each side and is dragged by three horses at a speed that takes no account of ruts and piles of stones and sharp corners, or that fact that the unstable passenger has nothing to grasp at in time of need, except his equally unstable fellow-traveller.[26]

It was also possible for tourists to hire such vehicles with a driver, allowing them to arrange their own itinerary and timetable, which may have been the case with the group depicted in Figure 3.3. The *Galway Vindicator* newspaper reported on the travels of such a group visiting Galway in 1896, describing the sites they visited, such as Inchagoill and Ross Errily abbey near Headford, as well as their stay in the Railway Hotel in Galway.[27] The photograph was taken close to Lough Shindillagh, on the road between Maam Cross and Recess. In his composition Welch captures the lake and Corcóg mountain. Both were encouragements to tourists to enjoy fishing or hill walking while visiting the area. Welch's skill in perfecting his compositions is highlighted.[28] He was careful to ensure that his work was always identifiable as he realised its value.

Welch's photograph, of the Leenane Hotel (Figure 3.4), while not included in the Balfour Album, was one of a series that he took depicting the modern and commodious hotels that had been built in Connemara during the latter decades of the nineteenth century. Several were used

26. Somerville and Ross, *Through Connemara*. p. 24.
27. *Galway Vindicator*, August 1896.
28. For further information on how Welch composed his images see Chapter 5.

in the railway company's *Handbook*.[29] Such establishments catered in particular for those engaging in the tourist pursuits, especially angling, for which Connemara was famous as is demonstrated by the following extract from Somerville and Ross's account of their stay in the Leenane Hotel in 1893:

> It was strange to feel at this hotel, – as, indeed, at all the others we stayed at – that we were almost the only representatives of our country, and casting our minds back though the maze of English faces and Babel of English voices that had been the accompaniment of our meals for the last fortnight, two painful conclusions were forced on us; first, that the Irish people have no money to tour with; second, that it was Saxon influence and support alone that evoluted the Connemara hotels from the primitive feather-bed alluded to earlier.[30]

Figure 3.4
Leenane Hotel (MGWR *Handbook*, 2nd edition, 1900)

Figure 3.5
The Limpet Shell midden Dog's Bay (*Balfour Album*, James Hardiman Library Special Collections, NUI, Galway)

29. Other hotels depicted include those at Clifden and Galway.
30. Somerville and Ross, *Through Connemara*, p. 182.

Mr McKeon, the proprietor, was, in the days before mass advertising campaigns, an innovative and forward-thinking character. His facilities were sufficiently regarded by the railway company to be included in the second edition of the *Handbook* despite the fact that his hotel was at least thirteen miles by road from the railway station at Maam Cross. It was also noted that he converted Doolough Lodge, on the shores of Doolough, some miles from Leenane, into a hotel as well.[31]

Natural phenomena fascinated Welch, especially the seashore and its myriad life forms, (Figure 3.5). from biographical information we know that this was one of Welch's life long interests.[32] Plate 18, for example, is a fine study entitled the 'The Limpet shell midden, Dog's Bay'. Welch's own scientific preoccupations are very successfully demonstrated in a significant number of pictures in the Balfour Album highlighting either natural history or archaeological subjects. This photograph of a prehistorc 'kitchen midden' of limpet shells exemplifies how Connemara was regarded as a rich source for the study of both subjects. Welch's photographs, as well as providing accurate depictions of monuments and sites, encouraged like-minded tourists to travel to see them. The photographs of archaeological remains on the island of Inchagoill in Lough Corrib are of special importance as the earliest photographic depictions of these monuments. Inchogoill was a favourite destination for visitors interested in archaeology or natural history. The appeal of sites like Dog's Bay to naturalists is evident from the accounts of trips to the West of Ireland organised by groups such as the IFCU, which have been documented by Timothy Collins.[33] The caption to the Balfour Album photograph of the IFCU landing at Arranmore specifically mentions that this excursion was to take advantage of the new railway. Trips organised by such learned societies provided safe opportunities for travel to hitherto remote regions, especially for women. Rosamund Praeger, sister of R.L. Praeger, was one of the party visiting Connemara in the mid-1890s, as is evidenced by her sketch of Welch attempting to cope with the Connemara climate in his photographic endeavours (Figure 1.7).[34] Organisations such as the IFCU and the Belfast Naturalists' Field Club provided Welch and others with opportunities for publishing. The latter society, for example, produced a comprehensive hand-

31. MGWR *Handbook*, p.80.
32. W.A. Maguire, *A Century in Focus: Photographs and Photographers in the North of Ireland, 1839–1939* (Belfast: Blackstaff, 2000); Evans and Turner, *Ireland's Eye*.
33. Collins. 'Praeger in the West'.
34. Evans and Turner, *Ireland's Eye*. p. 17.

book entitled *Belfast and the Counties of Antrim and Down* in 1902, on the occasion of the visit to Belfast of the British Association for Advancement of Science.[35] This latter publication contains twenty-three plates by Welch illustrating chapters on antiquities, botany and geology.

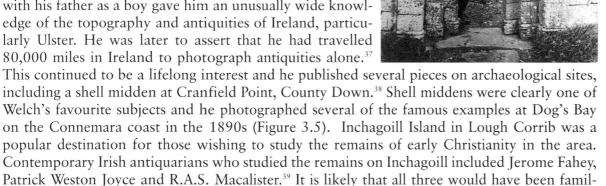

Figure 3.6
Cyclopean door and masonry at Temple Phaidrig Inchangoil (5th or 6th century) (*Balfour Album*, James Hardiman Library Special Collections, NUI, Galway)

There is also much evidence for the photography of antiquarian remains in Welch's work. Since the publication of the Earl of Dunraven's *Notes on Irish Architecture* in 1875, the use of photography in the study of what were essentially archaeological monuments had been developing.[36] As W.A. Maguire has pointed out, Welch's excursions with his father as a boy gave him an unusually wide knowledge of the topography and antiquities of Ireland, particularly Ulster. He was later to assert that he had travelled 80,000 miles in Ireland to photograph antiquities alone.[37] This continued to be a lifelong interest and he published several pieces on archaeological sites, including a shell midden at Cranfield Point, County Down.[38] Shell middens were clearly one of Welch's favourite subjects and he photographed several of the famous examples at Dog's Bay on the Connemara coast in the 1890s (Figure 3.5). Inchagoill Island in Lough Corrib was a popular destination for those wishing to study the remains of early Christianity in the area. Contemporary Irish antiquarians who studied the remains on Inchagoill included Jerome Fahey, Patrick Weston Joyce and R.A.S. Macalister.[39] It is likely that all three would have been familiar with the work of R.J. Welch.

The examples here provide only a flavour of Welch's photography, particularly as regards attracting tourists to Galway and Connemara. His involvement with the railway companies, notably the Midland and Great Western Railway, provided him with a significant showcase for

35. Belfast Naturalists' Field Club. *Belfast and the Counties of Antrim and Down* (Belfast: McCaw, Stephenson and Orr, 1902).
36. Earl of Dunraven, *Notes on Irish Architecture* (London: G. Bell, 1875–7).
37. Maguire, *Century in Focus.*, p. 88.
38. R. Welch, 'Kitchen-midden at Cranfield Point, County Down', *JRSAI*, 16 (1906), p. 85.
39. Jerome Fahey, 'The Shrines of Inis-an-Ghoill, Lough Corrib', *JRSAI*, 11 (1904), pp. 236–45; P.W. Joyce. 'On the Headstone of Lugna, or Lugnaed, St. Patrick's Nephew, in the Island of Inchagoill, in Lough Corrib', *JRSAI*, 16 (1906), pp. 1–10; R.A.S. Macalister, 'The Inchagoill Inscription, Lough Corrib, Co.Galway' *JRSAI*, 16 (1906), pp. 297–302.

his output. The impact on potential tourists of pictures as well as words was not lost on those marketing the railway company's services. The second edition of the Midland and Great Western Railway company's *Handbook to Connemara* contains many more photographs than the first, published only four years earlier in 1896. Two thirds were taken by Welch.

It is clear that he derived enjoyment as well as professional advancement from his visits to Connemara and the West. Perhaps the most important and far-reaching commission he was to undertake there was his involvement, between 1909 and 1911, with the Clare Island Survey, sponsored by the Royal Irish Academy, of which he was a member. This has been described as the most ambitious natural history project ever undertaken in Ireland. Welch was part of a team of experts in the fields of archaeology, botany, geology and zoology, who carried out the first comprehensive survey of a specific land area. The monumental three-volume work published as a result remains one of the great achievements of early twentieth-century Irish scientific publishing.[40] As with the Balfour Album, the many photographs in the Clare Island Survey publication contributed by R.J. Welch are a testament to his dedication and his appreciation of the unique natural surroundings to be found in Connemara and the West.

40. Royal Irish Academy, *A Biological Survey of Clare Island in the County of Mayo and of the Adjoining District*, Vols I–III (Dublin: Hodges, Figgis and Co, 1911–15).

CHAPTER FOUR   # Ireland – in Birmingham

MAGGIE BURNS
Librarian in Local Studies and History, Birmingham Central Library

It may seem strange that Birmingham Central Library, in the English West Midlands, holds a large collection of photographs of Ireland from about a century ago. Many people came to Birmingham from Ireland during the nineteenth century, some to flee the Famine, some to set up highly successful businesses, such as the newspaper proprietor John Feeney, who founded the *Birmingham Post* in 1857. But the collection of more than six hundred Irish photographs in the library does not owe its existence to the Irish in Birmingham, but to a local Conservative MP, Sir John Benjamin Stone.[1]

The Irish photographs are part of the Sir Benjamin Stone Collection, presented by Stone's trustees to Birmingham Public Libraries in 1921. The entire collection comprises some 22,000 mounted prints, along with 17,000 surviving glass negatives for the photographs that Stone took himself (he also purchased many images from commercial photographers worldwide). In addition, there are over six hundred stereoscopic prints and more than a hundred albums of commercial prints and newscuttings. The entire collection has been filmed and can be viewed on microfiche in the Local Studies and History section of the Central Library. The Irish collection includes photographs by the Belfast photographer Robert Welch, which Stone had purchased in 1904, and Stone's own photographs taken in 1899 when he visited the South of Ireland.

Stone was born in Aston, just north of the centre of Birmingham, in 1838. He went to the free grammar school, King Edward's, which was then in New Street in the centre of the city. His father was a glass manufacturer; J.B. Stone went into the business and eventually succeeded his

1. It is not always possible to give a precise source or date for newspaper cuttings, of which Sir J.B. Stone made a very large collection. While he was meticulous about recording the dates, locations and sometimes the names of the subjects on the mounts of his photographs, he did not do so for the newspaper cuttings. The name of the newspaper is not normally included, nor is the date.

father as director, having also established a wide range of other commercial interests. In 1867 he married Jane Parker; she was ten years younger than him, and they had a family of six children. He purchased a house and estate, The Grange, in Erdington in 1877. Erdington was still a village in the country although only four miles to the north of Birmingham, and J.B. Stone was able to extend both the house and the estate.

Stone was rich enough to be able to lead the kind of life he wanted, and he did not need to spend all of his time on business. He was involved in politics – this also did not entail total commitment for a Victorian gentleman. In 1869 he was first elected as town councillor for Duddeston in east Birmingham. Unusually for Birmingham, a predominantly Liberal city, he was a Tory. Some of his comments, for example his speech suggesting to young women in Duddeston that they should only have sweethearts who were good Tories, caused much satirical comment in local papers, in cartoons, prose and verse. From the Birmingham paper *The Dart* in 1877:

> ... Break, break, break
> This club-law, O Stone, and see,
> That it would doom the girls of Duddeston
> To endless celibacy [2]

He was knighted by Queen Victoria at Windsor in 1892, and in 1895 was elected Member of Parliament for East Birmingham.

The fact that he managed to keep his seat despite Birmingham's strong support for the Liberal Party suggests that he was a man whom people liked, even if they mocked him on occasion. One newspaper report described him as follows:

> Personally Sir Benjamin is distinguished by a friendly manner and an unfailing smile. He is always chatty and vivacious and has a pleasant word for everybody ...[3]

2. *The Dart*, 31 March 1877.
3. *Birmingham Mail*, 16 September (year unknown).

Another, from an unknown newspaper, probably in 1888, recorded his generosity, commenting: '... he has supported every social and philanthropic movement, irrespective of the class, creed or condition of life of its promoters'.[4] This quality was not only regarded as a virtue but had almost come to be expected in Birmingham, a city where many rich industrialists had given both land and money to improve the life of the poor.

Stone gave a talk to the Erdington Literary Association in 1881, in which he spoke about the problem for men such as themselves (rich and middle-class): '... how to spend their spare time to the best advantage'.[5] He recommended travel, to which a natural concomitant was the new hobby of photography. He had collected photographs from an early age, when he was still at school, and in 1868 he began to take his own. One of his very early photographs shows the side of a three-storey house in central Birmingham completely covered in posters; the image is so clear that it is possible to read much of the lettering. Photography was still a new and expensive pastime, and there were very few amateur photographers. A considerable quantity of equipment – including a tent to serve as a darkroom for immediate development – had to be transported to a site near where the photographer was working. Later Stone had a darkroom at The Grange, and employed two men working full-time to develop and print his photographs.

A press cutting, undated but included in a volume with others from 1905, quotes Stone's explanation of why he considered photography to be important: '... to show those who will follow us, not only our buildings, but our everyday life, our manners and customs. Briefly, I have aimed at recording history with the camera, which, I think, is the best way of recording it.'[6] Another aspect of his photography was his belief that, to be useful as a historical record, photographs needed to be accompanied by clear notes. Thus his images are always dated, and in many cases the names of the subjects are given. He said as much in an address given to the Royal Photographic Society in 1900:

4. Stone Collection of Newspaper Cuttings (paper and date unknown), BCL.
5. See B. Jay, *Customs and Faces: Photographs by Sir Benjamin Stone, 1838–1914* (London: St. Martin's Press, 1972).
6. As note 4.

'... pictures should have explanatory notes to make them intelligible, for, however good the pictures may be in themselves, they will be more valuable if used in conjunction with literary matter, condensed as much as possible, and of perfectly reliable character ...'[7]

Sir J.B. Stone and Robert Welch held different positions in society, the main distinction being that Robert Welch had to earn money whereas Stone had inherited it. Although Stone associated with the upper classes he did not belong with them – when he gave lectures, accompanied of course by lantern slides, there were comments on his thick Birmingham accent. However, he and Welch did share many interests apart from photography. Stone was a Fellow of the Geological Society, of the Royal Geographical Society, and of the Linnaean Society. Welch was a member of the Belfast Naturalists' Field Club (President 1909–10), of the Belfast Natural History and Philosophical Society and of the Conchological Society of Great Britain and Ireland (President 1922–3). Stone wrote about the need to record ancient customs in *The Amateur Photographer* in March 1900:

I have myself been interested in taking records of ancient customs, which still linger in remote villages. These have an important bearing on the earlier history of our country ...[8]

Directory entries for Robert Welch state that his photographs are of landscapes, but advertisements for his images add that many are 'Antiquarian, Geological and Ethnographic'.[9] Ethnography – the scientific study of races – was a popular subject for study across Europe in the late nineteenth and early twentieth century. As a description it could encompass both Stone's photographs of festivals and Welch's images of ancient tools still used by people in the Irish countryside.

A substantial number of the photographs of Ireland held in Birmingham were taken by Benjamin Stone himself. In 1899 he joined the tour of a Parliamentary Party, arranged by the Irish Tourist Association, to the South of Ireland in the Whitsuntide recess, 20 May–17 June

7. See Jay, *Customs and Faces.*
8. *Amateur Photographer*, 9 March 1900.
9. E.Estyn Evans and Bryan Turner, *Ireland's Eye: The Photographs of Robert John Welch* (Belfast: Blackstaff Press, 1977)

1899. His name was not included on the original list of fifteen MPs, so he must have been invited at a later date, or perhaps simply chose to accompany the party because of the opportunities it would offer for photography. MPs did not receive a salary, so all of those involved in the tour must, like Stone, have had money of their own to support themselves and their families. Several on the tour were accompanied by their wife or daughter. Other invitees included representatives from no less than ten British newspapers, as well as the Chairman of the Press Gallery in the House of Commons, so it was clear that this tour was intended to make the beauty spots of Ireland better-known. No Irish newspapers were represented, but Mr Curtayne Sullivan came as Editor of the *Birmingham Daily Mail*. Of the eleven 'Entertaining Companies', most (eight) were local railways and another was the City of Dublin Steam Packet Co., which took the group from Holyhead to 'Kingstown' [Dun Laoghaire]. The Parliamentary Party's route can be traced through the cards in one of Sir Benjamin Stone's many scrapbooks held in Birmingham Central Library: 'Invitation Cards etc. 1895–1901'.[10]

In this scrapbook Stone pasted five mementoes: the invitation from The President and Council of the Irish Tourist Association, the First Class Free Pass for the Dublin Wexford & Wicklow Railway, the ticket for the Special excursion to Bantry and Glengariff, the menu card for the dinner in Limerick, and the Itinerary. The Itinerary is the only card to include words in Irish, the traditional 'Cead Mile Failte'. It lists the many members of the Council of the Irish Tourist Association, which had first been registered in 1893. The President in 1899 was 'The most noble the Marquess of Londonderry K.G.'. The Secretary was Arthur E. Moran, of the Royal Dublin Society, and the Honorary Secretary, photographed by Stone during the tour, was W.T. Macartney Filgate, J.P. This was a tour for the British upper class.

Stone noted in his diary for Saturday 20 May 1899, '... Norman and I joined the Parliamentary Party for tour in Ireland. Left Birmingham at 8.40 in the evening & crossed to Ireland the same night. In Ireland until June 2 1899'.[11] During the next ten days the group trav-

10 Stone Collection, Invitation Cards etc., vol. 6, 1895–1901, BCL.
11. Parliamentary Diaries, Sir J.B. Stone,1899–1900, BCL.

elled for the most part by 'Special train'; Stone took a photograph of the Cork–Bantry train, and noted on the card on which the print was later mounted 'The interior of the carriage profusely decorated with flowers'. They stayed in Dublin, Cork, Glengariff, Parknasilla, Caragh Lake, Killarney and Limerick, returning to Dublin on 30th May. Stone stayed in Dublin until June 2 1900, as there is a letter from the Library of Trinity College listing the interior photographs he had taken there on 1 June 1900, including the Book of Durrow, the Book of Kells and the 'Harp of Brian Boru'.[12] He also took a photograph of the ornate state coach of the Lord Mayor of Dublin, who seems to have been a personal friend of Stone's, as there are several records in Stone's diary of meetings with him in London, for example for Thursday 7 June 1899 '... spent the evening with Henniker Heaton' and for Thursday 13 July '... Tea with Mr and Mrs Henniker Heaton'.

The Parliamentary group slept in stately homes and in hotels; Stone took photographs of the houses, gardens and staff. Various excursions were arranged, among them a trip round the harbour on a steamer at Cork, boating on the 'fjords' at Parknasilla and a visit to Shaw's Bacon Curing Works and Cleeve's Condensed Milk Factory in Limerick.[13] Several banquets were listed on the Tour programme. A card – one of five in his Invitation Cards scrapbook – proclaims 'Dinner at Cruise's Royal Hotel, Limerick, Monday 29 May 1899 Proprietor James Flynn' (Fig. 4.1). The card was printed especially for the dinner; the front included a sketch of the Treaty Stone, and of Limerick Castle. The menu was in French: it was a typical Victorian banquet, with seven courses: 'Potage – Poissions [sic] – Entrees – Releves – Roti – Entremets - Dessert'.

Stone took many photographs himself during this trip. There were the 'holiday snaps' – pictures of the dignitaries of the Ascendancy. These are stiffly posed, often in a doorway, and are similar to the many he took of MPs at Westminster. A number of these were taken at Killarney; for example, 'Mr. Filgate' stands by the 'Queen's Chair' in front of Queen's Cottage near Killarney House, Lord Kenmare's residence. He also took more relaxed photographs of the Parliamentary Party: for exam-

12. Stone, Transcripts and Photographs Documents 1894–1909, BCL.
13. As note 10.

Figure 4.1
Limerick dinner invitation

Figure 4.2
Lone Widow, Kerry

ple, having a picnic lunch sitting on the grass by Queen's Cottage, or setting off for a game of golf. Several of the press representatives appear in posed group in front of Killarney House.

In addition he took photographs of servants. From the Caragh Lake Hotel there are photographs of the maidservants, and a further picture of men and women on the staff. Stone took many photographs of turf-cutters, schoolchildren, women and houses, from which there is much to be learned. Hardly any of the children have shoes; nor does the elderly 'lone widow' (Figure 4.2), nor the 'female turf-seller' (Figure 4.5) standing on the road. The men do have boots to wear, and they are all wearing caps.

Stone's Parliamentary Diaries frequently include an entry 'took photographs ...'; and occasionally 'gave photograph ...' On Saturday 29 July 1899 he wrote, 'Very hot. Developing & printing photographs all day.' A week later on Saturday 5 August he recorded, 'Assorting & posting photographs all day with Roland & Norman'.[14] This may refer to the Irish photographs, among others, as there is no other reference to developing or printing in the two months since his return from Ireland. Stone chose a few of his Irish photographs to be included in the collection of prints that he lent to South Kensington Museum in May 1901, so it may perhaps be assumed that these were the ones in which he took the greatest pride:[15] Mansion House Dublin, turf-cutters in Co. Kerry, lone widow in Co. Kerry, Ballybunion single-track railway and schoolboys at Derrycreagh National School near Glengariff, Co. Cork. None of the boys were wearing shoes; however, in contrast with group photographs of children from the poorest areas of central Birmingham at the time, almost all of them had respectable clothes that fitted them (as opposed to ragged clothing cast off by adults).

Stone later purchased a large collection of photographs from Robert Welch, many of areas not visited by the Parliamentary Tour, the North and of the West, Ulster and Connaught. Almost certainly this was because of his desire to create a national collection for Britain. In 1897 he had launched his plan for a National Photographic Record Association at the Midland

14. As note 11.
15. As note 12.

Grand Hotel in Birmingham. The aim was to record the homes, public buildings, monuments, landscapes and customs of the time. The scheme was never completed, but many prints were deposited in the British Museum, and in local museums and libraries around the country. The selection Stone made of Welch's Irish photographs does not really reflect Welch's full range: there are none of street life in Belfast or Dublin, nor of any industrial subjects. Although Stone represented England's second largest city in Parliament he was not interested in city scenes; he was once quoted as saying, 'I quite fail to see what record of history is to be got out of an ordinary house or a regulation view from a bedroom window.'

The photographs in the Birmingham collection have been boxed together; they have not been separated according to whether they are by Robert Welch or by Benjamin Stone but have been indexed by location. Once Stone's photographs had been developed he had the prints mounted on cream-coloured card. Below the photographs he himself wrote on all the mounts the date (all 1899), the place and in some cases the names of people. Welch incorporated a brief title on the plate giving the location and the subject. Unfortunately he did not record people's names, nor a date; this has to be determined by a comparison between the number allotted to the image and his own notes.

The collection is rich because of the different qualities sought by the two photographers, in their choice of subject and in their preferred methods. While Stone and Welch held similar views on the importance and the purpose of the photographs, they differed in their view of the desired results. Certain conditions applied to all photographs at that time. Because a long exposure was required, most photographs had to be posed. (A newspaper report about the celebration of the Helston Furry dance in Cornwall, in May 1901, mentions that the dancers had been assembled in the street so that Stone could take pictures of them dancing. This article is glued to the back of one of the photographs of the Furry Dance; the title of the newspaper is not included.)

Welch waited some time to take one of his best-known photographs of Croaghmore (Figure

5.5) on Clare Island (he used it as a book–plate see Figure 1.3) so that a wisp of cloud would be in precisely the right place. Photographs of interiors rarely included people: because of low lighting the exposure needed to be exceptionally long. Welch positioned women outside their houses with their spinning-wheels and other household tools so that a pleasing picture could be composed in the light. Conversely he might ask workers to leave a room in the linen factory so that the machinery could be seen clearly. Many of his photographs have the composition of a still life.

Welch added to the artistic appearance of his photographs by working on them when developing them. The impressive capstone of the portal dolmen near Croagh, on the River Ballinderry, had had notices stuck on advertising farm sales. Some of these had been scraped off and by working on the glass negative Welch managed to remove all the last traces.

Stone did not use such methods: many of his photographs consist of people who appear to have assembled spontaneously – for example, the 'butter-girls' of Limerick, a group of men and boys sitting by the Treaty Stone in Limerick (Figure 4.3) – and frequently one of the group has moved, so the face is blurred.

Stone criticised the approach of professional photographers such as Welch when lecturing at the Royal Photographic Society in London in 1900:

> ... there is a lamentable custom resorted to of tampering with photographs either in the negative or in the process [of] reproduction, so as to insert artificial effects or to correct partial failures in the original negative, and oftentimes embodying distinctly fraudulent effects ...

He explained his objection:

> '... This degrading custom cannot be too much regretted, as faithful historical records

would become impossible, and the best pictures would be valueless, if it were permitted for one moment to take liberties of this character ...'[16]

Of course, he was not writing as a commercial photographer who needed to sell his photographs. And despite his stated principles he purchased many of Welch's photographs that had been posed and 'doctored' to present an aesthetically pleasing image. It might be asked whether Stone, and others, would have paid for images that included blurred faces, although he might have justified the quality of faithfulness to life in his own photographs.

Welch's photographs are immaculately clear, but Stone's do have the merit of spontaneity, as far as this was possible at the time. People stand in posed groups but there is no careful composition – the Treaty Stone photograph (Figure 4.3) gives the impression that Stone had simply asked everyone standing nearby to be in the picture. There are boys without shoes and men wearing caps, but also several boys wearing straw boaters that make them look from a higher social class. There is a photograph of a large crowd at Cahirciveen station, adults and children, who appear to be there solely for the purpose of saying goodbye to the Parliamentary Party. Stone himself appears in one group picture at Waterville, County Kerry – the substitute photographer was no expert, and the group is no longer in the centre but disappears off on the left-hand side of the image.

When Stone purchased photographs from Welch he obviously chose those that reflected his own interests – as mentioned above, no industrial workers – but he also selected those that would complement his own. He chose several types of image from the Welch collection. Firstly, antiquities: there are many beautiful examples by Welch, and his photograph of Newgrange long before it had been restored is still a moving work of art. Stone did take such images himself, for example the Waterville Stone Circle near the Hotel, but they do not compare. The collection in Birmingham includes many of Welch's photographs of Celtic crosses, ancient fortresses and churches from all over Ireland, and they are outstanding.

Secondly, Stone purchased landscapes. Again, he had taken some himself, but they were

16. See B. Jay, *Customs and Faces.*

Figure 4.3
Treaty Stone, Limerick

not of particularly high quality. Welch was keen to promote the tourist industry, and had taken many beautiful landscapes. Unusually for this collection there are two city views – looking along Patrick Street [sic] in the centre of Cork from two different viewpoints. In addition there are many of the North and the West, which Stone had not visited. A few are shots of plants, one of necklaces made from shells gathered near Cork.

There are a few images of the middle classes at play. Welch had had three of his friends dress up as cowboys, and photographed them standing in jaunty poses. The title of this one is 'Kerry cowboys' (Figure 4.4). There is a photograph of a female turf seller, unnamed, standing beside a road in Figure 4.5. Some of the images of antiquities include a child, more often a boy than a girl, and it seems probable that their principal role was to give a sense of scale. Cyclists are shown by the 'Tunnel' near Killarney. There is also a large group photograph of the Belfast Naturalists' Field Club on an a excursion.

Most importantly, there are Welch's 'ethnographic' portraits. including many images of women with their spinning-wheels, and series of photographs of different types of carts. All of these are carefully posed, some dramatically so. Welch did not only require larger household equipment such as spinning-wheels to be placed outside; other smaller tools might also be brought out and carefully arranged to achieve the best effect (see Figure 13.1). The impression given by these photographs is that Welch was trying to conduct a detailed scientific study of certain types of apparatus, the term 'ethnographic' requiring systematic observation. Because the picture is posed however, there is little feeling of involvement with the individuals, as compared with Stone's photographs of the 'female turf-seller' (Figure 4.5), the 'lone widow' (Figure 4.2) and the 'butter-girls' of Limerick.

Despite their difference in approach, both Stone and Welch were acutely aware of the need to record the traditions of their countries, and a way of life that was starting to disappear. A century ago photography was still an expensive occupation, requiring much equipment, and most of the photographs taken by Welch and Stone exist only because of their outstanding effort: no-

Figure 4.4
'Kerry Cowboys'

one else would have taken them. We are able to learn so much from these images of the lives of men, women and children in Ireland, rich and poor, for which we are indebted to Robert Welch and to Sir John Benjamin Stone.

Figure 4.5
Turf seller
(Benjamin Stone Collection)

CHAPTER FIVE

Technologies and Cultures:
Robert J. Welch's Western Landscapes 1895–1914

GAIL BAYLIS

This chapter seeks to situate Robert J. Welch's photography within the cultural context of its production. It will challenge a purely technical reading of photographic history, revealing it to be too limited in terms of our understanding of how photography operated in the nineteenth and early twentieth centuries. This is particularly true of commercial photography, in which practice is always mediated by issues of reception and circulation. The photographic image, as Susan Sontag notes, 'even to the extent that it is a trace ... cannot be simply a transparency of something that happened. It is always the image that someone chose; to photograph is to frame, and to frame is to exclude'.[1] In this context, the commissioned nature of much of the work that Welch undertook needs to be recognised in relation to the dictates of economic imperatives. As a professional photographer, his work was governed by the need to address a range of publics in order to make a living. This inquiry, in recognition of these working practices, will concentrate on Welch's representations of the West of Ireland in three sites: his photographs of the Aran Islands (1895), the Clare Island Survey (1909–11) and the work he undertook for the Congested Districts Board – CDB (1914).

Developments in camera technology in the late nineteenth century were contingent on the introduction of the half-tone process. This allowed, for the first time, photographs to be disseminated to a mass-audience, thus revolutionising the 'entire economy of image production'.[2] The resultant mass-marketing of the photograph is connected to the emergence of a new type

1. Susan Sontag, *Regarding the Pain of Others* (London: Penguin, 2004), p. 41.
2. John Tagg, *The Burden of Representation: Essays on Photographies and Histories* (London:Gill and Macmillan, 1988), p. 55.

of photographer, namely the professional photographer, of whom Welch is a prime example. Accompanying this new professional rank was a process of specialisation and a claim to status. For example, Welch could pursue his interest in natural history through photography, a preoccupation that would have been the preserve only of the well-to-do amateur earlier in the century but it was now possible for photographers to gain commissions from museums and to publish images in journals and magazines or produce them as lantern slides for lectures. He undertook a number of commissions from museums to photograph their collections (for example, amongst others, he was commissioned to photograph the collections of the British Museum, Manchester Museum of Science, Manchester Library and the National History Museum, Dublin). While there was a precedent in Roger Fenton's photographs of the British Museum's collections, what had changed by the turn of the century was the expansion of institutional commissions.

Early photographers in Ireland tended to be either amateurs (the landed classes) or commercial practitioners, the latter having their range of activities curtailed by the need for patronage or by the dictates of public taste. Portraiture had to be the stock in trade of commercial photographers due to market demand, even though they might specialise in other branches of photography, such as topography, as was the case with David Welch (the photographer's father).[3] The professional photographer, while still constrained by economic imperatives, had greater choice in the nature of commissions available.[4] *The Tourist* of 9 July 1898 refers to Robert Welch as 'The Traveller's Photographer', noting that he is one of the 'leading scenic photographers'. In addition, the writer notes that Welch does not take portraits.[5] As an independent, commercial practitioner the option to exclude commercial portraiture would not have been viable earlier in the century.

Welch also supported his interests with the other work he undertook: for example, views for railway companies, his work as official photographer for both Harland and Wolff and the Ropemaker's Company (both Belfast-based), as well as his many commissions from government bodies and industrialists. Far from these areas of commercial production being

3. W.A. Maguire, *A Century in Focus: Photography and Photographers in the North of Ireland 1839-1939* (Belfast: The Blackstaff Press and Ulster Museum, 2000), p. 35–7.

4. This is clearly indicated by the range of commissions he undertook. See E. Estyn Evans and B. S. Turner, *Ireland's Eye: The Photographs of Robert John Welch* (Belfast: Blackstaff Press and the Ulster Museum, 1977), p. 1.

5. Newspaper clipping pasted into R.J. Welch, *Excursions Diary*, 1898, p. 42.

unconnected, they were integral in terms of furthering his own areas of study. Given these types of connection, this chapter will outline how, in order to fully appreciate the way Welch represents the West of Ireland, that we need to consider both technical and cultural factors. In this, we will also resist the temptation to see the photographer's prodigious output as signalling a 'Welchian vision of Irish nature and culture'[6] and, rather, argue that how Welch represented the West was indexed by factors of cultural placement.

LAYING CLAIM TO THE LAND

An interest in antiquarian studies, flora and fauna, and the folk traditions of Ireland was established well before the Cultural Revival started in the last decade of the nineteenth century.[7] Indeed, natural history shared 'a good deal with other fields of activities such as folklore collection and antiquarianism'; all were 'motivated by a strong patriotic impulse: to provide a full, autonomous identity for Ireland while rejecting imposed models from outside, particularly from Britain'.[8] It is in these branches of study, with the drive to identify nomenclatures and find models in Ireland that have no counterpart in England, and in the taxonomical impetus to establish an Irish order of things, that the conceptualisation of a new idea of identity was nascent. Amateur field studies were particularly popular in the North-East of Ireland, where it reflected a strong Ulster Dissenting ethos. The growth of interest in amateur natural history (most marked by the success and longevity of the Belfast Naturalists' Field Club, of which Welch was a member from 1880, Secretary 1908–9, Chairman of from 1910–12 and made an honorary member in 1921) exemplified both 'one thread in a complicated weave of enthusiasm for cultural and local studies' and a means to assert a Presbyterian identity.[9]

E. Estyn Evans sees Welch's involvement in the natural sciences as being explicitly connected to his photographic practice: 'Welch brought the trained observant eye of the field naturalist to the perfection of his photographic skills'.[10] Cultural identity, as Luke Gibbons notes, 'does not

6. John Wilson Foster, 'Nature and Nation in the Nineteenth Century', in J. Foster Wilson (ed.) *Nature in Ireland: A Scientific and Cultural History* (Dublin: The Lilliput Press, 1997), p. 601.

7. Declan Kibberd dates the start of the debate about national identity to 1893, when Douglas Hyde established the Gaelic League, *Inventing Ireland* (London: Jonathan Cape, 1995), p. 7.

8. Sean Lysaght, *Robert Lloyd Praeger: The Life of a Naturalist* (Dublin:Four Courts Press, 1998), p. 12.

9. Ibid., p. 18

10. Evans and Turner, *Ireland's Eye*, p. 16.

11. Luke Gibbons, *Transformations in Irish Culture* (Cork: Cork University Press in association with Field Day, 1996), p. 10.

12. John Wilson Foster, *Fictions of the Irish Literary Revival: A Changeling Art* (Syracuse: Syracuse University Press, 1987, 1993), p. xvii.

13. Sean Lysaght, 'Contrasting Natures: The Issue of Names', in John Wilson Foster (ed.), *Nature in Ireland: A Scientific and Cultural History* (Dublin: The Lilliput Press, 1997), p. 440.

14. Foster, 'Nature and Nation in the Nineteenth Century', p. xvi.

15. Welch's father, a Scottish Presbyterian, moved to Ireland initially to take up employment in shirt manufacture in the North-East and later turned to photography as a profession (Evans and Turner: *Ireland's Eye*, p. 14).

16. Lysaght, *Robert Lloyd Praeger*, p. 26.

17. Ibid., p. 13

pre-exist its representations or material expressions, but is in fact generated and transformed by them'.[11] According to John Wilson Foster, what was 'ultimately at stake during the Irish revival were the nature and the identity of Ireland, and the extent of its legitimate power to define the nature and identity of the individual'.[12] The need to assert scientific objectivity as a sign of Protestant identity became even more pronounced as a counterweight to nationalist politics' insistence that Irish identity was Catholic and to the Literary Revival's claim to have found the essence of Irish culture in the ancient Gaelic tradition.

The appeal of the West of Ireland represented the promise of uncharted terrain and a recuperation of a pre-conquest identity of language, culture and nation. Photography, in this context, was not just a reflection of outer nature or simply a recorder of passing rural ways but also a means (as with natural history's discursive Irish programme) to register identity in the landscape, to lay claim to territory, so to speak. If giving names to natural phenomena and the species of nature was a way of 'controlling nature and subordinating it',[13] capturing the visibility of nature by the use of the camera was equally about asserting a stake in the Irish landscape. Foster defines the Revival as: 'By the Irish Literary Revival I would mean the work of those who sought to employ literature in a resuscitation of elder Irish values and culture that they hoped would transform the reality of the Ireland they inhabited.'[14] Such negotiations may have been even more marked in the heritage of the Ulster-Scots who could fit comfortably into neither an Anglo-Irish nor a Catholic-Irish tradition. This was a tradition that Welch both inherited and was a part of.[15] According to Lysaght, not only did the Belfast Naturalist's Field Club allow 'a cultural expression of a group within the Dissenter community which needed to define itself' but also a means by which 'history and locality could be appropriated through the nomenclature of botany, geology, palaeography and antiquarianism', which 'supplied an obvious atavistic dimension for a settler community conscious of its provenance in Scotland'.[16]

In this context, the field of natural history cannot be isolated from concerns of cultural and political identity and neither can the medium of photography within that project.[17] Lysaght, while he does not reference photography directly, points to 'the virtual monopoly enjoyed by Protestant Ireland of Irish image-making during the Cultural Revival'.[18] The methodological principles of objectivity, non-mediation and disembodied observation in natural history are articulated in photographic 'style' by the aesthetics of realism. Realism in photography works to mask the codes and structures, which give photographs meaning and affectively reduces the image to the 'immediacy of translation',[19] and it is in this context that we need to consider Welch's technical choices – how he chose to construct the image.

The photographer's *Excursions Diary* and *Notebooks* offer us information about the technical choices he made. Of note in these texts is an absence of direct political comment;[20] this omission, however, is not apolitical but concurrent with the discursive imperative of scientific inquiry that situates itself as outside the immediate. It is with this awareness of discursive enunciation that we need to critically engage with Welch's own pronouncements about his technical choices. He kept detailed references to photographic procedures and advances in technology in the form of his personal chemical recipes and pasted-in advertisements for new products in his *Notebooks*. However, in many respects Welch was a 'perfecter' of technique rather than an innovator. What he strove for (as was in accordance with the discourses of scientific rationality and his own cultural affiliations) was clarity and seeming objectivity.

An early reference in his *Excursions Diary* is indicative of the procedures that he undertook to seemingly construct neutrality. Undertaking legal work on the disputed path system at the Giant's Causeway, known as the 'Causeway Right of Way Case' Welch noted how his 8x6" prints offered more clarity than the opposition's larger photographs because the latter had been taken with 'long focus lenses <u>not</u> <u>stepped</u> <u>down</u>' thereby obliterating sharpness of detail.[21] Referencing his own practice (in retrospect) the photographer notes all views taken before 1894, and most before 1891, were taken with 'Ross' 7x10" portable symmetrical lenses, many of which being taken with a 'back combination of the 7" lens (all were 8½ x 6½ plates)'. He goes on to state:

This tho' slow I found to be a most excellent single landscape [and] indeed architectural

18. Sean Lysaght, 'Science and the Cultural Revival: 1863–1916', in P. J. Bowler and N. Whyte (eds), *Science and Society in Ireland: The Social Context of Science and Technology in Ireland* (Belfast: The Institute of Irish Studies, Queens University, Belfast, 1997), p. 153.

19. Roland Barthes, *The Eiffel Tower*, translated by Richard Howard (New York: Hill and Wang, 1979), p. 72.

20. Unless, in the case of photography it offered an opportunity for profitable image making, as on royal visits.

21. *Excursions Diary*, 1897, p.32.

22. *Excursions Diary*, 'Memos and Notes' , p. 20.
23. Naomi Rosenblum, *A World History of Photography* (New York: Abbeville Press, rev. ed. 1989), p. 443.
24. Evans and Turner, *Ireland's Eye*, p. 18.
25. Ibid., p. 17.
26. Michel Foucault, *The Archaeology of Knowledge,* translated by A.M. Sheridan Smith (London: Tavistock Press, 1972: 1974 English translation), p. 182.
27. In the case of its English expression it takes the form of nostalgia for a passing way of life caused by the experience of rapid industri-alisation. This type of artic-ulation could not have occurred in Ireland due to both a non-symmetrical industrial experience and because of the colonial lega-cy and the post-Famine con-sciousness, which meant that nature in Ireland could never be seen as purely benign. For a fuller account of this aspect of Irish nature imagery see Foster, 'Nature and Nation in the Nineteenth Century', pp.409–39.

lens, it never gave flare spot so like many of the rapid single lens … This one lens gave practically 3 lenses [and] with the 10" I had really 6 lenses of different F lengths available … I found too I could over-expose pretty well when in doubt, which made it still more useful. In later years I replaced it with Ross-Goerz of about same focal length (6") which I also used "split" a good deal. This of course was a much more rapid lens …[22]

This technical attention to producing apparent unmediated clarity was concurrent with his use of the platinotype process. 'This expensive material', as Naomi Rosenblum notes, 'appealed to the well-to-do amateurs and serious photographers who required a printing paper of permanence with a long tonal scale'.[23] Welch's preference for this process exemplifies both his technical exactitude and an eye on posterity. As Evans and Turner note: he sought to leave a permanent record of Ireland.[24]

This desire, at heart, is also about aiming to place oneself within a tradition. Welch was not averse to either 'doctoring' the negative or controlling the gradation of tonal distribution in the printing process. He did his own developing under, according to Evans, 'primitive conditions in the kitchen in Lonsdale Street' but also, as Evans goes on to note, 'many of the plates were elaborately doctored to remove blemishes and to bring out, for example by a portion of sky, the features he wished to emphasise'.[25] There is nothing new in such interventions in the history of photography. The seemingly objective image is tied into discursive practices of knowledge pro-duction: a 'domain constituted by the different objects that will or will not acquire a scientific status'.[26] The issue then is not to decry Welch's technical proficiency but to engage with how the technical choices and effects he made were inflected by cultural and historical factors.

For example, if we consider the adoption of the platinotype process in another site we can see how the Pictorialists, under different circumstances[27] and from a differing discursive impetus (art aesthetics), were adapting photographic technique for alternative ends. However, in this instance the comparison goes further: the Pictorialists were also reacting against the mass distribution of the image, which for Welch was the bulk of his livelihood. For the Pictorialists, the signs of human intervention in the photographic print were strategies to counter the mechanical process of photography as a medium in a mass-culture context.[28] For Welch, on the other hand, the construction of clarity was concordant with the notion of objectivity and autonomous vision, leading to a masking of interventionist acts.

GOING WEST

The appeal of the West of Ireland as an imaginative site for the construction of Irish identity reached its apotheosis in the islands off the west coast of Ireland. Not only did these islands represent the furthest that one could distance oneself from England while still being on Irish soil but they also held the promise (due to their isolation) of being the least tainted by colonial influences.[29] Such interest predates Synge's visits to the Aran Islands in the 1890s. For example, the antiquarians George Petrie and John T. O'Flaherty visited these islands in the 1820s, John O'Donavan (who worked on the first Ordnance Survey of Ireland) arrived on the islands in 1839; he was followed by writers, scientists and philologists 'many of them in pursuit of proof that Ireland had a pre-conquest civilization'.[30] A. C. Haddon and J. M. Browne (the photographer) were there in 1892 taking anthropological photographs of the inhabitants.[31]

According to Foster, what we witness in late nineteenth-century Irish cultural nationalism is a new version of island mythology, 'a creation myth for an imminent new order'.[32] At a symbolic level the 'island-state' offered a micro-version for fantasies of a macro-Ireland as a unitary nation. Such fantasies were not only to be found in nationalist rhetoric but also in natural history field studies.[33] In this, the intent of the naturalist did not differ from that of the cultural nationalist who sought in the islands off the West of Ireland a pre-conquest 'symbolic entirety of an undivided nation'.[34] Given this context, it is not surprising that the first Irish Field Club Union's excursion in 1895 was to the Galway region, with a three-day visit to the Aran

28 Rosenblum, *A World History of Photography*, p. 297.
29. Foster, 'Nature and Nation in the Nineteenth Century', p. 95.
30. Ibid., p. 94–5.
31. Maguire, *A Century in Focus*, p. 99. Welch, a member of the ethnography committee of the Belfast Naturalists' Field Club, also corresponded with, and provided photographs for, both Haddon and Benjamin Stone. See the *Excursions Diary* for a loose undated letter from Haddon to Welch and for Stone's praise of his ethnographic photographs (1904), p. 100.
32. Foster, 'Nature and Nation in the Nineteenth Century', p. 96.
33. Lysaght, *Robert Lloyd Praeger* p. 54.
34. Foster, 'Nature and Nation in the Nineteenth Century', p. 96.

Figure 5.1
Irish Field Clubs landing on
Aranmore, IFCU excursion,
W14/01/01

Figure 5.2
Canvas Currachs, Aran,
W14/01/10

Figure 5.3
Dun Aengus, W14/01/15

Islands.[35]   The significance of this western journey lay both in the discovery of new species of flora and a fashioning of a new type of identity.   The President of the Dublin Naturalists' Field Club summarised the excursion as comprising of a 'mixed assembly' so 'typical of the fauna and flora of Ireland, made up as they are of varying elements which have entered the country at different times and by different roads'.[36]   The appeal to inclusiveness here is unmistakable and no doubt held a particular resonance for the largely Protestant constituency of the field clubs.

Welch's photographs of this excursion are instructive of this cultural need for inclusion.   Of note is how differing techniques are employed to connote the field club investigator and the island dweller (with a high proportion of the latter being images of children).   As Justin Carville notes of Welch's field excursion photographs as a whole, they 'functioned as objects through which the middle-class naturalist's exterior presence in the natural world could be affirmed'.[37] Significant in terms of the excursionists' presence on Aranmore is a panoramic shot of their arrival that replays a discovery myth (Figure 5.1).   The field members are congregated at a harbour point with a pronounced inward group gaze to the island, which will be their point of discovery.   The focal viewpoint draws attention to the ship that has brought them, which is now returning while a smaller boat lands yet more field club members.   Welch has also chosen to include in this 'prospect' panorama a small disparate group positioned on an adjacent cliff. Their gaze is outward, in contrast to the larger group of excursionists. The overall effect is to construct a sense of voyaging and arrival, establish the presence of the group on the land and position their gaze as both outward looking and purposeful.

In contrast, in the images that Welch took of the Aran seafarers there is a strong emphasis on the horizontal plane, which not only serves to complement the line of the currach but also has the effect of foreshortening the vanishing point, thus situating the islanders as contained within the nature that surrounds them (Figure 5.2). This relegates them to the position of the surveyed rather than the surveyors (an authority position reserved for the 'objective' field club member). This subject positioning is augmented by the photographer's adept manipulation of contrasts

35. The excursion party was made up 'mainly of the Belfast and Dublin clubs, although the Limerick and Cork clubs were also represented', Lysaght, *Robert Lloyd Praeger*, pp. 41–2.
36. Lysaght, *Robert Lloyd Praeger*, p. 43.
37. Justin Carville, 'Photography, Tourism and Natural History: Cultural Identity and the Visualisation of the Natural World', in Michael Cronin, and Barbara O'Connor (eds), *Irish Tourism: Image, Culture and Identity* (Clevedon: Channel View Publications, 2003), p. 232–3.

HOLY WELL AND STATION, KILLEANY, ARAN IS. R.W. 2164.

Figure 5.4
Holy Well And Station, Killeany,
Aran Island, W14/01/03

of light and shade, together with his mastery of depth of field. The cumulative effect is to produce clarity of vision that positions the image within scientific discourses of objectivity. However, while this might be seen to indicate an effacement of the photographer's presence, the constructed vision seems to endorses the natural historian's authority over the landscape and positions the photographer as, correlatively, the objective recorder.

Other photographs of the field clubs' presence reinforce this relationship to landscape. The photographing of antiquities is a case in point. In Figure 5.3, field club members are represented as dominating the landscape: they are seen from the ramparts gazing down on all that surrounds them (See also: 'Dun Aengus', 'Chevaux de frise and three inner ramparts, Dun Aengus' and 'Inner ramparts, Dun Aengus'). In marked contrast, a representation of the same location ('Inner entrance, Dun Aengus'), with children of the island clearly posed, gives the impression that they are an outcrop of the ancient fort, in other words, part of that very landscape. In this way, the human element in the landscape divides between the expansive gaze of the natural historian and the localised vision of those who are subsumed into the natural environment, the latter becoming just another indigenous form to be observed and named. Welch's use of children is instructive regarding this process of articulating a relation to and control over nature. Such deployment not only adds 'local colour' and serves to give a sense of scale but also produces the effect of reducing the human element to a natural state. In Figure 5.4, 'Holy well and Station, Killeany, Aran Island', the children are positioned as if they grow out of the recesses and vegetation of the location. These 'little people' call into play folklore references to other-worldliness.

A different style of naturalising is to be found in a large formal group portrait of the children of Aranmore, similar to Figures 12.4, 12.5 and 12.6. Clothing indicates that this portrait may have been the outcome of an opportune moment, possibly after either Holy Communion or a special school event.[38] Welch has titled the photograph 'Descendants of the Firbolgs, Aranmore'.[39] This call to mythology, while holding scant relation to scientific 'fact', does position the inhabitants of the islands as both authentic and primitive: in other words, within an ethnographic frame

Figure 5.5
Croaghmore, Clare Island.
W16/04/26

38. Of note are the starched white dresses or pinafores worn by many of the girls and their generally tidy appearance, and the fact that a number of them carry books. A fair proportion of the boys also look dressed for an occasion.

39. The Firbolgs were a mythological pre-Celtic tribe who invaded Ireland and in turn were defeated and finally settled on the Aran Islands and surrounding coastland. The fort Dun Aengus, which Welch photographed (as I have outlined), was reputably the home of Aengus, king of the Firbolgs.

of reference. In addition to this it draws on a notion expressed in Celtic mythology (most notably in the early Irish *Book of Invasions*) of 'successive populations of Ireland'.[40] The choice of this type of historicising, which offered a means to 'root' successive incoming ethnicities as part of a pre-colonial history, may well have appealed to an Ulster-Scots tradition in Ireland.

NATURALISING HISTORY

By the time Welch was commissioned to take photographs for the Clare Island Survey (1909–11) he had established himself as a photographer of natural history and taken part in a number of important surveys.[41] He also contributed photographs to Praeger's *Tourist Flora* (1907) and *Tourist Fauna* (1908) and had been commissioned to take photographs for the *New Irish Drift Memoirs* (Dublin 1902, Belfast 1903 and Cork 1904). Clare Island represented 'for field studies what the Aran and Blasket islands became for students of Gaelic culture'; the Survey amounted to 'an attempt at projecting his own self [the scientist] on to the island of Ireland'[42] and, by extension, that of the photographer whose purpose was to visualize that endeavour.

An earlier Welch photograph, of Scarbo Cliffs (1903), is indicative of how this projection was communicated through photographic technique and style. In this instance, Welch, through technical interventions, was striving to produce a type of clarity commensurate with the discipline of geology.[43] Writing about this photograph, he points to how 'it shows the sills much clearer than usual'. In order to exploit the contrasts in rock stratum exposed by the previous wet night he 'underexposed to get all the contrast I could' and then 'printed on slightly contrasty paper'. The engraver additionally brought out the contrast between light and dark elements in the image, thus exaggerating features that would not normally be visible to the naked eye, so that 'the cumulative result shows the intrusions into the sandstones very clearly'. The addition of a human figure to the scene was intentional, in that it provided a 'good comparative scale'.[44]

40. Miranda J. Greene, *Dictionary of Celtic Myth and Legend* (London: Thames and Hudson, 1992), p. 99.

41. Welch made two trips to Clare Island (in 1909 and 1910) for this survey undertaken by the Royal Irish Academy. The photographs that he produced on these occasions both furnished the Royal Irish Academy's reports and were used for botanical, zoological and geological publications; others he took for Praeger (*Excursions Diary*, 1910, 76).

42. Lysaght, Rober Lloyd Praeger, p. 55.

43. The original photograph appeared as a print (Plate III) in the *New Irish Drift Memoirs: Belfast* (1903), where it was printed in half-tone. Welch has pasted a copy of this print into his *Excursions Diary* (1903, p.72).

44. *Excursions Diary,* 1903, 69.

Implicit in this account of production is a revelation of the means by which photography makes visible what had previously remained unseen, and as a practice of knowledge production serves to legitimise discursive authority (in this instance, the discourse of geology). Natural history, as Michel Foucault points out, was 'not merely the discovery of a new object of curiosity; it covers a series of complex operations that introduce the possibility of a constant order into a totality of representations'.[45] What is interesting in the account of the production of the Scarbo Cliffs image is how it reveals what traditionally science has aimed to mask – visibility is affective. In this instance, the construction of signs in the photograph becomes inextricable from the discourse of knowledge that it has been produced to serve.

Technological difficulties (camera work) also speak of specific historical and cultural signification. Dorinda Outram, who takes issue with Foucault's universalising reading, points to the need, in terms of Irish science, to recognise the 'embeddedness of the natural order in a particular land'.[46] Welch's need to photograph flora *au naturel* was indicative of this embeddedness, wherein within the universalising rationale of scientific inquiry a specifically Irish register was sought through landscape. For example, during a trip to North Clare in 1907 for Praeger's *Tourist Flora* Welch records how high winds caused him considerable difficulties. To combat this, he adopted a cumulative exposure plan, even though photographing some plants then took five to fifteen minutes from first exposure to last.[47] Such difficulties were compounded by the type of plant photography he was producing (namely, close-up views on location) where the need to achieve 'the maximum sharpness possible' involved him having to slow down the exposure time to sometimes between ten and thirty seconds in order to produce fully exposed negatives at close quarters. In order to achieve this type of photograph he made a special camera stand, which 'could be inclined at any angle easily, close to the plant' and in addition could be 'fixed' firmly on very uneven ground.[48]

He recounts numerous other instances of such difficulties, even during successful photographic encounters. For example, on a trip to Lough Derg, where he was photographing for Praeger's *Tourist Fauna* (1908), he had to make four or five exposures due to there being just

45. Michel Foucault, *The Order of Things* (London: Tavistock Publications, 1966; 1970 English translation), p. 158.
46. Dorinda Outram, 'The History of Natural History: Grand Narrative or Local Lore?', in John Wilson Foster (ed.), *Nature in Ireland: A Scientific and Cultural History* (Dublin: The Lilliput Press, 1997), p. 470.
47. *Excursions Diary*, 1907, 115.
48. Welch has drawn a sketch of this machinery in his *Excursions Diary*, 1907, 118.

sufficient 'puffs of wind to make a single long exposure impossible'.[49] At Croaghmore Lough he had difficulty photographing plants. In order to do so, rather than explicating them to a neutral extemporal backdrop (the previous taxonomical precedent), he chose to stand with his camera in mid-drift, on the edge of still deeper water. There is an intrepid note of adventure and pitting oneself against the natural elements in this sort of testimony: 'You cannot hope to get plain sailing always in plant photography anymore than you can when on the cliffs after sea birds … I found this out later on Clare Island cliffs'.[50] In this type of self-projection the colonial appropriation of photographer as explorer is discernible.

Welch's photograph of Croaghmore on Clare Island (Figure 5.5) is impressive not merely for his careful manipulation of light and shade, which emphasises the geological strata of the foreground cliff face, but also for how by careful adjustment of focal length the distant cliff (less distinct in outline) is made to provide the scene with a sense of scale. However, these visual signs also carried wider registers as prerequisite Irish qualities of landscape. The representation of shrouded mistiness and rugged elementalism drew on the aesthetics of Pictorialism, which came to carry the cultural signifier of landscape during the Irish Revival. In Welch's representation of the land's end we witness both a good photographer at work in poor weather conditions and the articulation of a scientific and cultural location.

Not only did this photograph appear in Praeger's *The Way That I Went* but Welch chose it for the basis of his bookplate (Figure 1.3).[51] The bookplate is revealing of how natural history was part of a larger cultural programme in Ireland.[52] In the change of medium (from photograph to bookplate) a number of decorative elements have been added. These reference Welch's personal interests (a variety of shells serve as a motif for his conchological interests, an axe head symbolises antiquarianism and the addition of flowers at the cliff face, which are not in the original, the naturalist's pursuits). Other additional decorative elements specifically draw on Celtic iconography to frame the meaning of nature in Ireland. The bookplate speaks both of naturalism in Ireland and the desire to claim identity within the nature of Ireland.

49. *Excursions Diary*, 1908, 135.
50. *Excursions Diary*, 1908, 134.
51. Evans and Turner, *Ireland's Eye*, p. 20.
52. Ibid., reproduced p. 13.

CONTOURING THE LANDSCAPE

One of the outcomes of the work of the Congested Districts Board (CDB) was the opening up of the West of Ireland. This, along with the Light Railways Act (1889), was fundamental to the development of the field club movement in Ireland and to the extension of tourism in the West of Ireland.[53] In addition to this, the advent of motor car transport meant that the potential for travel, and for photography, was greatly expanded. In an eight-day excursion with Mr Kempster to show him 'the condition of the West' and the work of the CDB, Welch estimated that he and his companion covered some eight hundred miles by car. Also, the introduction of Hydra plate, which Welch started using in 1912, gave the photographer greater latitude and assurance of results.[54] It is in the context of these social, cultural and technical changes that we need to consider the photographs that Welch produced for the CDB.

Prior to Welch undertaking this commission, the CDB gave an album of photographs documenting the conditions in the West to Queen Victoria when she visited Ireland in 1900. The majority of these photographs were by Welch and those selected for inclusion were of 'peasant life, industries, and unique antiquities', together with views taken on Belfast Naturalists' Field Club excursions [55] While the ethos of the CDB programme lay within social improvement, it becomes evident from this selection process that Welch's ethnographic and field club photographs were also considered as appropriate genres for communicating the effectiveness of the Board's work.[56] The precedent set by the album (for which Welch was awarded the Royal warrant) indicates that the inflection of natural history discourses, as a means to delineate landscape and change, would permeate the representation of social conditions.[57]

Discussing William Bulfin's photographs in *Rambles in Eirinn* (1907), Spurgeon Thompson notes how in Bulfin's photograph 'The smiling midlands' we see 'Ireland from the perspective of the soil' and he concludes that this perspective 'de-aestheticises the landscape by reading its

53. Lysaght, *Robert Lloyd Praeger*, p. 155).
54. Welch refers to the Hydra plate as being 'a real god-send to anyone undertaking such a very varied class of work as mine … Their latitude is wonderful. I gave 4 & 5 times correct exposure, when in doubt, with success' (*Excursions Diary,* 'Memos', 228).
55. Newspaper clipping from the *Northern Whig*, 11 June 1900, pasted into *Excursions Diary*, p. 218.
56. Among the institutional bodies that gave assistance on the Clare Island survey was the Congested Districts Board (Lysaght, Robert Lloyd Praeger, p. 92).
57. The comparison with Jacob Riis here is instructive: both as an indicator of the different approach that Welch takes and because it highlights how notions of urban and rural poverty may in themselves impact on what type of realism is constructed.

history' and thereby politicises the land by revealing a history of dislocation.[58]   In this way, Bulfin's work references land clearance and evictions as part of a history of colonial imposition. Interestingly, Welch employs a variant on this technique in his photographs of congested villages. The vantage point offered is from a middle distance (the field or rough ground) or, in some cases, from a higher, more distanced point. In some photographs it is clear that Welch has adopted a high vantage point, some distance away, in order to photograph not only the whole village but also the surrounding environment (in particular, the marks on the land evincing the remains of the rundale system of farming). This strategy is to be seen in his photographs of Cappagh village where Welch notes: some 'dreadful rundale holdings' are indicated by the 'great stone dykes in a hillside' and by the houses being 'all close together'.[59] In this type of photograph people seem almost incidental in the larger vista of landscape, suggesting that Welch was not primarily making an identification of land and people.

The effect, however, is not to make the image picturesque but to draw attention to how the material environment has been contoured in terms of human geography (see, for example, Figures. 10.1 and 10.2). The result is that the land is seen as analogous to the geologist's perspective, which in turn serves to neutralise an overtly political reading. This avoidance becomes even more marked when we consider the anterior context of the eviction photograph, which was used to great effect in nationalist rhetoric. Technical terms reinforce the visual codes that Welch is employing to signify improvement: villages are 'migrated', the land 'stripped' and 'redistributed'.[60] Images produced to provide evidence of the Board's modernising agenda exploit perspective to infer an opening-up of the land; roads run on to the receding horizon line, houses are dotted among expansive cultivated terrain or are evinced by the tidy cottage garden of the migrated tenant (Figure 6.4).

Revealingly, Welch makes only one passing comment on the issue of ownership and improvement of the land. On a holiday jaunt when he was showing friends the work of the CDB as well as antiquarian sites and spots of natural interest, the party stopped at Garumna,

58. Spurgeon Thompson, 'The Politics of Photography: Travel Writing and the Irish Countryside, 1900–1914', in L.W. McBride, *Images, Icons and the Irish Nationalist Imagination* (Dublin: Four Courts Press, 1999), p.128.
59. *Excursions Diary*, 1914, 189.
60. Ibid.

where the CDB's work included improved housing and schools. Welch compared the original situation with that at another location (Gweedore, in Donegal) before a reforming landowner 'bought the estate and altered the condition of things'.[61] Improvement in this context speaks of a particular tradition of land usage and ownership.

There is a curiously festive mood to Welch's reminiscences of the period when he was undertaking photography for the CDB. This, in part, is likely to be related to the fact that when he was undertaking this commission he was also engaging in a number of excursions in the West of Ireland by motor car. Contained within an album entitled 'Irish Motor Trip July 1914', are two intriguing photographs. Taken at Costello, Co. Galway, when Welch was photographing for the CDB, the first shows the 'Lord Lieutenant, dressed as Irish Colleen with shawl, standing next to a creel laden donkey'; the second, a view of R.J. Welch 'dressed as an Irish peasant with bainis and waistcoat standing next to a laden donkey'.[62] Jokes, in a Freudian sense, are never solely innocent affairs; rather, they speak of repressions and desires.[63] Both images reference the processes of 'Othering' at a specific historical location. However, as Lacan makes evident, the imaginary is always a misrecognition of unity and wholeness. If, as suggested, Welch's photographs for the CDB, by locating vision within the gaze of material environment, aim to avoid the politicisation of the land that preceded them in eviction photographs (see Figure 11.1), these two pictures speak of how difference is always premised on a desire to contain the Other. In many respects these photographs speak not simply of the jest of masquerade, involving gender, class and identity, but also poignantly of differences that were not to be negotiated – the desire is prescient.

This chapter has sought to consider Robert J. Welch's use of camera technique within a context of cultural practices. It has acknowledged that developments in the technology of photography extended the range of what could be represented and has also stressed, through a critique of Welch's photographs of the West of Ireland, that these developments cannot be explicated from a cultural context. This is not to deny the relevance of Welch's images to various branches

61. *Excursions Diary*, 1914, 193–4. George Hill's improvement of the land at Gweedore, through the introduction of sheep farming, which involved land clearance and evictions, was contentious, to say the least. This type of 'improvement' fuelled nationalist stereotypes of the venal landlord, which were further exploited to considerable effect during the Land Wars of the 1880s and 1890s.

62. Y22699 and Y22700, Welch Collection, Ulster Museum. Miss Sheila Dolan originally owned the album, which comprises thirty-one prints. At the age of ten, Sheila Dolan and her mother and father accompanied Welch on this leg of his tour of the congested districts in the west of Ireland.

63. Welch had a penchant for joke photography (Evans and Turner, *Irelands Eye*, p. 7). An early combination image of male field club members as mermen references both the nature of field club interests (nature) and a projection of identification with natural states.

of scientific investigation.[64] It is, though, to highlight how the choices any photographer makes are dependent both on the technologies available and referenced by cultural and historical location. On this point, it is worth quoting John Tagg:

> Photographs do not carry their meanings in themselves, nor can a single range of technical devices guarantee the unity of the field of photographic meanings … Images can signify meanings only in more or less defined frameworks of usage and social practice. Their import and status have to be produced and effectively institutionalised, and such institutionalisations do not describe a unified field or the working out of some essence of the medium: they are negotiated locally and discontinuously and are productive of meaning and value.[65]

By situating Welch's practice within the broader frame of cultural politics in Ireland, this chapter has sought to consider photography as a form of cultural production. If we miss this aspect of his photography, we also miss the full richness that Welch's photographs hold for a deeper understanding both of the negotiations at play in the construction of one type of identity at a specific point in Irish history and of the role that photography plays in visualising these possibilities.

64. For example, Evans acknowledges how Welch's photographs stimulated his interest in geography and Martyn Anglesea insists that as scientific resources Welch's negatives 'should be regarded as one of the national treasures of Ireland' (1997, pp. 513–14). To these acknowledgements I would add, however, that we must also recognise the ways in which photographs communicate. Martin Anglesea, 'The Art of Nature Illustrations', in J. Foster Wilson (ed.), *Nature in Ireland: A Scientific and Cultural History* (Dublin: The Lilliput Press, 1997).

65. John Tagg, 'Totalled Machines: Criticism, Photography And Technological Change', *New Formations*, No. 7, Spring (1989), p.30

CHAPTER SIX

Picturing Poverty: Colonial Photography and the Congested Districts Board

JUSTIN CARVILLE

School of Creative Arts, Institute of Art, Design & Technology, Dun Laoghaire

1. J.M. Synge, *The Aran Islands* [1907] (London: Penguin, 1992), pp. 33–4.
2. For an account of the market conditions of kelp manufacture during this period see C. Breathnach, *The Congested Districts Board of Ireland, 1891–1923: Poverty and Development in the West of Ireland* (Dublin: Four Courts, 2005), pp. 80–5.
3. J. Clifford, 'On Ethnographic Authority', in *The Predicament of Culture: Twentieth-Century Ethnography, Literature and Art* (Cambridge, Mass.: Harvard University Press, 1988), p. 24.
4. Synge, *The Aran Islands*, p. 34.

Writing in his book *The Aran Islands* in 1907, the playwright John Millington Synge gives a brief account of the process of kelp burning on the island of Inishmaan.[1] Charting the process from manufacture to sale,[2] Synge's description demonstrates the type of ethnographic authority identified by James Clifford as having emerged in Western anthropological field-work around the turn of the nineteenth century.[3] At the end of the account, however, Synge diverges from his ethnographic observation to convey an overall impression of the scene:

> In Aran even manufacture is of interest. The low flame-edged kiln, sending out dense clouds of creamy smoke, with a band of red and grey clothed workers moving in the haze, and usually some petticoated boys and women who come down with drink, forms a scene with as much variety and colour as any picture from the East.[4]

Synge's romanticisation of the ethnographic enterprise has been identified in a number of studies of his account of the Aran Islands, and such remarks are not uncommon in the

5. See S. Ashley, 'The Poetics of Race in 1890's Ireland: An Ethnography of the Aran Islands', *Patterns of Prejudice: Institute for Jewish Policy Research*, 35, 2 (2001), p. 6 and G. Castle, '"Synge on Aran": The Aran Islands and the Subject of Revivalist Ethnography' and 'Staging Ethnography: Synge's "The Playboy of the Western World"', in *Modernism and the Celtic Revival* (Cambridge: Cambridge University Press, 2001).

6. This is reminiscent of Edward Said's description in *Orientalism* as discourse of, and on, the Orient, which rather than being passively reflected in scientific knowledge, the social sciences, literary texts and visual imagery etc., is actively produced geographically, politically and imaginatively. See E. Said, *Orientalism* (London: Penguin, 1995), p. 3.

7. See J. Lennon, *Irish Orientalism: A Literary and Intellectual History* (Syracuse: Syracuse University Press, 2004), pp. xxvi–xxviii, 205–370.

Cont.

description of his overall impressions of island life.[5] In his comparison of kelp manufacture with a 'picture from the East', however, another dimension of the romantic imaginary of Aran begins to emerge. Not only are the social and physical aspects of the labour process reduced to visual spectacle, the resulting image is framed by an already circulating set of colonial and, in this particular example, 'Oriental' imagery.[6]

Synge's visual analogy between Aran and the 'East' could be identified as yet one more example of what has been described in recent Irish literary criticism as Revivalist 'cross-colonialism': the identification of familiar experiences and representations between colonies as an anti-colonial strategy aimed at destabilising the dominant relations between imperial centre and colony.[7] The merits of such post-colonial interpretations aside, what interests me about Synge's 'cross-colonial' comparison is its wider implication for the consideration of the broad spectrum of representations of the western seaboard produced throughout the late nineteenth and early twentieth centuries. Such a comparison is of particular relevance to the study of the photographic representation of Ireland during this historical period. Photography quickly became an established technique for visualising the West of Ireland as real and 'imagined' geographical and social space throughout this historical juncture. By the time photography had been incorporated into fields such as the social sciences and colonial administration during the closing two decades of the twentieth century, however, the techniques, methods and methodologies of using photography within such disciplines had already been refined through their use across the European colonies.[8] Indeed the historical parallels between photography and colonialism are such that is hard to imagine that the techniques and methods developed for its incorporation into such fields would have become so clearly defined.

It is with the intersections of photography and the colonial enterprise in mind that this chapter will examine the Congested Districts Board (CDB) photographic archive. Their description as an archive is important to the discussion that follows. Although individual photographs may be identified as providing specific technical data about the clothing, technology or labour practices of a particular historical period, the CDB photographs were not produced to be read as discrete, historical documents. Photographs, as John Tagg so persistently and forcefully reminds us, 'are never evidence of history' – they are not passive reflections of real events transferred onto the geometric surface of paper, nor are they a transparent window onto the world – 'they are themselves the historical'.[9] As it will be demonstrated, it is by examining the CDB photographs as an archive within the historical context of the very institutional structures that commissioned, accumulated and categorised them that we can begin to identify the history that these photographs enact. Examining the representation of poverty and housing in a cross-section of imagery, the chapter will explore the intersection of the aesthetic and political in the archive's visualisation of the CDB's policies of progress, development and reform. From this perspective the chapter will argue that, much like Synge's conflation of the ethnographic and the romantic, the visual itself has a history and an ideology.

PHOTOGRAPHY, THE ARCHIVE AND THE GEOGRAPHICAL IMAGINATION

Established by the Land Act of 1891, the CDB appears to have had very little official use for photography within its routine administration and data collection. Unlike many other state institutions that incorporated photography into their systems of administration, there were no official published guidelines for the taking, acquisition or distribution of photographs. Nor, it would appear, was there a set of defined criteria for the types of subject-matter that should be photographed. Photographs did not feature in the CDB annual reports, and there are no statements by inspectors suggesting that photographs formed part of their routine collection of statistical data. Beyond the commissioned work of Belfast photographer Robert John Welch, J.D. Cassidy of Ardara, County Donegal and, most likely, a number of other local photographers from the bigger towns along the western seaboard whose work comprises the CDB archive, photography appears to have been no more than peripheral within the overall administration of its activities.

Cont.

8. The literature on colonial photography is voluminous. For a cross-section see J.R. Ryan, *Picturing Empire: Photography and the Visualization of the British Empire* (London: Reaktion, 1997); N. Monti, *Africa Then: Photographs 1840–1914* (London: Thames & Hudson, 1987).

9. J. Tagg, *The Burden of Representation: Essays on Photographies and Histories* (London: MacMillan, 1988), p. 65.

While the use of photography may have not been officially defined, however, it is apparent that it played no insignificant role in the history of the CDB. Although photography was not officially submitted along with the other data collected by the inspectors who contributed to the baseline reports – compiled according to a defined set of 'headings of inquiry'[10] – a number of inspectors took photographs during their investigations into the condition of rural industries and housing. Major Ruttledge-Fair, whose photographs were collected in an album by James Hack Tuke, long-time campaigner on poverty in the West of Ireland and advisor to the then Chief Secretary to Ireland Arthur Balfour,[11] took photographs during his inspections of the congested districts in 1892 as part of the process of producing the Board's baseline reports (see Chapter 2).[12] J.W.D. Walker, an inspector and amateur photographer who contributed photographs to the Dudley reports on district nursing in rural Ireland, also took photographs during his duties as an inspector – see Figure 12.1.[13]

Outside of the use of photography by CDB inspectors, that photographers were commissioned to document their involvement in the agricultural and fishing industries, and an archive was compiled to demonstrate the improvement of rural housing and land distribution, suggests that photography had a clear function within the administration of the CDB. The use of photography within the CDB can thus be identified as operating within two distinct spheres of social life: the personal and the private sphere of the individual – in the form of albums compiled for personal reference – and the professional and public photographs commissioned for the organisation's official records. Such differentiation is significant not because of a distinction between amateur and professional, or because it implies different intentions, uses or choice of subject-matter. The distinction between the personal albums created by individual inspectors from those officially compiled by the Board is important because it is through the authority of the institution that the photographs came to accrue their meaning. This is not to suggest that photographs taken by inspectors or other interested parties could not find their place within the CDB's official archive. On the contrary, it is precisely through the qualitative accumulation

10. See Breathnach, *The Congested Districts Board*, p. 36.
11. Ibid., p. 35.
12. Ibid. p. 22. The Tuke Album is held in the National Photographic Archive. See Chapter 2.
13. I would like to thank Ciara Breathnach for this reference. The annual reports of the Lady Dudley Committee are held at the NLI.

of photographic imagery by the CDB rather than the authorship of individual photographers that the archive is invested with its authority.[14] As Allan Sekula notes, the photographic archive is both an enclosed discursive system and a collection of material objects in which photographs are incorporated or excluded in relation to similarities or differences to other photographs in the archive.[15] Differences in style, technique and subject-matter, while important to any discussion of the photographic archive, are not the issue at stake here. Rather, it is the ownership and administration of the archive that confers the photographic image with authority as truthful and realistic representation.[16]

In order to identify the role of the photographic archive within the administration of the CDB, it is necessary not to examine the photographs produced by the Board as illustrative of the organisation's initiatives or as documentary records of its achievements. Nor is it correct to read the photographs against the backdrop of the history of the CDB. What is required is a careful consideration of what might be termed the archival project of colonial administration, as well as the examination of the role of photographic archive in projecting the Board's policies of progress, development and reform. That is to say, the photographic archive should not be read as merely a repository for dusty sheets of photographic paper, passively and transparently reflecting the past. In order to read the photographic image historically, it is important to acknowledge the CDB archive as an active rather than a passive instrument of colonial administration. The establishment of photographic archives is rarely motivated solely by the desire to preserve records for posterity: they are more likely to be driven by the desire to be productive – not in terms of producing the material documentation of administration that fills the physical space of the archive – but rather the production of knowledge of its subject and how its subject is defined.[17] In order to explore the administrative and ideological motivations behind the CDB's use of photography it is important to situate it as a working archive, actively and deliberately producing a body of useful information on the territory, housing and labour practices of the congested districts. As a departure point for examining the archival project of colonial administration within the

14. See A. Sekula, 'Photography Between Labour and Capital', in Benjamin H.D. Buchloh and R. Wilkie (eds), *Leslie Shedden: Mining Photographs and Other Pictures, 1948–1968*, (Halifax: The Press of the Nova Scotia College of Art and Design, 1983), pp. 193–68.

15. A. Sekula, 'The Body and the Archive', in R. Bolton, (ed.), *The Contest of Meaning: Critical Histories of Photography*, (Cambridge, Mass.: MIT, 1989), p. 352.

16. See Sekula, ibid. 187; Tagg, *The Burden of Representation*; and J. Tagg, 'The Proof of the Picture', in *Grounds of Dispute: Art History, Cultural Politics and the Discursive Field* (London: MacMillan, 1992).

17. M. Foucault, *Discipline and Punish: The Birth of the Prison* (London: Penguin, 1991), pp. 27–8, 189–91.

Figure 6.1
Panoramic view of Lissaniska,
Castlebar R28,190 and
R28,189, NLI

context of the CDB, this chapter will now turn its attention to a specific type of photographic image. This image is atypical within the overall range of photographs produced by the CDB, but is useful precisely because it visually demonstrates in material form the ideological use of the photographic archive.

Within the CDB collection in the National Library of Ireland are several panoramic views. Constructed from joining together two separate photographs to form a sweeping vista of rural space, the images expand human, and even the camera's, normal range of vision. In one such panoramic photograph of Lissaniska, Castlebar (Figure 6.1), an arching, almost semi-circular view of the village is produced through the combination of the flat surfaces of two photographs. In the panoramic picture the same group of local villagers is represented twice. In the left-hand foreground they are gathered around a small thicket of trees, and in the right-hand background they are lined up in a dutiful and orderly fashion against the gable end of a white-washed cottage. Some villagers are not only represented twice, they also duplicate their poses.

As if automatically yielding up the uniformity of pose desired by the photographic archive, one girl, standing out from the rest of the group in a dark pinafore and white sleeves with hands clasped in front of her body, duplicates her pose in both photographs, while another slightly taller girl, in a grey pinafore, hides her hands behind her back, replicating her position within the group. Such duplication of bodily pose suggests not so much a familiarity with being photographed, an ability to present oneself 'to be represented', but rather conformity and obedience to the scrutiny of the camera. This image, then, can take its place alongside those other photographs that display the characteristics of social power relations between photographer and subject, identified by Tagg and others as being linked to the instrumental use of photography by institutions of the state.[18] As an example of the type of representation produced through what Mary Louise Pratt has defined as the 'contact zone' between peoples normally separated geographically and historically, the photograph can be read as the result of coercion and inequality between photographer and villager.[19] Beyond the social relations between photographer and subject, however, what might the photograph in the form of a panoramic view tell us about the broader workings of the CDB archive? How might the expanded vision of the panorama provide a departure point for examining the visual rhetoric of the CDB's photographic representation of rural space? The answer, I want to suggest, is to briefly examine the panorama historically as a social as well as an ideological phenomenon.

Originally devised as a popular form of entertainment bridging the divide between high art and mass culture, the idea of the panorama has now come to suggest a general overview of something or, on a visual level, a particular style of pictorial representation. Throughout the nineteenth century, however, the technology and visual effects of the panorama had quite a specific social meaning. First exhibited commercially in London in 1791 by the Irish artist Robert Barker, the panorama was a large painted canvas exhibited on the interior wall of a circular room, providing a 360° view of the subject depicted in the painting.[20] In the middle a platform was constructed providing the viewer with an unrestricted vantage point from which to see the

18. Drawing on the work of French historian and philosopher Michael Foucault, the 'social power model' has become a dominant model within photographic historiography for discussions of colonial, ethnographic and social science photography. See, for example, Sekula, 'The Body and the Archive' and D. Green, 'Classified Subjects' *Ten.8*, 14, (1985), pp. 3–37.

19. M.L. Pratt, *Imperial Eyes: Travel Writing and Transculturation*, (London: Routledge, 1992), p. 6.

20. The most comprehensive account of the technological and social impact of the panorama can be found in S. Oetterman, *The Panorama: The History of a Mass Medium* (Cambridge, Massachusetts: Zone Books/MIT, 1997).

painting in its entirety. The most popular subject-matter depicted in panoramas from the late eighteenth century on were elevated views across the roof-tops of cities and spectacular displays of historical battles. Panoramas were toured across Europe and North America so that from the many purpose-built Rotundas the public could view the cityscapes of Rome or Paris with as much ease and familiarity as they could their own. Panoramas thus allowed the viewer to visually experience geographical spaces from which they were separated by great distances. They contributed to the geographical imagination of distant places, deriving their significance in shaping public perception not through the realistic depiction of the paintings but through the technological illusion created by the panoramic display of the image.

The panoramic photograph of Lissaniska is by no means as grand a visual display as the architecturally constructed panoramas exhibiting the spectacular cityscapes of London, Rome or Paris, but the same formal principles have been applied. The joining together of the two photographs to form a composite view of the village constructs a similar sense of illusionary depth out of the flat, one-dimensional surface of the photographic image. Expanding the singular photograph's normal range of vision, the panoramic image allows the viewer to visually access the village in its entirety. Scanning across the surface of the image, the viewer is able to identify geographical landmarks and property boundaries while also establishing a sense of the village's overall spatial layout. It provides the viewer with a visual frame through which to 'imagine' the village geographically as place.

To concentrate solely on the technological effect of the panorama as a form of pictorial representation, however, is to overlook the significance of what the concept of the panorama means as a philosophical model for seeing the world. Stemming from the Greek words *pan* 'all' and *horama* 'view', meaning a 'complete view', the panorama is merely one material example of a wider discourse of Western vision encapsulated by the idea of a 'world view'. The concept of a world view proposes that objects, societies and systems of belief can be 'visually mapped' in their entirety by 'anyone with an adequate overview'.[21] In effect it suggests that there is a

21. C. Classen, 'McLuhan in the Rainforest: The Sensory Worlds of Oral Culture', in D. Howes, (ed.), *Empire of the Senses: The Sensual Culture reader* (Oxford: Berg Publishers, 2005), p. 147.

privileged position from which to observe and survey the world. Among the models of vision emerging in the late eighteenth century that conform to the idea of the world view, Jeremy Bentham's 'Panopticon' has been identified by the French philosopher and historian Michel Foucault, as demonstrating most clearly the intersections of vision and ideology embedded in philosophical discourses of seeing and producing knowledge of the world.[22] As Foucault argues, Bentham's penal design of permanent visibility with its central tower surrounded by a circle of divided, backlit, open faced cells, illuminating every square inch of space so that the incarcerated body is permanently visible from the watch tower, is more than an architectural structure.[23] It was an 'event of the human mind' in which a 'whole type of society emerges' through it. A society 'not of spectacle, but of surveillance'.[24]

It is the intersection of these visual and ideological concerns raised by the panorama that are at play in the function of the photographic archive within the administrative procedures of the CDB. On the one hand the photographic archive expands the normal range of vision of the administrator, the politician, indeed anybody who cared or had reason to examine the photographic representation of the congested districts. It allows the viewer to inspect every detail of the subject recorded on the rectangular frame of the photograph. From the technical detail to the overall view, the photographic archive allowed the viewer to visually access spaces from which they are physically denied access. The combinations of photographs from landscapes to housing, agrarian labour to the maritime industries, constructed an imaginative geography of the territory defined as the congested districts. In this respect, the methods and aims of the photographic archive are exactly congruent with that of the inspectors' reports, with their combination of statistical data and overall impressions of the lives of those measured in the accompanying statistical tables (see, for example, Chapter 10).

On the other hand the photographic archive functioned as an administrative tool to produce knowledge of the condition of the congested districts, and of the workings of the Board to improve the housing, agriculture and fishing industries in these areas. Through its mapping and

22. Foucault, *Discipline and Punish*, pp. 195–28.
23. Ibid., p. 200.
24. Ibid., p. 216.

surveying of the geographical territory in its jurisdiction, the photographic archive established how the congested districts came to be seen. It produced a purely visual, transparent form of knowledge (the phrase 'seeing and knowing' springs to mind), through which the viewer could glean any and all information on the congested districts they required. The CDB photographic archive is then yet another instrument of the society of surveillance identified by Foucault, invested with power relations that produce a correlative 'field of knowledge' of its subject.[25] However, as an instrument of colonial surveillance, the photographic archive was not solely invested with the observing and recording of the congested districts, it was also charged with monitoring the administration of this territory by the Board. In a passage that includes a citation noting the material and ideological similarities between Bentham's 'Panopticon' and Barker's panorama, Foucault notes that, in such a system of surveillance, anybody, from official inspectors to the general public, will be able to observe not only the object of the gaze but also the observers themselves.[26] In this regard it is perhaps worth noting here Francis Sheridan's remarks in his report of 1915 on the aims and objectives of the CDB's initial survey of the territory designated congested under the terms of the Land Act of 1891, and identified by Balfour as requiring state intervention during his tour of the western seaboard a year earlier:

> the first step taken by the Board in 1892 was to institute a comprehensive survey of the economic condition of the scheduled districts – to form a baseline from which progress could afterwards be measured, as well as to indicate the course of action which might be best suited for the different circumstances of the various districts, for the special characteristics of the localities have to be borne in mind in framing schemes of improvement.[27]

Sheridan's remarks demonstrate that the data produced, accumulated and categorised by the inspectors had a specific function in defining and determining the type of activities undertaken by the Board. Schemes of improvement required specialised knowledge of particular districts

25. Ibid., p. 27.
26. Ibid., p. 207.
27. F.S. Sheridan (1915), 'The "Congested Districts" and the Work of the Congested Districts Board', reprinted in J. Morrissey (ed.), *On the Verge of Want* (Dublin: Crannóg Books, 2001), p. 4.

which could be identified by referring to the information contained within the statistical data collected in the baseline reports.[28] Initiatives undertaken by the Board, from schemes of improvement to financial loans, were based on a system of constant reference and referral to the accumulated economic and demographic data. More significantly, however, these reports became the yardstick by which 'progress' could be 'measured'. This progress was measured not only to determine the cyclical, economic modernisation of the congested districts, but also to determine the success and progressiveness of the CDB's policies and schemes of improvement. It became a mechanism to measure its own success and failures in administrating the economic development of the western seaboard.

The photographic archive played a significant role in demonstrating this modernisation of the congested districts through the Board's schemes of improvement and economic reform. It produced a traceable, visual record of the development and modernisation initiated by the Board's schemes while also functioning as a regulatory system to measure, through the unquestionable veracity of the photographic image, its own progressiveness as an administrative body. In this sense it is congruent with the CDB's use of the baseline reports to measure the progress of its development schemes. However, the use of the codes and conventions of photographic realism, in combination with colonial practices of representing rural space, measured this progress in purely visual terms. Progress was measured in terms of the visual idealisation and aestheticisation of the landscape. Nowhere in the CDB archive is this demonstrated more clearly than in the photographic representation of housing, to which this chapter will now turn its attention.

COLONIAL PHOTOGRAPHY AND THE VISUALIZATION OF PROGRESS

As part of his commission for the CDB, Robert John Welch photographed a great deal around the agricultural districts of Mayo and Galway. Views of grass farms identifying the lines of

28. For a detailed discussion of the baseline reports see Breathnach, *The Congested Districts Board*, pp. 30–46.
29. On the CDB's land purchase schemes see ibid., Chapter 5.

undivided holdings are combined with detailed images of the newly acquired farmhouses purchased by the Board as part of its consolidation and redistribution of agricultural land.[29] Through this archival combination of photographs a conjuncture is established between the undivided plots, signifying the communal land tenure of the rundale system, and the newly formed, single holdings established under the CDB's land purchase scheme. What is most striking about this conjuncture of images is the use of photographic codes and conventions to convey this process of agricultural modernisation. Through the framing and viewpoint of the camera, progress is visualised on the geometric surface of the photographic image. Social and economic change is signified through the abstract aestheticisation of rural space.

Amongst Welch's photographs of rural housing is a 'View of unsanitary house in Monivea, County Galway' (Figure 11.2). Accompanying the photograph is a short note stating that the 'tenants of this house were soon to be migrated to new holdings'. The dwelling is typical of those often described in the inspectors' reports as 'built of stone, roofed with "scraws" and straw or rough mountain hedge' and consisting of 'one room and a kitchen' shared with cattle and fowl.[30] The photograph depicts a group of tightly clustered buildings that fill the middleground of the image. In the foreground there is a barren, muddy yard strewn with stones and to the right a dilapidated stone wall. The differently coloured patches of thatch on the roof of the cottage and unkempt appearance of the yard and surrounding buildings signify the haphazard, shabby nature of the rural peasant's dwelling. Apart from the shadowy presence in the doorway of the middle building the yard appears almost devoid of human presence, although the turf stacked against the gable end of the thatched cottage and the wooden cart suggest that this is an inhabited and working farm.

The tight framing of the photograph, cropping out parts of the adjacent buildings, fills the space of the image, conveying a sense of a densely built environment. Indeed the truncated representation of the buildings suggests that this space is so congested, so crowded, that the photograph is unable to incorporate the dwelling in its entirety within its frame. The pictorial

30. Ruttledge-Fair, Major R. 'District of Belmullet', reproduced in Morrissey, *On the Verge of Want*, p. 103.

organisation of space, with the buildings appearing at different angles to
one another within the frame of the
photograph, reinforces the sense of
the dwelling being over-crowded and
unsanitary. The buildings crowd in on
one another as if encroaching upon
each other's space. In this photograph, then, the incorporation of the
cart signifies the represented space as
rural and pastoral, with the tools of
agrarian labour clearly visible. The
absence of livestock, combined with
the barren, untidy yard, however, suggests that this is not a functioning
farm. There are no signs of productive

Figure 6.2
View of congested village of
Cappagh, Castlerea district
County Galway, CDB20

labour. Everything about the photograph connotes social and economic stagnation, the stop-
time exposure of the photograph reflecting the stasis of agricultural development and economic
progress.

Compare this photograph with that of 'New house of John Commons, farmer and tailor,
Ryehill, Monivea, County Galway' (Figure 11.5). Immediately one is struck by the differences in
composition between the photographs. Here the framing of the scene incorporates the adjacent
field, possibly farmed by the owner of the dwelling. The adjoining building, possibly a shed or
workshop, newly whitewashed with modern roofing, is set back away from the house. Social and
working spaces are clearly defined by hedgerows and boundary walls. There is a clear separation
of the spaces of labour from those of family life. The framing and point of view of the photo-

graph, drawing the viewer's eye along the boundary wall that recedes into the distance, not only suggests the demarcation and careful management of agricultural land but also connotes private property. Indeed, the textual description accompanying the photograph – John Commons' new house – reinforces a sense of ownership. In the photographs of congested villages or unsanitary houses, there is always a sense of anonymity about the owners conveyed through the captions, while the families who have migrated to new holdings constructed by the CDB are frequently clearly identified by name.

There are others signs in the image that suggest progress. In contrast to the barren yard in the previous photograph, the field to the left hand-side of the image, with its long grass, connotes productivity and modernisation. As W.J.T. Mitchell suggests, such open spaces are 'not just a spatial scene but a projected future of "development" and "exploitation"'.[31] The children, sitting along the boundary wall gazing back at the camera, reinforce this sense of future development. Contrast this image of childhood with that of 'View of congested village of Cappagh, Castlerea district, County Galway' (Figure 6.2), one of the worst congested villages the Board had to deal with, in which a small child is barely visible among the jagged boulders that cut through the foreground of the photograph. Even Commons's new house itself, jutting up out of the landscape, signifies social, economic and moral development, as if the two-storey house is a symbol of social and class mobility. The symbolic improvement of housing did not simply convey a sense of economic progress, it also carried with it moral imperatives. Henry Doran, in his report on Kiltimagh, remarked on the practice of children of both sexes sleeping together that;

Reflecting on the habits of the people of this and neighbouring districts, who are born and reared in the same room as their cattle; where brothers and sister occupy the same sleeping apartment, insensible of any violation of human decency; living in such foul surroundings, in such close association with the brutes of the field, I have often marvelled how they are

31. W.J.T. Mitchell, 'Imperial Landscape', in W.J.T. Mitchell (ed.), *Landscape and Power* (Chicago: University of Chicago Press, 1994), p. 17.
32. H. Doran, 'Kiltimagh baseline report', reproduced in Morrissey, *On the Verge of Want*, p. 109.

so moral, so well disposed, and so good in many ways as they are.[32]

The conjuncture of the two photographs in the CDB archive, visually demonstrating the modernisation of rural housing, can thus be read not only as indicating economic and social mobility but also moral amelioration. For the new owners the elevated dwelling, the two-storey house, clearly identifiable in the landscape, was no doubt a symbol of their improved social status. However, as the sociologist Eamonn Slater has observed, the construction of single dwellings in the rural landscape, replacing the small villages of the communal rundale system, made it easier for the authorities to identify and monitor the social and moral behaviour of the rural peasantry.[33]

This interconnection of economic and industrial progress, combined with social mobility and moral improvement, is represented through the abstract visualisation of rural space. Not only are new houses built and the rural landscape managed, it is visually cleansed. Aestheticisation becomes a signifier of progress and social reform. The codes and conventions of the photographic image are deployed to visualise the modernisation of rural life through the CDB's agricultural and housing schemes. Terry Smith has identified such practices of aestheticisation as part of the visual regimes of colonisation.[34] Smith identifies three major components of colonial vision: practices of calibration (the measuring of peoples and property boundaries and their surveillance); practices of obliteration ('the erasing of the habitus, imagery and viewpoints and eventually, the physical existence of indigenous peoples'); and practices of aestheticization, (the transformation of experience into an abstract process of symbolisation).[35] The visualisation of progress in the CDB's photographic archive incorporates aspects of all three of these visual regimes of colonisation. The photograph defined property boundaries, recorded details of its subject and, as discussed above, functioned as a form of surveillance. Through the aestheticisation of rural space constructed using the codes and conventions of the photographic image, viewpoints were adopted that projected a specific image of the congested districts. Through this process of visualisation the photographic archive became a mechanism to visually demonstrate to the viewer, in the clear and unambiguous visual language of the photograph,

Figure 6.3
House of Mrs. Bridget Kelly Lisvalley, Vesey, near Tuam, County Galway, CDB1

33. E. Slater, 'Marx on Achill: Can Marx's Methodology Help Us Explicate the Material Existence of Nineteenth Century Irish Peasantry through Photography', Unpublished paper delivered at *Into the Light: Photography in 19th Century Ireland*, IADT, 2 November, 2005.
34. T. Smith, 'Visual Regimes of Colonization: Aboriginal Seeing and European Vision in Australia', in N. Mirzoeff (ed.), *The Visual Culture Reader*, 2nd edn. (London: Routledge, 2002).
35. Ibid., pp. 483–4.

Figure 6.4
View from the new dwelling
house of Mrs Bridget Kelly
(fig. 6 CDB2)

36. Sheridan, 'The "Congested
Districts"', p. 4.

the progress and modernisation initiated by the CDB's policies, in words of Sheridan 'to raise the mode of life from the submerged condition to which it had been reduced to that of a virile, progressive, self-supporting and self-respecting community'.[36]

The extent of the connections between visualisation, progress and self-improvement is demonstrated quite clearly in two photographs relating to the migration of Mrs Bridget Kelly from the congested village of Curraghan, County Leitrim, to a CDB house in Lisvalley, County Galway. The first photograph depicts a newly built house with a group of people gathered at the doorway (Figure 6.3). The presence of the horse and cart with the cabby suggests that the men are possibly CDB inspectors, but beyond this the photograph is rather banal and utilitarian in its documenting of the dwelling. The textual information accompanying the photograph, however, suggests that there is something more going on here. The notes record that 'the bay window seen in the photograph was added at her own expense'. The reasons why the notes draw attention to this window become clear in the next photograph, 'View from the new dwelling house of Mrs Bridget Kelly' (Figure 6.4). The construction of the bay window was not to add space to the property, to increase the square footage of the holding, but rather to allow visual access to the idealised, picturesque landscape beyond the property boundary of the house. The frame of Welch's photograph replaces the frame of Mrs Kelly's window, which constructs a picturesque view of the Irish countryside. The abstract aestheticization of rural space to connote progress and modernisation has been incorporated into the very process of constructing dwellings. The fact that Mrs Kelly has contributed financially to this visual amenity merely serving to reinforce the idealised visualization of rural space as a signifier of modernisation.

CONCLUSION

At the beginning of this chapter, Synge's description of the Aran Islands was introduced to demonstrate the extent to which representations of Ireland collapse into romantic aestheticisation. More importantly, however, Synge's ethnographic description reflects the overlapping discourses of colonialism, the social sciences and romanticism in the visualisation of nineteenth- and early twentieth-century Ireland. The photographs produced for the CDB archive, established to document the housing, agriculture and fishing industries, also reflect these colonial practices. It is important to stress, however, that there is nothing innocent about this idealisation of the Irish landscape. Photography's visualisation of the congested districts had a clear ideological function. As suggested above, the aestheticisation of rural space was bound up with the practices of calibration and obliteration identified by Wright as the visual regimes of colonisation. In the CDB photographs these practices where incorporated into measuring the Board's modernisation of rural space, the romanticised, picturesque rural space signifying progress. The visual idealisation of the congested districts through the aesthetic codes of photographic realism was employed to produce visible evidence of social and economic progress. The result was to reduce the social realities of the people affected by the CDB's schemes to a series of visual appearances. The effect of Bridget Kelly's migration from Leitrim to Galway, resulting, no doubt, in separation from friends and family and dislocation from her community, is reduced to the abstract visualisation of an idealised landscape. Progress is equated to purchasing a room with a view.

Allan Sekula has argued that archives serve as a 'kind of clearing house of meaning', through which it (meaning) is 'liberated from the actual contingencies of use'.[37] Thus the original uses and meanings of the archive can be supplanted by new ones. Historians may find the CDB photographs useful in providing technical details of housing, agriculture, clothing and transportation, but to read these photographs as documentary evidence of a bygone era is to overlook the context in which they were put to use. Foregrounding the CDB photographs as an archive, this chapter has set out to read the photographic image as the historical. By examining the photographic archive as active instrument of colonial administration, producing, accumulating and distributing visual evidence of the progress initiated by the CDB schemes, we can begin to identify the photographs produced by Welch and others not as objective, documentary evidence but as representations specifically constructed to project the ideology of the Board's policies of modernisation and reform.

37. Sekula, 'Photography Between Labour and Capital', p. 194.

CHAPTER SEVEN

Robert John Welch, the Accidental Folklorist

CIARÁN WALSH

1. The Department of Irish Folklore, *UCD News*, May 1995 http://www.ucd.ie/ucd-news/may95/folklore.html, accessed on 21 June 2006. '*The Department of Irish Folklore at University College, Dublin (holds) information in 14 main topics on which information has been gathered (between 1935 and 1971 under the direction of James Hamilton Delargy): Settlement and Dwelling; Livelihood and Household Support; Communications and Trade; The Community; Human Life; Nature; Folk Medicine; Time; Principles and Rule of Popular Belief and Practice; Mythological Tradition, Historical Tradition, Religious Tradition; Popular 'Oral Literature'; and Sports and Pastimes.*'

2. See Kevin O'Neill, *Looking at Pictures*, in Adele Dalsimer (ed.) *Visualizing Ireland: National Identity and the Pictorial Tradition* (London: Boston, Faber and Faber, p. 4, cont.

This chapter deals with the Welch collection from a 'folk' perspective. Standard studies on folk life in Ireland concentrate on the traditions of rural communities between 1850 and 1950[1] with the emphasis on the preservation of orally transmitted native knowledge, customs and beliefs collected at source: the authentic voice of the people and the spirit of the nation. Folk usually refers to pre-literate and pre-capitalist agrarian communities which, in an Irish context, constitute the cottiers and smallholders of the western seaboard, the class that has become synonymous with the native Irish and whose members are traditionally, if inaccurately, referred to as the Irish peasant.

Historically very little emphasis has been placed on the visual components of folk culture, which it is generally accepted to be exclusive of what we regard as art. Although this assumption has not been tested to any great extent,[2] there is anecdotal evidence that supports it. Synge surmised that no art was unknown in the simple lives of the Aran islanders,[3] despite a native artfulness and distinctive visual quality evident in their everyday objects. Paul Henry concluded that art was alien to the native Irish, on the basis of his experience of life on Achill Island, compounded by institutional and public indifference to the arts in the Free State.[4] In the absence of evidence to the contrary, most enquiries into the visual aspects of folk culture inevitably default into a study of the representation of the common people in the visual culture of the elite, whether in art or, increasingly, a wider range of visual sources.[5] It follows that a study of the visual record of the common people has to be a second-hand affair, the collection of evidence on the material conditions of rural populations from sources external to those com-

Cont.

3. John M. Synge, *The Aran Islands, Illustrated by Jack B. Yeats* (Mineola, New York: Mineola, 1998) in an unabridged republication of the work published by John W. Luce and Company in 1911, p. 29.

4. See Paul Henry, *An Irish Portrait, the Autobiography of Paul Henry R.H.A.* (London, New York, Toronto, Sydney: B.T. Batsford), 1951,

5. Since the 1990s the nature of the search has changed. Nudged out of the comfort zone of orthodox narratives of Realism, the search for a national art and the first Irish modernist, art historians have begun to acknowledge the complexity of visual culture, grappling with critical models developed in other disciplines.

6. See W. A. Maguire, *A Century in Focus: Photography and Photographs in the North of Ireland 1839–1939*, (Belfast: Blackstaff Press, 2000), p. 54. F.J. Biggar was a member of the Belfast Field Club and an enthusiast for all things Irish. He was a member of the Gaelic League and revived the Glens Feis or *Feis na nGleann* in 1904.

Cont.

munities: from the pictorial record of the elite; the anecdotal evidence of the traveller; the enlightened enquiry of the private scholar; the ethnographic gaze of the stranger; the folkloristic endeavours of the Revivalists; and the documentary record of campaigners and colonial administrators concerned with social conditions and the politics of distress. It constitutes an ethnographic retrospection of sorts with a firm focus on artefacts and living conditions as the visible markers of folk life in the 'West'. The Welch collection offers the possibility of an authentic visual record of life in the townships and a benchmark against which other forms of representation can be assessed.

Robert John Welch was not a folklorist. He would have come in contact with the folk component of the Gaelic Revival in County Antrim[6] but there is no evidence of an active engagement with the Revival or any sympathy with its aims. If anything, Welch personifies the Anglo-Saxon attitude that provoked the development of folklore as a counter-hegemonic measure in the culture wars of the late nineteenth century. His documentation of the peasantry is one component of a complex practice, the bulk of which was focused on commercial work in the industrial and tourism sectors. His scientific outlook and practice was Victorian. His work for the Congested Districts Board (CDB) earned him a Royal Warrant and ultimately a royal pension. He was, in a very real sense, a member of the establishment and a loyal servant of the Crown; not the profile one would associate with the folklore movement. Yet his photographs have been incorporated into conventional folk narratives as authentic representations of folk life in Ireland in the nineteenth century. Welch embraced the age of mechanical reproduction and was instrumental in the production and dissemination of images of old Ireland in the first decade and a half of the twentieth century. Others translated his photographs into the first generation of folksy images of 'auld' Ireland. Since then reproductions of his photographs have slipped sideways into visual culture and continue to function as authentic images of the real Ireland of long ago. Welch, the quintessential Victorian gent, a private scholar and member of the colonial establishment, has been transformed into an accidental folklorist.

The abiding image of Welch is of an intense looking man in tweeds on the left of the a group of conchologists photographed by W.H.W. in May 1897 on a field trip to Mulrough Bay, Co. Antrim (Figure 7.1). Welch and his friends stare at the camera, deeply conscious of the act of representing themselves 'in photography'. It is this look, the objective posture of the gentleman enquirer active in the field in the cause of popular science, that defines the Victorian gaze. Welch's own photograph (Figure 7.2) of an old woman squatting beside a crude stone cabin on a beach in Co. Antrim is a perfect example of that gaze. It records the practice of harvesting seaweed that is so associated with life along the western littoral. The careful arrangement of pots demonstrates a keen interest in artefacts as the material markers of the cottier class and their primitive way of life. There is a strong sense of the past in the present, a sense that we will never see the like of this woman again.

The Victorian fascination with primitive societies was channelled into the developing field sciences of ethnology, ethnography and anthropology. Photography became an effective way of collecting and disseminating specimens of otherness. Welch quickly developed a reputation as an ethnographer and his photographs were much in demand by those involved in field sciences.[7] He was closely associated with Dr Alfred Cort Haddon, a zoologist turned ethnographer whose work had considerable influence on the development of anthropology as an academic discipline in Britain. The photographic collection of Cambridge University's Museum of Anthropology contains a large collection of Welch's photographs, one of which is used on the museum website to illustrate the use of photographic reproductions in the dissemination of images of otherness within colonial networks of exchange. It is a postcard of an old woman spinning that Welch sent to Haddon in 1931

cont.
Having restored a tower in Ardglass in the style of a traditional Irish chieftain's he organised traditional music and dance performances by people in 'fancy dress', Gaelic costumes which he personally designed. Welch must have witnessed these early versions of folk theatre. He was a regular visitor to Ardglass and photographed 'Shane's Castle' for Bigger.

7. E. Estyn Evans and Brian S. Turner, *Ireland's Eye: The Photographs of Robert John Welch*, Ulster Museum series 201 (Belfast: Blackstaff Press, 1977), p. 99. 'He sent on request over a hundred Irish ethnological photographs to General Pitt-Rivers of Rushmore, Salisbury in 1897, and in the following year he contributed to the collection of anthropological photographs sponsored by a British Association committee of which Professor J. L. Myres was secretary. In addition nearly a thousand of his pictures went to the association's Geological photographs committee.'

Figure 7.1
Janet W01/28/14

Figure 7.2
Snail Hunters
W01/56/48

Figure 7.3
CDB 96 Tuke, Girl
Running

8. Postcard, R. Welch. Ireland. Haddon Collection. P.490683.ACH22, Photographic Collection of the Cambridge University Museum of Archaeology and Anthropology. It features, as per the caption, a woman (Irish peasant in traditional shawl) spinning by the roadside. http://museum-server. arcanth.cam.ac. uk/home/collections

9. Marie Boran, 'The Ireland That We Made, A Galway Tribute to Arthur J Balfour', *Journal of the Galway Archaeological and Historical Society* (2002), p. 168.

10. Evans and Turner, *Ireland's Eye*, p.7. Excerpt from a report in *Northern Whig* of 11 June 1900 on 'The Queen's Visit. Interesting exhibit of west of Ireland Photographs'. The exhibition was held in the Vice-Regal Lodge, Dublin, as a showcase for the work of the Congested Districts Board. The report in the *Northern Whig* is focused on Welch's appointment as photographer to Queen Victoria, but contains a useful summary of his Connemara portfolio.

with the greeting 'how's this for ethnog' written on the verso.[8] In 1895 Welch produced an album of photographs of Connemara as 'a gift to the former Chief Secretary of Ireland Arthur J Balfour in recognition of his support for the building of the Galway-Clifden Railway'.[9] The Balfour Album is made up of fifty plates that show 'the character of the congested districts of the western seaboard, and the peasant life, industries and unique antiquities, as far as photographs could show them'(and see Chapter 3).[10] It is a project that reveals much about his practice, his methodology as a photographer and his status as an ethnographer. The Album is assembled from a back catalogue of around two hundred photographs of Galway, Connemara and the Aran Islands. There is none of the close observation that characterises

11. See Sarah Rouse, *Into the Light: An Illustrated Guide to the Photographic Collections of The National Library of Ireland* (Dublin: National Library of Ireland, 1998), p. 7.

12. Ibid, p. 19 for reference to the Congested Districts Board Collection.

13. Henry, *An Irish Portrait*, p. 52.

14. Tuke's activism in the West was central to the establishment of the Congested Districts Board. He commissioned Major Ruttledge-Fair to document conditions in Connemara. People, especially adults going about their daily lives (and avoiding the camera), feature much more than in Welch's photographs.

15. Ibid., 170. Mick McQuaid was ' a well known Irish humorous character' whose exploits were penned by William Francis Lynam in *The Shamrock* periodical from 1867 until its demise in 1920, long after Lynam's death in 1894.

16. Tallon / Mansion House Committee Collection, National Photographic Archive, National Library of Ireland, Dublin. Tallon, Lord Mayor of Dublin, reported to the Mansion House

cont.

Browne's documentation of the people of the Mullet Peninsula.[11] In fact, people are an unstable element in Welch's photographs. They move and when they move, they expose the limitations of his equipment and antagonise his dislike of imperfection in the printed image. But there is another dynamic at work. There is little evidence of any engagement with the people of the place, even if it that been possible for the gentleman photographer dressed in tweeds and speaking with a strange accent. In a photograph of members of the CDB in conversation with a woman on Old Head, County Mayo[12] a local man can be seen in the background acting as an intermediary. Paul Henry describes how local people would run away and hide from the 'sketcher' during his time on Achill Island.[13] This fugitive quality is perfectly captured in the Tuke collection[14] and especially in Figure 7.3, a photograph of a young woman running away from the stranger with a camera.

Much more damaging to Welch and his reputation as an ethnographer is the nakedly political nature of the Balfour project. Plate 23 of the Balfour Album is entitled 'A Bog cabin, Ben Lettery' but it is catalogued in the Ulster Museum as W14/05/83 'An Evicted tenant's cabin', a more accurate description of the type of temporary accommodation constructed by cottiers after eviction. Another squatter's home is described as 'Mick McQuaid's Castle' (Figure 11.1), a humorous reference to a character from popular fiction.[15] 'Mick McQuaid's Castle' is a clever device in terms of the political sensitivity of the project in hand, but one that denies the evidence of dispossession and reinforces the narrative of the feckless Irish with their primitive cabins and the benevolence of the architect of the policy of improvement. Also, Welch was selective, with a noticeable preference for the picturesque. There was evidence of extreme poverty to be found on the island of Gorumna, not far from the sites he visited. Some of the most harrowing photographs of distress were taken here and published in the Report of the Mansion House Enquiry in 1898.[16] They reveal the dark interiors of the cabins and the wretched conditions of the impoverished populace. The difference between these photographs and the Balfour Album condemn Welch as a spectator who was deeply complicit in the politics of improvement.

GIRLS 'SETTING' SEED-POTATOES, BREAKING CLODS WITH SPADE, GLENSHESK, CO. ANTRIM. R.W. 1164.

cont.
Committee in 1898 on distress in the West and South-West of Ireland. There are thirty images in the collection, most notably photographs R27,399, R27,390 and R27,449.

Figure 7.4
Setting potatoes W01/56/25

It would be wrong to dismiss Welch entirely. His documentation of the break-up of the run-dale systems in the West of Ireland is a remarkable record of the transformation of the rural Irish landscape. There is an ethnographic element to his work but it should not be confused with an exaggerated pitch for sales to curious Victorians or his clients in the travel business and the colonial administration. Nevertheless it is this element that makes Welch interesting in a contemporary folk context – not as a conditional record of folk life so much as the way his collection is used and the second life achieved by his images at the hands of others.

E. Estyn Evans, Professor of Geography and Director of the Institute of Irish Studies at Queen's University, Belfast, describes how he met Welch very soon after he 'came to Queen's in 1928 to establish a department of geography. "He gave me old prints of a number of his photographs, many of them with his annotations scribbled on the back and I got from him a set of lantern slides which I used in lectures"'. Evans had begun to turn his back on the Anglocentric orthodoxy of Queen's University Belfast and, with the support of the Belfast Naturalist's Field Club, had concentrated on the ethnology of the living 'peasant culture still lingering in the hills', on folk life and folklore and 'the unrecorded traces of cultural history' that survived in the aftermath of the Great Famine of 1845–9. Welch provided Evans with a documentary record of that lingering culture and Evans incorporated Welch's photographs into an authoritative narrative of folk life in Ulster.

Evans wrote the introduction to the principal catalogue of the Welch collection that was published in 1977.[17] He annotated each of the photographs that were reproduced in twelve thematic photo essays. According to Evans Plate 41, 'Setting potatoes', is 'probably the best known photograph in the collection'. It records the McAllister sisters 'setting seed potatoes, breaking clods with spade, Glenhesk, County Antrim'.[18] Evans states that 'there are very few illustrations of the way in which the spade ridges whose traces can be seen on many hillsides were made, but Welch saw the value of recording a very ancient method of cultivation'. In *Highland Landscapes: Habitat and Heritage*'[19] Evans traces the system of ridge cultivation to the Neolithic and

17. Evans and Turner, *Ireland's Eye*.
18. Maguire, *A Century in Focus*, p. 98.
19. E. Estyn Evans, *The Effect of Man on the Landscape: The Highland Zone*, ed. J. G. Evans, Susan Limbrey, Henry Cleere, Research Report No. 11, The Council for British Archaeology, 1975, p. 4.

the describes the spade used by the women as the ancestor of the long-handled Atlantic spade, which can be traced to the Mesolithic. Evans uses artefacts in the context of settlement patterns and land use to argue 'that the inter-action of prehistoric societies with upland environments has long-lasting effects on both habitat and inhabitants', which could still be gleaned in the contemporary folk life of Ulster at the end of the nineteenth and the beginning of the twentieth centuries.

Evans' treatment of the Welch collection reveals the ideological impulse and political effect inherent in most folk strategies. He is in search of an origin myth that would refute the nationalist emphasis on conquest and settlement as the basis for Ulster Protestant heritage. The McAllister sisters may seem like a world away from the destitute old woman on a beach in County Antrim but they are linked in Evans' view by the charm of rural industry and the narrative of the lingering presence of an ancient culture. The nationalist view is quite different. Images of women and children beside their hovels had become something of a shorthand for poverty in the representation of distress throughout the nineteenth century. In the 1830s a Royal Commission of Enquiry into the Conditions of the Poorer Classes identified widows with children as particularly vulnerable and described how some were left to scavenge on the seashore in order to survive.[20] As a visual trope, the image has a pedigree. James O'Mahony, in his writings for the *Illustrated London News* in its reports on distress in Ireland in 1849, embodied the effect of famine in the South-west in the wretchedness of Bridget O'Donnell and her children,[21] an image that represents the folk memory of the Great Famine more than any other.

These competing constructions of Irish folk life in Ireland point to a problem with the study of folk culture in Ireland. Traditional folklorists have tended to deal in certainties fixed in time by survival and continuity in transmission within culturally defined communities, with an attitude that is invariably nationalist or counter-hegemonic in character. Evans upsets that presumption and suggests a mobility of subjectivity and context over time. Images become dislo-

20. With introduction by Niall Ó'Cíosáin, Dept of History, U.C.G., Poverty Before the Famine, County Clare, 1835, Appendix (A) to the First Report from His Majesty's Commissioners for Enquiring into the Condition of the Poorer Classes in Ireland, CLASP Press, Ennis, 1996, p. 23.

21. *Illustrated London News*, XV, 1849. See Margaret Crawford, *The Great Famine 1845–9: Image Versus Reality: Art into History*, ed. Raymond Gillespie and Brian Kennedy (Dublin: Town House), 1994, p. 81–2.

22. Michel Frijot, *States of Things, Image and Aura: The New History of Photography*, (Cologne: Könemann, 1994), p. 381. Michel Frijot quotes Ernest Lacan's response to the new art of photography in the Paris Universal exhibition of 1855 with reference to Tiffereau's photographs of Mexico: Lacan '...clearly saw the way (photography) could de-contextualise and isolate' not just the archaeological object and the physical environment, but also 'human beings and domestic objects' (E. Lacan, *Esquisses photographiques á propos de l'Exposition et de la guerre d'Orient*, Paris, 1856), p. 19–20.

Figure 7.5
Turf Slide Car W01/54/12

23. John L. Stoddard, *Lectures, Ireland I, Ireland II, Denmark, Sweden*, suppl. vol. (Boston: Balch Brothers Co. and Chicago: Geo. L. Shuman & Co.), p. 53.
24. Evans and Turner, *Ireland's Eye*, Plate 20, 'At the Fireside', p. 41.
25. Benjamin Stone Collection, Birmingham Central Library, taken in 1895 on a combined field club excursion to County Kerry. See Evans and Turner, *Ireland's Eye*, Plates 94 (Farm Inn) and 151 (Ice Sculpture).
26. *San am fado:* long ago.

cated and assume new identities as they function in altered contexts.[22] Language is critical. Images are contextualised in nuances of narrative – words like cottier, peasant, folk, the common people, hovel, cabin, house, destitute, dispossessed, primitive, residuum and so on - locate subjectivity in a range of contexts. Terminology is contentious. Peasant may be synonymous with folk but it is a terminological import from another discourse. It is widely used by nationalist and colonialist alike but is essentially inappropriate in an Irish context. It is the language of the ethnographer, the stranger and the official but not of *an pobal*, the people. All of this suggests an instability in folklore. It is not the fact of the past or its recreation in the present that matters but the process of translation over time that makes sense of the fact in traditional folk narratives. The conventional systems of retrieval, categorisation and representation within a defined chronology and ethnological context need to be replaced by radical folk perspectives that deal with folklore as part of a broader cultural narrative. 'Setting seed potatoes' is a case in point. In 1915 the photograph was published in Stoddard's *Lectures on Ireland* with the caption 'The crop that failed'. It was used to illustrate a text on Daniel O'Connell in the context of the calamitous failure of the potato crop in 1846 and 1847.[23] Published in America, this is essentially a popular history and distinctly nationalist in tone, heavily illustrated with reproductions of photographs, many of which are taken from Welch's catalogue. His 'Irish Views' had begun to slip sideways into visual culture where, even today, they function as signifiers of an idea of Ireland. Benner's Hotel in Dingle has a photograph of a fireside[24] and an enlarged half-tone print of the kitchen of the Loo Bridge Inn.[25]

The former is also featured in T. Walsh and Co.'s public house on Brunswick St. North in Dublin. Betty's 'traditional' bar in Tralee has a photograph of a slide car that is attributable to Welch. This is the soft centre of contemporary cultural nationalism. These reproductions function as references to a 'real' Ireland, an imaginative province of certainty and secure identities. They connote tradition and continuity. They are 'folk' images of a time beyond the chronology of the clock and the narratives of official history … Ireland *san am fado*.[26]

27. Evans and Turner, *Ireland's Eye*, Carts and Curraghs, Plate 70, Turf Slide-Car, p. 95. The postcard was posted on the Website of Maggie Blanck, http:www.mag-gieblanck.com/Mayopages/People.html. It is shown alongside another image taken from Stoddard. The website also features a hand-tinted postcard of the photograph Welch sent to Haddon in 1931. Blanck has gifted her postcard collection to Mayo County Library in Castlebar, Co. Mayo.
28. The Balfour Album was illuminated and bound by Marcus Ward Ltd.
29. Claudia Kinmouth, *Irish Rural Interiors in Art* (New Haven & London: Yale University Press, 2006), p. 30.
30. Michel Frijot, *Photography and the Media: Changes in the Illustrated Press. The New History of Photography*, (Cologne: Könemann, 1994), p. 362–9. See also W. A. Maguire *A Century in Focus* p. 129–37.

Cont.

The second life of Welch's photographs as tokens of the real Ireland reveal a lot about folk strategies and the construction of identity. In the wake of the Revival the Victorian gaze is turned on its head as photography enters the age of mechanical reproduction and ethnography is commodified in a wave of popular consumption. Welch photographed a turf slide car (Figure 7.5), a primitive form of transport still in use in the Sperrin Mountains in the 1890s. A similar car was featured in a display of transport organised by Welch for the British Association for the Advancement of Science in Queen's University Belfast in 1902. Shortly afterwards his photograph of the turf slide car was published as a hand-tinted postcard.[27] It seems like a minor point but it is a milestone in many ways. In 1902 post office restrictions were lifted and the picture postcard was introduced. Postcards quickly became a very lucrative business and the craze continued until the outbreak of the First World War. Welch's photographs were taken up by publishers like Marcus Ward Ltd. of Belfast,[28] who commissioned a mass of detailed photographs of 'Irish life' for publication as postcards. These were 'manipulated'[29] in the studios of printing firms in Germany, where up to 1914 the bulk of the printing was done.[30] At a minimum they were hand tinted. Others were edited and some were transformed from photographic images with an ethnographic or topographic origin into stereotypes of Paddy the Farmer, the Irish Colleen and the Old Woman on the Donkey-Cart. A useful example is supplied by Paddy Mac Monagle in his catalogue of vintage postcards:[31] a series of three postcards published by Anthony of Killarney.[32] In a scene from Irish life, a 'rail' fine old type complete with top hat is shown standing on a donkey-cart outside O'Donoghue's Pub in the 'original genuine' photograph. The farmer and donkey-cart are then cut out and pasted into a photograph of bothereen in front of a thatched cottage. The overall tone of the image is sharpened through increased contrast and some editing of fine detail. The third image is a hand-painted transcription in colour of the farmer, cart and donkey with Ross Castle, one of the main tourist attractions in Killarney, used as a backdrop. 'Auld' Ireland had just been invented and was going down a treat with tourists and returned emigrants.[33] Welch provided the raw material for the production of popular devices that were used to depict an exaggerated image of peasant Ireland cast as Gaelic Catholic Ireland with a whole host of recognisable characters and situations: the old woman spinning; the hearth; the thatched cottage; the ass and cart; the poitin still;currachs being carried ashore; and so on – imagery that has remained in currency for over a century. Indeed, John Hinde's iconic image of the red-headed children with their donkey and creels of turf is but one variation on a theme established by Welch long ago.

It seems a long way from the old woman and her cabin on the beach. Welch left us what is probably the only record of her existence but there is a sting in the tail of that story. He informs us that Janet was 'Washed out and old woman drowned in the Great Cyclone of 22–23/12/94'.[34] Destitute and marginalised, the woman is caught between unyielding land and unforgiving sea, a cruel fate that is the perfect metaphor for a shattered community doomed to extinction. This is where folklore comes from. Welch was many things, but he was not a folklorist. He is qualified to be: he has left us a with an authentic record of a way of life on the point of eclipse, his images have been translated into markers of identity and they remain relevant to contemporary folk narratives, to the origin myths of nationalists in Ireland and Ulster alike. Welch has until now been largely ignored outside of Ulster, although his achievements rank alongside those of Petrie and Henry in terms of their roles in the visual construction of Irishness. These men had much in common and there are many parallels in their lives and careers. Petrie did the fieldwork that provided the Young Irelanders with a set of symbols that could be translated into popular images of 'patriotic fervour'.[35] In a similar way Welch anticipates Paul Henry. Welch was obviously enthralled by Connemara. His images of the Twelve Bens show an awareness of pictorialism and pre-empt the compositional devices of Henry. Both were Belfastmen who went 'West' to document the peasants: Henry in search of work as a 'black and whiter',[36] Welch in the service of tourism. Both worked for the Congested Districts Board and each produced images of Ireland for rail companies; and those images have entered popular culture as potent signifiers of the 'West'. But there is a crucial difference between Henry and Welch. Henry was

Cont.

31. Paddy MacMonagle, *Paddy Mac's Collection of Vintage Postcards* (Killarney: Mac Publications, 2006), p. 130–1.

32. Ibid., p. ix. Originally from Alsace, Louis Anthony established a studio in Killarney that supplied Lawrence with scenic views. He also developed a photographic service for tourists, which he based in the Gap of Dunloe.

33. See Maggie Blanck, 'A Letter from Pat in America', 'The American Letter' and the photograph reproduced from Stoddard show an old couple holding a letter. http:www.maggieblanck.com /Mayopages. There is a diasporic component to tourism and the dissemination of these postcards which needs further research.

34. E Estyn Evans and Brian S. Turner, *Ireland's eye*, Plate 67. Janet, p. 91.

35. Jeanne Sheehy, *The Rediscovery of Ireland's Past: The Celtic Revival, 1830–1930* (London: Thames and Hudson, 1980), p. 41.

36. A 'Black and Whiter' was the trade name for a graphic artist who worked for illustrated newspapers and periodicals.

an *avant gardist* with aspirations to be *the* painter of the Revival but he has become a model of formal conservatism and nationalist orthodoxy. Welch was personally and professionally conservative, a loyalist who was proud of his Protestant heritage, yet he has produced a body of work that remains in the public domain as an authentic representation of Corkery's hidden Ireland. It is ironic that it is Welch's photography that now performs the function that Henry's posters once did, the anonymous images of an accidental folklorist.

CHAPTER EIGHT

Fisheries in the West

NIAMH CONNOLLY

This chapter deals with maritime industries that pre-existed or were encouraged by the Congested Districts Board (CDB) from 1891 to 1915. In the absence of organised markets and the consequent dearth in archival material, the James Hack Tuke and Robert J. Welch images help to reconstruct maritime life and livelihoods and give us an idea of the gender division of labour in both the traditional context and, comparatively, in the era of modernisation. In the 1890s the population for the most part was not actively engaged in fishing, and seldom in fishing alone as a means of subsistence, with smallholders favouring the land over the sea. In coastal areas where people did participate in fishing the reliance was generally on the return their small plots of land could provide, supported by sporadic sea fishing from canvas canoes or open yawls.[1]

The reasons for this are abundant. The history of fishing was turbulent: prohibitive legislation imposing duties on vessels, salt taxes and more recently the introduction of a bounty system that served to have a negative effect on the industry.[2] The unpredictable nature of the sea, the exorbitant cost of boats, tackle and salt, the want of a steady income, the poor state of infrastructure required for fishing (lack of steamers or a rail network to transport fish, the scarcity of suitable harbours and piers) and little training were all determining factors in the lack of a commercial industry in the west of Ireland. Another significant barrier to commercial fishing was the stigma attached to eating fish, to consuming both shellfish and fresh fish, which was seen as a mark of poverty, and it was noted that death caused by eating contaminated shellfish along the sea-coast during the Famine 'persisted in folk memory and turned people against them'.[3] If no natural local market existed for fresh fish it had to be cured, packed and transported all adding

1. W.L. Micks, *An Account of the History of the Congested Districts Board of Ireland from 1891 to 1923* (Dublin: 1926), p. 35. Both classes of boats were lightweight and could be lifted onto the shore if needed.
2. C. Breathnach, *The Congested Districts Board of Ireland, 1891–1923: Poverty and Development in the West of Ireland* (Dublin: Four Courts Press, 2005) p. 72–3
3. L. Jones, 'Food and Meals in a Congested District: County Donegal in 1891', in A. Fenton, and T. Owen (eds), *Food in Perspective* (Edinburgh: Donald 1981), p. 162.

to the costs to the fisherman and, with no government lending system in place, it was a prohibitively expensive business to be in.

In the years leading up to the formation of the CDB the numbers of men employed in fishing, not only as a primary income source but also as a secondary supplement to farming, were in decline. Allied to this was the fact that fishing had not developed as an industry in any notable way in the previous fifty years. However, the potential for a successful fishing industry existed in many areas along the western seaboard, a fact recognised by the CDB, established in 1891 to alleviate 'congestion'. A congested district was deemed to exist where more than 20 per cent of the population lived in an area where the rateable value was less than 30s. per person.[4] Reiterating the findings of the CDB, the Department of Agriculture and Technical Instruction for Ireland later established that the fishing districts could loosely be divided into two categories: the first having inadequate transport and marketing amenities, generally speaking the coastal areas of Galway, Mayo and Donegal; and secondly the coastal zones of Cork and Kerry, where construction of piers and slips were a more pressing need.[5]

The period between 1890 and the first quarter of the 1900s brought about much change and modernisation in the fishing industry. The people of Donegal in particular wholeheartedly embraced the ethos of the CDB and the changes it suggested and implemented, with the result that viable fishing communities grew and prospered. All along the western seaboard piers were built and loans provided for boats, nets and the necessary equipment. It was identified by the CDB that financial input, training and development of subsidiary industries to fishing were the necessary components for the successful development of the industry, and subsequently these industries, such as boat-building, curing stations and cooperages, were fostered. The CDB did much to turn the tide of poverty in the West of Ireland and, although it looked like being a monumental task in 1890 the Board achieved considerable success in developing the sea-fishing industry in the congested districts, most significantly in Donegal. Areas such as Teelin and Downings underwent substantial social improvement due to the advance in sea-fishing implemented by the Board.

4. Section 36 of the Purchase of Land (Ireland) Act, 1891.
5. Department of Agriculture and Technical Instruction for Ireland, *Ireland Industrial and Agricultural*, (Dublin: Browne and Nolan, 1910) p. 268.

6. CDB, Second Annual Report, (1893), p. 24-5.
7. P. Bolger, 'The Congested Districts Board and the Co-ops in Donegal', in W. Nolan, M. Dunleavy nd L. Ronayne (eds), *Donegal History and Society: Interdisciplinary Essays on the History of an Irish County* (Dublin, 1995) p. 655.
8. Micks, *The History of the Congested Districts Board of Ireland*, p. 39.
9. W.S. Green, 'The Sea Fisheries of Ireland', *Ireland Industrial and Agricultural*, (Dublin: Browne and Nolan, 1902), p. 376.
10. P. O'Sullivan, *Field and Shore. Daily Life and Traditions, Aran Islands 1900.* (Dublin: O'Brien Press, 1977, repr. 1985), p. 108.

About twenty curing stations were set up between Donegal, Mayo and Galway in the Board's first year of operations. William Lawson Micks, the CDB secretary, was initially responsible for the erection of curing stations in Donegal, due to his previous experience in that county, and since immediate executive supervision of Donegal fisheries was assigned to him. He travelled to Scotland, where curing had been underway for some time, to gain from their experience. In the Shetland Islands Micks arranged for thirteen proficient curers to come to Donegal to train the locals in the art of cod and ling curing. It was predominately the younger generation who received instruction from the Scottish curers, as the men were mostly out fishing.[6] Men were then brought from Mayo to learn from the success of the Donegal curing stations, thus spreading the knowledge gained even further. Alexander Duthie, a Scot very much involved and experienced in the development of Scottish fishing and curing, became acquainted with Micks and was appointed CDB fishery inspector for Donegal. One of his best-known achievements was the exchange of these curers from Scotland for the training of Donegal girls in the Scottish curing stations.[7] Eventually many fish curing stations were purchased from the CDB by local merchants, from whom the fishermen received better prices for their fish. The Board often remained very consciously on the scene as a fallback and to ensure that merchants did not give a lower price than it had set, thus endeavouring to secure a future for the industry.[8]

At the turn of the century the Department of Agriculture and Technical Instruction estimated the number of large deep-sea fishing vessels on the coasts of Galway and Mayo in the region of 75, placing the value of each boat at about £300–600.[9] The types of fishing in which the men of Aran engaged at this time included drift net fishing, long line fishing and setting pots. Long line fishing was used for catching fish, such as cod, pollock and flat fish. Drift net fishing involved floating nets near the surface, creating a barrier into which herring and mackerel would swim. From 1892 Aran men abandoned currachs in favour of large sail-powered wooden drifters when drift net fishing.[10] These drifters were introduced by east coast fishermen brought to Aran on a training endeavour by the CDB in an effort to modernise and improve the efficiency of the fisheries. When catches were abundant fish were cured for the American market by packing fillets head to tail into barrels filled with a brine of salt and fresh water, work in the main undertaken by women.

As is portrayed in the Tuke and Welch images, the involvement of women in shore-based fishing work was standard practice, often fish gutting, packing, curing, gathering bait, baiting lines or carrying seaweed. Evidence of the physical work in which women participated is provided by many of the Welch photographs, such as Figures 8.4 and 8.5. Hill and Pollock note that 'Male respect for women's roles in the success of fishing was such that it was extremely rare for men to take a wife who was not part of a fishing tradition'.[11]

The building and improvement of the sea-fishing industry by the CDB may have been extremely rapid, but the foundations were solid. The research had been thoroughly executed, and the recommendations expertly implemented. The fishermen had acquired superior equipment and boats, and markets had been opened. By the turn of the century the CDB had accomplished many of the recommendations of the Base-line reports, specially those laid out for Co. Donegal. The Board had enabled the fishermen to purchase boats and advanced equipment through a loan system. Fishing had come a long way in the first ten years of the CDB's existence, and was conferring on the people of the west coast of Ireland periods of prosperity hitherto unknown. The success of the industry was praised by Micks:

> I never saw such a sudden alteration of circumstances in a short time, a lightning change all over the districts, from depression and hopeless poverty to happiness and comfort. Many a man said to me in private that he had 'a good bit of 'dry' money laid by.[12]

Fishing was not always a prosperous business, however. Despite the extensive financial input and the training facilitated by the CDB for the development of the industry, there was one factor to which fishermen were always vulnerable. Takes were greatly affected by bad weather conditions, which restrained the use of the newly acquired fishing boats.

11. M. Hill and V. Pollock, *Women of Ireland: Image and Experience c.1880–1920* (Belfast: Blackstaff Press, 1999), p. 57.
12. Micks, *The History of the Congested Districts Board of Ireland*, p. 36.

The success of one industry affiliated to fishing was completely dependent on adverse weather conditions, namely the industry of kelp-burning, which involved the cutting and gathering of seaweed after storms at particular times of the year. In the 1890s seaweed was gathered for personal use as a fertiliser for the land, sold inland to farmers and in some localities sold to dealers for iodine as a cash income. In areas where access to the shore was prohibited by nature the practice of gathering rods, a species of seaweed, was almost non-existent but in some maritime districts on the north coast of Donegal it was the principal source of income for the coastal people. One such district was that of the Fanad region (Mulroy Bay), where it was noted that in the early 1890s it would be difficult for the people to exist without this industry. The seaweed was harvested after spring and autumn storms. A successful yield depended on the drying conditions, and consequently it is no surprise that this harvest has often been equated to the saving of the hay. According to the CDB baseline inspector for Fanad, after a storm 'every man, woman, and child in the place is in the water saving the weed, any who have carts, back them into the water, and any who have no carts must creel it up on donkeys, or on their own backs to the grass or sand above high water mark'.[13] This usually went on for two or three days, after which the seaweed was laid out to dry, with space often being a problem for collectors. A kiln, made of earth and stones, was filled with turf over which the seaweed was burnt. The kelp was then stacked awaiting the dealer and payment in the region of £4 a ton in 1890– averaging 4 tons of kelp per man per year, more if there was a large family employed in the reaping.[14] CDB inspectors observed that the price given to the kelp collectors on the Inishowen peninsula could have been almost double the amount paid by the dealers but a monopoly of several established Scottish firms reigned along the Irish coast, thus keeping prices low. An Irish iodine manufacturer set up in Ramelton in 1880, with the consequence of increasing prices paid to local collectors – only to be closed shortly thereafter by the payment of £300 to the entrepreneur by threatened Scottish firms.[15]

Carring heavy loads of seaweed was a shore-based task in which women could be involved.

13. Baseline report, district of Fanad, 1893, pp. 6–7. For further information on the Baseline reports see Chapters 2 and 10.
14. Baseline report, district of Fanad, 1893, p. 7.
15. Ibid.

BRINGING HOME SEAWEED, CONNEMARA. R.W. 2357.

Figure 8.2
Bringing in the Seaweed,
W14/05/80

The men, with knives sharpened on stones on the shore, were usually involved in cutting the weed, a skill requiring the ability to utilize the knife in either hand. When men or donkeys were not available to carry the weed women would transport it to dry, as illustrated in Figures 8.2 and 8.3. Robinson estimates that a creel of weed weighed about a hundredweight. The women often wore animal hide on their backs under the creel to protect their clothing. He also remarks that at times Aran women had to work at the seaweed until late in their pregnancies. An old Aran saying runs, 'Is é moladh na mná óige, a dhroim bheith fluich' – 'Praise of the young woman, that her back be wet'- wet, he observes, with the brine from a basket of weed.[16]

Another of Welch's photographs 'Digging "sand-eels" for bait- Mulroy Bay' (Figure 8.3) is located on the northern seaboard of Co. Donegal. There is a narrow opening to a long, convoluted bay. The channel varies in width and depth with many small rocky islands; the north of the inlet is sheltered by hills. The tides in the bay are affected by the tight entrance, which delays the times of both high and low tides, and reduces the tidal amplitude. These conditions in the bay are amenable to the survival of the sand lance, more commonly known as the 'sand-eel' (though bearing no relation to true eels). The sand-eel generally avoids areas with strong tidal currents and make its home by burrowing into the sand on the sea bottom.

Larval forms of this fish serve as a major food source for salmon, cod, pollock and other species in the North Atlantic and have long since been used as bait for long line fishing of cod, ling and also flat fish such as plaice, sole and turbot. Long lines were of up to 300 m in length, with more than 100 hooks attached, baited with sand-eels or other suitable organisms (such as slugs). These lines would be buoyed by an inflated cow-bladder.[17] Sciaths, a type of basket, were traditionally used for holding long lines. There were usually about 100 cm long and 41 cm wide, with one rounded end and the other square. The depth was approximately 20 cm at the rounded end, with holes left for carrying the basket.[18] The lines were traditionally left anchored overnight and lifted the following day, with markers to signal where the lines were set.[19] Generally there would be two takes of fish, one at each end of the day, though if the market

Figure 8.3
Digging 'sand-eels' for bait, Mulroy Bay W04-69-53)

16. T. Robinson, *Stones of Aran– Pilgrimage*. (Dublin: Lilliput Press in association with Wolfhound Press, 1986), p. 144–5.
17. Baseline report. p. 187.
18. John de Courcey, Ireland, *Ireland's Sea Fisheries: A History*, p. 64.
19. O'Sullivan, *Field and Shore*, p. 108.

Figure 8.4
Curing Mackerel for America,
W/04/45/7

for fish was poor, or if they had already had several good catches, there would only be one take. In the morning, the lines set the previous evening were lifted, and the lines to be lifted that evening were set. When the lines were lifted the fish were taken from the hooks, and kept at the bottom of the boat until it had docked. A good catch would constitute two dozen fish to each line, and since there would be one line per fisherman and about seven men per boat, the catch would amount to fourteen dozen fish. According to Hill and Pollock it was not uncommon for women to be involved in all stages of of long line fishing processes, except the fishing itself.[20]

In Figure 8.3 men, women and children are pictured working the harvest of the sand-eels. As in the harvest of the weed, all hands were employed in the digging of the eels. Women for the most part are carrying small woven baskets, which were used to gather the eels after they were dug up by men brandishing extraordinarily long handled shovels, essential for extrapolating the sand-eels from the sandy or gravely sea bottom. There are also horses in the background which were most probably used for transporting the creels of eels.

The digging of eels for bait was not a pursuit exclusive to Donegal inhabitants. Tim Robinson also observes a history of digging eels for bait on the Aran Islands, most on notably 'Trá na Lugaí, the beach of the lugworms', which he notes 'provides bait for the Corrúch lads' fishing lines'.[21] A CDB inspector in the early 1890s remarked of this area that there were very few families solely employed in fishing. There were twenty-eight second-class boats and fifteen third-class boats registered in addition to the currachs. In all, there were 103 men fishing intermittently, usually seasonally when fish were in.[22] By and large the majority of fish caught were herring, flake or plaice, turbot and sole. With no curing station in the region fish was transported to market in Rathmullen or Buncrana. Salted glasson haddock or whiting were occasionally consumed at home. In addition to the registered boats there were many unregistered vessels that were not employed for fishing but rather for the transportation of turf or seaweed.

In a further photograph taken by Welch entitled 'Curing mackerel for America' (Figure 8.4),

20. Hill and Pollock, *Women of Ireland.*
21. Robinson, *Stones of Aran*, p. 186.
22. Baseline report district of Fanad, 1893, p. 46 These second-and-third class boats were rated lower in other districts.

the trough on the left-hand side serviced by a pump would have been for gutting–work, in this instance carried out completely by women and supervised by the two men at the end of the trough. The table, surrounded by men working in groups of three, would have been for curing. The barrels in the photograph would most likely have been made with materials imported from England or Sweden and sold to local curers.[23] They were sold for 3s. 9d. to 4s. each.[24] Some cooperages were founded and run (at a loss) by the Board and some continued under private business: it was commercially cheaper to buy components and assemble than to buy completed product.There is some evidence in the photograph that children participated in the work – while the two boys on left-hand side are just mischievously posing for the photographer, a young boy in the background can be observed working at the gutting trough, and another at a barrel near the curing table. The three men at the rear of the photograph were almost certainly buyers or fish dealers.

From the late 1880s America was the principal market for mackerel caught in Irish waters. Prices obtained were high, which John Molloy attributes to the passing of the Wilson Tariff Bill that eased the import duty on pickled mackerel from Ireland by 50 cents per barrel.[25] While it was predominately mackerel from fisheries on the southern coast of Ireland that was exported to America, the western and north-western fisheries did take part, if to a much lesser degree in the succeeding decades. This was due to the pattern of the mackerel – they did not often come close enough to shore along the northern coast. It was noted in the baseline report for Teelin that, despite the fact that an abundance of mackerel came close to the shore between Teelin and Rathlin Island the waters were too deep to enable the fishermen to take advantage of their close proximity.[26]

For this reason in Killybegs curing mackerel for America would not have been as common as the practice of curing herring. In 1890 mackerel were taken in large numbers in Killybegs and it is reported that all catches were salted or cured and exported.[27] It is noted in the baseline report, however, that despite the fact that in the following years the mackerel were still

23. Fourth Report of the
   Congested Districts Board
   for Ireland, p. 17–8.
24. Sixth Report of the
   Congested Districts Board
   for Ireland, p. 21.
25. Molloy, John, *The Irish
   Mackerel Fishery and the
   Making of an Industry*
   (Killybegs, KFO and Marine
   Institute, 2004), p. 39.
26. Baseline report, Teelin,
   p. 10.
27. Baseline report, Killybegs,
   p. 6.

plentiful there, the men were more interested in the work provided by the building of the railway, probably as this supplied a more consistent income at the time. The establishment of this railway in Killybegs did much to encourage the fishing industry in the area, opening up access to markets in Derry and subsequently Dublin. After five years in operation a total of 3,328 tons of fish had been carried on the Donegal Railway line.[28]

There were two separate, but concurrent, fishing industries well established by 1900: the fresh fish trade and the cured fish trade. Competition between the two industries enabled high prices to be attained for the fish. The curing trade took different forms: salting, curing and pickling. The latter process took off with regard to herring in particular. The difference between curing and salting was that in the process of curing a combination of both salt and water was used like a brine, where as in the process of salting only salt was used to preserve the fish. Figure 8.5 illustrates the process of curing herring.

There were four different classes of herring boats fishing off the Donegal coast in the early years of the twentieth century: steam drifters, motor boats, sailing boats of Zulu lugger rig and open Greencastle yawls.[29] Examples of these boats can be observed in the background of Welch's photograph overlooking a busy Rosapenna pier (Figure 8.6). Steam drifters were slowly being introduced, with a total of five steam-drifters by 1914. These boats were effectively able to fish twelve months of the year, and because of this they were able to follow the fish, rather than waiting for the fish to come closer inshore. Long trains of nets, and trawling, were the fishing methods used on these types of boats.

The herring fishing off the Donegal coast experienced a decline in the few years leading up to the First World War due to unfavourable weather conditions and also increased fishing by larger foreign boats in the region. Investors and fishermen alike were reluctant as a result to take the risk of investing heavily in such boats, especially since there was no guarantee that the herring fishery would improve.[30] The disincentive for many fishermen was that in order to repay the large loans required to purchase steam drifters they had to undertake fishing as a full-time

Figure 8.6
Rosapenna pier, W/04/69/46

28. *Thom's Directory of the United Kingdom of Great Britain and Ireland for the Year 1900* (Dublin: Alex Thom and Co., 1900), p. 700.
29. Twenty-Second Report of the Congested Districts Board for Ireland, 1914, [Cd. 7865], HC 1914–16, xxiv, p. 12.
30. Twenty-Second Report of the Congested Districts for Ireland, p. 13.

profession, to travel great distances from the shore, and also to remain at sea for long periods. These practices were alien to fishermen of the time and they were apprehensive and of adopting them.

While it is not borne out in the images, it is worth noting that the new Free State government could not support commercial fisheries nor was their development prioritised. Unfortunately CDB help coincided with rapid change and modernisation in this field, particularly with the advent of motor boats. As a result the costs associated with commercial fisheries rose exponentially, which ensured that CDB-funded schemes were rendered obsolete and fishermen could no longer compete in sail vessels. The Tuke and Welch images are of paramount importance to the maritime historian. They highlight the gender division of labour and the hardships of maritime work. These images showcase regional successes and full-time engagement in fisheries at particular times of the year. In the name of caution it was still preferred to combine fishing with farming or other activities such as kelp burning. So the Congested Districts Board did not succeed in creating full-time fishermen out of maritime dwellers but the level of development that occurred, as evidenced in the Tuke and Welch photographs, was unparalleled for some considerable time.

CHAPTER NINE

Welch's Claddagh Images

LORNA MOLONEY

1. James Hardiman, *History of the Town and County of Galway* (London, 1820), p. 30. In etymological terms the word *Claddagh* is derived from the Irish word *cladach* meaning 'stony beach'.
2. O'Brien's bridge was located on the site of a fourteenth century structure but the Salmon Weir of later construction in 1818 was so named after the abundance of salmon lying on the river bed.
3. Roderick O'Flaherty, *A Chorographical Description of West or h-Iar Connaught* (1684), ed.James Hardiman (Dublin, 1846) p. 40.
4. *AFM* as cited in M.D. O'Sullivan, *Old Galway* (Cambridge, 1942), p. 17.
5. The term tribe was first used by Cromwell's soldiers, who applied it to define the important families in Galway town.

Traditionally the Claddagh[1], located within the parameters of Galway City, is famed as being one of the most remarkable fishing districts in Ireland and has recently become a symbol of quintessential Irishness. Three bridges – O'Brien's Bridge, the Salmon Weir Bridge and Dominic Bridge – linked Galway with the Claddagh fishing quarter.[2] While it is not unusual for fishing quarters to be located near commercial centres and city centres, the Claddagh is unique, because of a complex set of exclusive fishery laws.[3] This chapter traces the origins of the unusual legal arrangements synonymous with the Claddagh and outlines its maritime heritage, which is inextricably linked to its identity. Throughout this work a selection of Robert J. Welch's images, which capture a day in the life of the Claddagh community, are contextualised.

The origins of the Claddagh's maritime history can be traced back to a fortress in the fourteenth century.[4] A passage from the Claddagh area, a few hundred yards wide, led to the only fordable part of the River Corrib, which made it a suitable position for such a fortification. Galway became a walled town during the reign of Edward I. Fourteen families gained civic control, retained up to the era of Oliver Cromwell, from which time they became commonly known as 'the tribes of Galway'.[5] A distinctive pattern of isolation exhibited by the tribes has often been put forward as a primary reason for the separateness of the Claddagh fisher folk. In the late middle ages trade between the Claddagh inhabitants and Spain, importing wine and exporting fish, provided the impetus for a thriving medieval herring trade, which also encouraged the 150 days' abstinence from eating meat in the ecclesiastical calendar. The town's charter confirmed by Queen Elizabeth I in 1579 appointed the Mayor as Admiral with jurisdiction over Galway Bay and the Aran Islands. In the seventeenth century, the city walls with their fourteen towers and fourteen gates were still intact: now just a fragment remains, lying, in the proximity of the Claddagh. This is the famous Spanish Arch, once leading to Spanish Place. Among other traditions, Claddagh inhabitants refused to marry outsiders. This exclusivity posed such problems for attempted plantation that, in 1518, the Corporation highlighted the boundaries to be observed by Galway inhabitants: that no Galway inhabitant should allow entry into his house or

> ...at Christmas, Easter, no feast, else, any of the Burkes, MacWilliams, Kellys, nor any sept else without licence of the Mayor and council on pain to forfeit £5, that neither O nor Mac shall strut nor swagger through the streets of Galway.[6]

6. Edmund Curtis, *A History of Medieval Ireland 1110–1513* (Dublin: Maunsel and Roberts, 1923), p. 149.
7. D.H. Moutray Read, 'Folklore and History in Ireland', in *Folklore*, vol. 29 (1918), p. 285.
8. Hardiman, *History of Galway*.
9. Testimony of John Leslie Foster, MP, before a Committee of the House of Lords, quoted in George Cornwall Lewis, *On Local Disturbances in Ireland* (London, 1836), p. 75.
10. Thomas N. Brown, 'Nationalism and the Irish Peasant', in *Review of Politics*, vol. 15, No. 4. (1953), p. 2.

They also elected their own representative, the renowned 'king of the Claddagh'. Moutray Read notes the custom of self-regulation, making the Claddagh community 'exempt from all government taxes'.[7] In later times this tax exemption for the Claddagh community ceased to exist. At the feast of the nativity of St John the Baptist, 24 June, the Claddagh people made a processional march through Galway, headed by their king, who decided the hierarchical order of the procession, and on their return held a festival lasting through the night.[8] The centralising act of creating the king of the Claddagh, provided a major focal point to their communal activities

Early nineteenth-century observations cited a great disparity between Irish regions: 'different districts ... almost as unlike as any two countries in Europe'.[9] Noticeable regional variation meant, to outsiders, that familiarisation with native customs was an even more difficult process, especially when the inhabitants exhibited 'a severe aloofness ... ignoring outsiders'.[10] The Claddagh is an extreme example of 'aloofness' as there was no otherplace like it in Ireland. The notoriety of the Claddagh fishermen drew the attention of nineteenth-century anthropologists, such as Edward Wakefield, an Englishman well versed in agronomy.[11] In 1808–10 he toured Ireland recording his observations and rebuked the natives for their 'indolence and inactivity', suggesting that if they would not exploit the rich fisheries at their disposal, more deserving subjects could be found. Such low opinions of the industriousness of the population of the west coast fed into an existing negative discourse on Irish customs, perpetuating it for the rest of the century.[12] Ironically Wakefield, whose views were widely circulated and are often cited, failed to set foot in the places that he criticised.[13] Reports of inspectors[14] and engineers, such as Alexander Nimmo (instrumental in the survey of the Western District) and Richard Griffith, are more truthful and detailed.[15] Various Royal Commissions on the state of the Irish fisheries were appointed throughout the nineteenth century. They noted the wealth of the Irish coastal waters and commented on the inability of the fishermen to avail themselves of it. Moreover, little was done to improve the situation.

Despite general desegregation and the general paucity of the Irish commercial fisheries, it was found that, in 1836, 820 fishermen were based at the Claddagh using 105 sailing craft and 80 rowing boats. This was a proportionately high figure given that it was estimated that the banks surrounding the entire west coast could supply two thousand vessels per season. In contrast with poor participation elsewhere the Claddagh supported a number of secondary service industries, employing carriers, helpers, basket-makers, sail-makers, cordage production and boat-builders.[16] Although the Claddagh relied heavily on fisheries, its local consumption of fish was questionable and the area was clearly hit hard by food shortages. Starving was nothing new for Claddagh people. Before the famine, in 1842, the Galway starvation riots were caricatured in *The Illustrated London News*. Women and children spearheaded the riot with 'an imposing reserve in the rear of the Claddagh fishermen'. The authorities did not punish the rioters and the disturbance dispersed fairly peacefully.[17] With the onset of the Potato Famine, the Claddagh fishermen pawned their fishing equipment to buy food. At the beginning of 1847, when the Famine was at its worst, remnants of their boats were at the quay, 'not a sign of tackle or sail remaining'. James Hack Tuke

11. Ibid., p. 46.
12. Edward Wakefield, *An Account of Ireland, Statistical and Political*, vol 1 (London, 1812), p. 45.
13. Kathleen Villiers-Tuthill, *Alexander Nimmo: The Western District* (Clifden, 2006), p. 109.
14. *Commission of Inquiry on State of Irish Fisheries. First Report, Minutes of Evidence, Appendix.* [C1-9550]H,C. 1837 xxii.i, 95. Inspectors were frequently employed to keep the peace, and enforce local legislation. It was noted that such a role in Ireland was reserved for half-pay military officers with little knowledge of the fisheries, where bribery for bounties was also in evidence.
15. J. H. Andrews, *A Paper Landscape: The Ordnance Survey in Nineteenth-Century Ireland* (Dublin, 2002), p. 30.
16. Hely Dutton, *A Statistical and Agricultural Survey of the County of Galway* (Dublin: Royal Dublin Society, 1824), p.110.
17. *The Illustrated London News*, June 25, 1842.

THE CLADDAGH, GALWAY, GIN. R129

noted that 'nets and tackle had been pawned or sold'.[18] This was the case for every fishing port along the coast of Ireland.

The Claddagh residents protected their traditions fiercely: for example, the government asked the Society of Friends to help the Claddagh community during the Famine but the society found them 'exasperating … next to incorrigible'.[19] It was noted that they would go out fishing only on certain days and were violently protective of their fishing rights and grounds. In 1848, the Quakers focused on providing longer-term assistance, such as fishing tackle, seeds and farm implements, but the fierce, vigilant nature of the Claddaghmen meant that William Todhunter, the Society of Friend's representative in the Claddagh, eventually advised that a government boat should be positioned at Galway Bay to protect the rest of the other fishermen. Often, where any assistance was concerned, the prevailing consensus was that to give alms to them would be 'damaging to the fishermen's morale'. and could also lead to the 'habits of chicanery'.[20] This, it was felt, could potentially have a domino effect, with fishermen being unable to pay back loans on time and so on. The notions of deserving poor and undeserving poor were clear benchmarks within the ideological parameters of many philanthropists in the nineteenth century. Fishing communities tended to be viewed as less deserving. For decades after the famine, limited monies from public and private funds were sporadically lent to the fishermen to redeem their equipment. The Claddagh fishermen were also given suitable clothing. Fish curing stations were set up as government initiatives. They were positioned along the coast and employed skilled Scottish fish curers who could teach the trade. Scotland was frequently compared to Ireland: as the principal seat of British fishery, it had harbour facilities and a larger number of curing establishments.[21] Scottish efforts were always held as a template for how the Irish fisheries should proceed: this unfair assessment did not consider the advantage of strategic port-to-market locations like the Clyde and Firth of Forth.[22]

The concept of exclusion is an important element in the Claddagh maritime heritage and, in 1850 when two external fishermen introduced two fishing trawlers into Galway Bay, the

Figure 9.1
The Claddagh, W14/02/11

18. Cecil Woodham-Smith, *The Great Hunger, Ireland 1845–1849* (New York: Harper & Row, 1962), p. 289.
19. Foster, *On Local Disturbances in Ireland*, p. 80.
20. Smith, *The Great Hunger*, p. 90.
21. Richard Valpy, 'The resources of the Irish Sea Fisheries', in the *Journal of the Statistical Society of London*, 11 (1848), pp. 55–72.
22. L.M. Cullen and T.C Smout (eds), *Comparative Aspects of Scottish and Irish Economic and Social History 1600–1900*, (Edinburgh: John Donald, 1977), p. 228.

Claddagh fishermen instantly attacked them. Alexander Synge, from Aran, landed his catch in Galway, then a crowd of over a hundred tried to force him to stop trawling. In 1851, Browne, the other trawler owner, had his boat destroyed by the Claddagh fleet at the Galway fishery of Black Head. While the boats in Welch's photographs seem inoffensive, the trawlermen, who retaliated with gunfire, failed against stones and other missiles. Due to the sheer weight of numbers against them, a Claddagh fleet of seventy-two boats of the type appearing in Figure 9.1, the trawlermen had to cut their nets and flee to the Aran Islands. The coast guard assembled. Eventually opposition to the Claddagh fishermen spread out over a ten-mile area across the bay. All the boats were searched, and twenty-five men were arrested. But anyone who gave evidence against the Claddagh fishermen came to regret their decision and the magistrate noted that 'the Claddaghmen have hitherto escaped because of the terror that they have always struck in the mind of witnesses'.[23] The fishermen eventually pleaded guilty to assault and were finally released without penalty, promising to stop opposing trawling.

The Claddagh fishermen were regularly criticised for continuing to use small boats (as depicted in Figure 9.1) but this failed to take local considerations into account. Markets were unstable, excess fish could not be refrigerated or transported and rather than cause a glut in the market the unsold/excess fish would have been dumped. The lack of resources put into fish curing compounds and salters was not reflected in populist accounts that denounced the ways of the Claddagh fishermen. Communication routes were impossible to navigate so, though excellent fishing was available, transporting the fish was frequently impossible. [24]

A cursory glance at Figure 9.2 takes in fishermen sitting around staring aimlessly at their boats. The tide is out and the figures in the distance appear to be queueing as if to go somewhere. Contrary to the initial impression of idleness further examination of this image shows that they are clearly waiting to trade. This is evidenced by the horse-drawn carts, probably belonging to outside traders who would travel from distant places to buy fish. The Claddagh fishermen called these people 'cadgers' and 'hawkers'; they were very welcome visitors as they

Figure 9.2
In the Claddagh, W14/02/10.

23. *Fourth Report of the Bog Commissions*, as cited in Kathleen Villiers-Tuthill, *Alexander Nimmo*, p. 108.
24. Hely Dutton, *A Statistical and Agricultural Survey of the County of Galway* (Dublin, 1824), p. 5.

stabilised prices, sparing the need for the Claddaghmen to dispose of an unwanted catch back into the ocean. Yet, it is the men depicted as lounging by the walls of the distant whitewashed houses, recognisable by their attire, that claim our attention. The image supports and is in keeping with the frequently undeserved negative views held of the Claddagh fishermen. It fails to take account of the fact that these men have already completed a day's work. Fishing expeditions were nearly always dictated by the ecclesiastical calendar. The Claddagh fishermen never fished between Saturday evening and Monday morning except for winter herring, which lasted only a few days. In their evidence to fisheries inspectors they admitted to keeping more holy days than were fixed for religious purposes, protesting that 'Fishing is never stropped to lessen the supply of fish brought in'.[25] Juxtaposing their Catholicism led to various superstitions being attributed to Claddagh fishermen.[26] They were perceived as backward and fitting of the rubric 'if Ireland was but an island in the South Pacific, it is safe to assert that it would be the happy hunting ground of the ethnographer, anthropologist and folklorist'. However, some minuted reports noted 'There are not any superstitious observances known to exist among the fishermen here'.[27]

Claddagh fishermen were enterprising and dealt in herring, mackerel, skad, turbot, haddock, sole, hake, cod, ling, bream, gurnet and pilchards. To a lesser extent they took hake, cod and ling to the fishery on Boffin Island, where a great deal of it was 'salted and sold wet in Galway'. More obscure and less reliable species were also caught: for example, sunfish were taken for their much-needed oil but were not seen on an annual basis and were periodically scarce during the nineteenth century. Five to seven barrels of oil were obtained from the annual catch. In 1855 shark oil was more expensive than paraffin, the oil from the liver was valuable and sources note that it was sold for as much as £90 per shark. [28]

Welch's images of boats docked at the Claddagh tell a very poignant survival story: everyone in that community had an important function and the division of their labour is clear from the photographs. The Claddagh fishermen preferred hookers to 'decked boats of larger dimensions,

25. *Commission of Inquiry on State of Irish Fisheries. First Report, Minutes of Evidence,* 108.
26. D.H. Moutray Read, 'Folklore and History in Ireland', in *Folklore,* 29 (1918), p. 289.
27. *Commission of Inquiry on State of Irish Fisheries. First Report, Minutes of Evidence,* Appendix. [C1-9550] H, C. 1837 xxii, 178.
28. MacNally (1976).

with row-boats on board',[29] though the cost of £5 to fit out hookers was a deterrent. Claddagh sail boats were all open hookers, ranging from 6 to 13 tons. They were principally made of oak and minus cabins. The Claddagh fishermen customarily repaired the boats twice a year and cleaned the bottom of the boats four times a year. Twelve ships' carpenters were resident at any one time in the Claddagh; their wages per day with food were 3s. With or without a meal allowance, they were entitled to three to five glasses of whisky daily. Ownership of a boat made a great difference to a Claddagh fisherman: without it, security for loans could not be realised. As part of the annual economic cycle some fishermen pawned their fishing equipment at slack fishing times and redeemed it in anticipation of a good fishing season.[30] It is worth noting that Claddagh fishermen were better off than fishermen from Connemara, who purchased the second-hand Claddagh boats when they were two to three years old.[31]

Each Claddagh hooker held six men, but at times in the summer there might be eight men in a boat. Each was expected to provide a portion of the fishing gear and in return would receive a share of the catch. In some reports differences between the fishermen of Galway and Connemara emerge. The Connemara boats held just five men and they fished only for herring, using their boats at other times for transporting turf. Often after the winter fishing season was over the Connemara fishermen sought employment on the land. Other fishermen from nearby Menlo dealt entirely in seaweed, which was primarily used as a fertiliser for the land.

After the feast of the Assumption of Our Lady on 15 August, crowds traditionally assembled at the Claddagh to bless Galway Bay and its fishermen. The ceremony involved the reading of a passage from the gospel of St John (21:6), where Jesus on the Sea of Galilee tells the fishermen to 'Cast the net on the right side of the boat and you will find. Then they cast it , but they were no longer able to draw it in because of the multitude of fishes.' This might explain why the Claddaghmen were so against trawling, as it is only when Peter, a chosen fishermen and apostle, throws the net that the fishing is successful and the nets are not broken (21:11).[32] It was also a rule of the Claddagh fishermen not to start the herring harvest until 4 September,

29. *Commission of Inquiry on State of Irish Fisheries. First Report, Minutes of Evidence*, 178.
30. Ibid., 114.
31. Ibid.
32. *The New Testament.*

'when the Fair of the Hill was held in Galway', and it would not commence unless all the boats were prepared. Two reasons were given for this: firstly, that it would help control the market and drive the price for fish higher; secondly, that it prevented isolated, inexperienced fishermen going out until the entire community was ready.[33]

The nets used were usually made of flax and some of the Claddagh fishermen barked them. Nets were made with the twine spun by the fishermen's families, which was considered women's or children's work.[34] The nets' meshes had the dimensions of a penny and a halfpenny. Sometimes the nets were tarred which was seen as a terrible method of preserving them and injurious to the fish. [35] Work on the nets would have been undertaken in the Claddagh fisher folk homes.

Small boats with small nets found it hard to compete with trawlers. Fishery reports in the 1870s attest to the problems caused by trawling in Galway, though many reports cite them (incorrectly) as having abated. In the 1870s the number of coast guards was reduced, which meant that certain parts of the coast were no longer visited at all and gaining information from the unexamined areas proved impossible. Fishing companies were not proving successful, exemplified by the failure in 1873 of The South of Ireland Fishing Company, located in Kinsale, due to the shoals moving further from the shore. The Claddaghmen were again arrested for their violence against those operating trawlers and a gunboat, the HMS *Orwell*, had to protect the trawlers, remaining there for some time.[36] Further investigation showed that it was still as hard to gain information on trawling as

> No evidence was adduced on the part of the trawlers to contradict or rebut the evidence of those against trawling, the men engaged in the latter mode of fishing having made affidavits that their lives would be in danger if attempted to come into court to give evidence.[37]

33. *Commission of Inquiry on State of Irish Fisheries. First Report, Minutes of Evidence, Appendix.* [C1-9550]H,C. 1837 xxii.i, 104.
34. *Commission of Inquiry on State of Irish Fisheries. First Report, Minutes of Evidence, Appendix.* [C1-9550]H,C. 1837 xxii.i, 116.
35. *Commissioner of Public Works in Ireland. Fourth report,* [HC, 1836], xxxvi, 491.
36. Inspectors of Irish Fisheries Report, 1872 C. 758, xix. 607, p. 105.
37. Ibid., p. 105.

The tangible fear that fish would be too plentiful and drive down prices meant the Claddagh fishermen stayed at home when they felt the market was threatened.[38] This fed into the indolent stereotype surrounding the Claddagh fisherfolk and was evident in them being photographed in inactive states. It can be seen especially in Welch's photograph of the docked boats (Figure 9.2), with a number of menfolk standing and sitting around. In all the photographs the Claddagh residents are seated staring, motionless figures.

Numerous nineteenth-century sources reiterated the notion that fishermen on the west coast were not true fishermen, i.e. full-time fishermen. This ignored the Claddagh community, which exhibited all the traits fulfilling true fisherfolk status.[39] In the summer English boats were employed in the Irish fisheries for herring and had complete control of the market but the Claddaghmen persisted. The summer market was still lucrative because of demand. Herrings were worth three times more at 10s. per hundred, in the summer, becoming less valuable in the winter, down to an all-time low of 2s.6d. per hundred. The resources of the Claddagh fishermen, and the resulting profits, were capped from the beginning and they had to give way to colonial enterprises.[40] Unlike rural fishermen, who usually had the fall-back cushion of plots of land Claddagh fisherman fished in the winter out of necessity.

The differences in number between first-class and second-class boats is worth mentioning as often the Irish were sailing in boats that were unseaworthy. First-class boats had fixed masts and rigging while second-class vessels had none. Earlier in the nineteenth century there had been an absence of safe and well-placed harbours and piers. The piers depicted in Welch's photograph (Figure 9.2) had been needed for decades. Widespread poverty was not blamed on colonial enterprises or perpetuated frauds but on the notion that the Irish were feckless, ignorant and idles, especially the fisherfolk of the Claddagh. Though the Claddagh fishermen often tried to assimilate and are on record as applying for the freedom of Galway town as they considered themselves tradesmen, this request was refused, thus increasing their – by the mid-nineteenth century- undesired isolation.[41] Modernisation of commercial fisheries met the same problems

38. *Select Committee on Industries (Ireland) Report, Proceedings, Minutes of Evidence*, (268) p. 797.
39. *Commission to investigate Existence of Corrupt Practices in the town of Galway, report, minutes of evidence*. C.2291, H.C. 1857–58, xxvi, 340.
40. Valpy, 'The Resources of the Irish Sea Fisheries', p. 60.
41. *Commission to investigate Existence of Corrupt Practices in the town of Galway, report, minutes of Evidence*. [C.2291], H.C. 1857–58, xxvi, 335.

as the reform of agriculture. Communications were sadly lacking: 'the roads between the coast and the neighbouring villages and towns are few and bad'. Many localities, that could command a supply of fish were unable to do so. Communal ownership of fishing rights, boats, seaweed and wrack meant that the Claddagh was always involved in communal economics, especially where agricultural concerns were not dominant.[42]

While they paid no tolls on incoming fish, as strangers did, all paid outgoing tolls on fish retailed. Conditions for the Claddagh fishermen during the nineteenth century were poor. In the first half of the century, no harbour existed for them in Galway Bay, though parliamentary reports written in 1884 show infrastructural development at nearby Cleggan Pier involving large sums of money, as much as £2000.[43] The deep sea fishing industry required 'good harbourage, abundant docks and large markets with excellent communications', which the West of Ireland was devoid of, is largely omitted in nineteenth-century accounts. There was no lighting when they arrived at night. In inclement weather they had to make sure they reached Casleh or Costello Bay twenty miles from Galway.

The Claddagh women's influence in family economics was paramount. Women depicted in the Welch photographs were clearly involved in marketing. Claddagh fishermen left 'the sale of all fish, except Herrings, to their wives and daughters who sell to dealers by the dozen or score, and also sell to private buyers'.[44] Carrying fish by the headload and balancing such baskets would have been commonplace in the Claddagh. (However, selling herring was often a male-dominated enterprise, as the women were not known to be involved in this market.) Sales of fish were also traditionally on site and according to the Claddagh fishermen, 'The only fish sold by weight was salmon'. In addition, pre-arranged contracts were never made: sales were made at the best price that they could obtain on the day.[45] Women returning from market would be in charge of distributing the profits. Older women would have had more status in the fishing communities than younger, unmarried women. Married Claddagh women needed to be independent: they were in charge of the purse strings and it is likely that subconsciously a contingency fund was

42. C.R. Browne, 'The ethnography of Garumna and Lettermullen', *Proceedings of the Royal Irish Academy.*, 3rd series (1897), pp. 317–70; Thomas Fitzpatrick, *The King of Claddagh: A Story of the Cromwellian Occupation of Galway* (London, 1899), p. 39.
43. 1884–85 (266) *Return by Secretaries by Grant Juries of Sums presented for Erection, Improvement, Repair or Maintenance of Piers and Harbours, 1846-84;by harbour constables of amounts paid out of Tolls; Statements by County Surveyors of Conditions of Piers and Harbours,* [HC 1884–85] (266) C. 167, lxx. 21, p. 16.
44. *Commission of Inquiry on State of Irish Fisheries. First Report, Minutes of Evidence,* 100.

kept to deal with the untimely fatality of their menfolk. Often, even in close-knit communities, being widowed, in the absence of a social welfare safety net, meant destitution for women and children. Fishing studies show that women gave daily pocket money to men and, should men get into debt, they were responsible for repaying. If the women had lacked character such an onus of responsibility would have been futile. When twenty-five of the Claddagh men were arrested in 1852 for attacking trawlers, it was the women who came to act as security and who eventually helped them to escape.[46] Because they were directly involved in earning an income, they wielded power within the community. Despite the limitation of the herring season, the women did not encourage men to go out fishing in bad weather as the loss of a life could cast a family into a life of total poverty.

Children also played a very important economic role in the Claddagh. In 1837 educational records showed low school attendance, with only sixty male children at a public school in Galway. Absenteeism was blamed on the lack of proper clothing.[47] Earlier sources described a small school in the Claddagh, run by a Pat O'Brien, with payments from thirty-five children in full attendance at 1d.–2d. weekly. This teacher's income (£7 per year) was higher than that of the fishing school of Barna (£5 per year). He also held a house rent-free at the bequest of Rev. Fr Morney, parish priest.[48] Educational establishments in the area were sensitive to maritime needs: for example, there is evidence of a 'piscatory school in Galway', where netting was taught with great success in 1848–9. 'Many of the men emigrated and formed a colony not far from Boston, which is called New Claddagh', where they carried their newfound skills with them.[49] Attempts to replicate this success involved the set up of a similar operation instructing women in net making and men in the best fishing techniques.[50] Unfortunately, it was too late and sustained emigration from the Claddagh meant the continued decline of fishing skills.

The Welch photograph 'Cabins in the Claddagh' (Figure 9.3) testifies to a healthy Claddagh population of children. An unusual incident concerning the Claddagh children highlights school funding mechanisms and their manipulation. In 1868, the Sisters of Mercy ran a school

46. *The Illustrated London News*, July 25, 1852.
47. *Commission of Inquiry on State of Irish Fisheries. First Report, Minutes of Evidence*, 113.
48. *1835 Royal Commission on State of Religious and other Public Instruction in Ireland*. First report, Appendix, second report.
49. *Select Committee on Industries (Ireland) Report, Proceedings, Minutes of Evidence, Appendix*. C.2671, [HC 1884-85], p. 62.
50. Ibid.

at the Claddagh, which was entered as a mixed (Catholic and Protestant) school, and thus giving it access to state funding. However, senior officials became suspicious about such a school having Protestant pupils and decided to investigate further. The Royal Commissioners found that contrary to regulations the enumerating constable had failed in his duty to count the students properly, being 'too bashful' to question the nun's word when assured of the pupils' religious denomination and number within the school. In fact it was found that one child from the Established Church had attended for just a single day and matters had been 'grossly misrepresented': the child with the valuable status had failed to cross the threshold for a couple of years. The constable was fined £1 but did not lose his post, though his future was uncertain for a time. This attests to the strong and support given by religious educators in the Claddagh area.[51] In the 1890s, sources enumerating grants from the National Education Commission showed that the

Figure 9.4
A Galway fishwife, W14/02/09

51. *Royal Commission on Nature and Extent of Instruction in Ireland for Elementary or Primary Education, and working of System of National Education, Volume VI.* Educational census. [HC, 1870], C.6.

52. *Return from Schools in Ireland receiving Grants from National Education Commissions of Numbers of Roll; Average attendance number; Religion and Classification of teachers; Amounts received by Teachers from Coms...and by School from Local Aid.* [HC, 1892], C-323-LX.427, p. 224.

53 *Commission of Inquiry on State of Irish Fisheries. First Report, Minutes of Evidence,*100.

54. Eustas O'Heidain 'The Blessing of Galway Bay' in *Spirituality* (Galway: Dominicans Publication, January 1996).

55. *Royal Commission on Ecclesiastical Revenue and Patronage in Ireland.* Second report, [HC, 1834] (589) p. 113.

56. *Select committee on Industries (Ireland) Report, Proceedings, Minutes of Evidence, Appendix. [HC, 1884–85] C.2671,* p.351.

57. Ibid. p.1027.

58. Edeltraud Drewes [Report] *Three Fishing Villages in Tamil Nadu: A Socio-Economic Study with Special Reference to Role and Status of Women.* Bay of Bengal programme: Development of small scale fisheries.(Food and Agriculture Organisation of the United Nations), p. 42.

Claddagh school was totally Catholic and had 120 pupils, with two teachers, which on a comparative level was still a high number.[52]

A curious symbiotic relationship existed between the Catholic church and the Claddaghmen. Reference is made to a religious source in 1730 noting in the accounts that a Dominican priest, courtesy of a generous donation of Maddam Ffrench, dispensed 10 quarts of strong water to the Claddaghmen. Sails for the boats were made on the floor of the Claddagh church; 'each boat owner paid sixpence' for this right and in 1837, the location for making the sails was the floor of the courthouse whereupon they paid the same charge.[53] This changed in the middle of the nineteenth century with the introduction of a navigational industrial school directed by the Church.[54] This exposed the annual amount owed as ecclesiastical revenue from the Claddagh and Clonbern of £36 18s. to the See of Tuam.[55]

Reports regarding the survival of Cladagh's special arrangements were often inconsistent. By the 1880s, 'the Claddagh and its system' was described as 'almost done away with' and the population was reportedly down to 200 families.[56] A source of 1885 contradicted this noting that the Claddagh fishermen were still adhering to 'their peculiar customs'.[57] The photograph 'A Galway Fishwife' (Figure 9.4) shows a woman standing next to a mule- drawn cart. Her warm woollen shawl and lace-up boots were distinctive attire for Claddagh women. The mode of transporting goods, by the headload, is most unusual compared with other Welch images of women bearing creels on their backs (see Figure 8.2) meant that women could carry small amounts quickly to market. It could also have been linked to a marketing ploy: the pretence of a small take could potentially earn a higher price. Loads were normally sold early in the morning but, if the catch arrived too late or there was a glut, the fish would be taken home, and spread out in a shady, airy place or on the dry, cobbled ground. (Spaces for this purpose are evident in front of the Claddagh houses). Fish were also sold at an evening market. It might have been against the Claddagh women's interests to promote larger vessels or increased fishing activity.[58] It can be argued that women controlled the market to deter the arrival of bigger fish traders and auctioneers who dealt with all types of fish. Small, manageable catches meant the women could transport what they needed by the headload and keep control of resources.

The traditional world of the Claddagh seemed isolated from rapidly changing economic conditions. The photograph by Welch depicting the Claddagh's cabin housing (Figure 9.3) highlights the extent to which the Claddagh heritage embodied much of the rural tradition: old, low, thatched, whitewashed cottages dotted about in an irregular pattern. In the background the outside world with its newly slated roofs dominate the neighbouring quarters of Galway. Welch's images show women in traditional dress sitting outside the doors of their houses. The additional chimneystacks provide the extra heat needed for domestic work on nets and tarring boats. According to certain sources, some held their cabins rent free, under Mr Daly of Dunsandle; it is not clear why he was so benevolent. None of the fishermen had land or hired land for growing potatoes. In the photographs by Welch the houses are all devoid of gardens; the stony ground would not in any case have been suitable for growing vegetables. They purchased goods through the market in Galway. One public house existed but it was noted that Claddagh fishermen 'frequented houses in another part of town'.[59]

This contrasts directly with other minuted records. Mr Lynch, MP for Galway, was a landlord and carried out numerous improvements on cabins with small gardens for the fishermen in neighbouring Barna, where vessels were landed. The yearly rent was 10s 6d.,[60] very different from rents of £1–2 annually mentioned in certain cases by the Claddagh fishermen. Sources cite them using the outside of the walls to dry fish and at one stage living in black beehive huts. Such walls exist in Welch's photographs and could well have been used for this function. The falling numbers of families needing housing must also be noted. Clear evidence of once-adjoining houses can be seen Welch's photograph of the cabins (Figure 9.3). Clamps of turf exist beside other dwellings, but housing needs were declining. The four hundred families with two thousand occupants, giving an average of five for each family, were reduced to two hundred families by the end of the nineteenth century. The Famine, emigration and changes in fishing

59. *Commission of Inquiry on State of Irish Fisheries. First Report, Minutes of Evidence*, 112.
60. *Commission of Inquiry on State of Irish Fisheries. First Report* i, 102.

patterns all took their toll on the Claddagh community.

Welch's images coincide with a period of immense change. The advent of and wider use of motor boats at the beginning of the twentieth century escalated the decline in fishing, which had started with the Famine. Some progress occurred with the successful introduction of beau trawlers and side trawlers. However, the disincentives of hard work and uncertainty of payment meant that many of the Claddagh fishermen eventually joined the British Navy on the outbreak of the First World War. The Claddagh community provided ready-made seafaring skills but also had no recourse to other employment, 'Three-quarters of its excess population entered the merchant navy and merchant service.'[61]

To conclude, this chapter demonstrates that while the Claddagh people and their often belligerent nature earned many entries in Irish historical records, much remains uncaptured. In this respect, Welch's images serve to supplement documentary evidence but in many other ways it captures more than words. His pictures point to the ironical contrast of newly built piers and a declining skilled population. The inactivity of the fishermen in the photographs inadvertently reflects the cynical view of the 'idle' Claddagh fisher folk. Poignantly, the abundance of children featured in these images are the final generations of a once populous fishing settlement. The economically controlling Claddagh womenfolk, with their traditional dress, carrying headloads in an ancient fashion, present a strange face of Irish culture, one now largely forgotten. All of Welch's pictures provide invaluable glimpses of this unique urban maritime settlement remembered for romance and superstition, thus revealing another layer of Claddagh history.

61. J. Stanley Gardiner,'
    Geography of British
    Fisheries', in *Geographical
    Journal*, vol. 45, no. 6.
    (1915).

CHAPTER TEN

The Agricultural Work of the Congested District Board

JONATHAN BELL

Agriculture was the main source of income for most people living in the areas defined as congested districts, and its improvement was identified as the Congested Districts Board's (CDB's) main area of work. An Agricultural Committee was established at the first meeting of the Board in 1893.[1] CDB officials were clear that most farms in the West of Ireland were too small and too badly managed to be viable:

> The great majority of inhabitants were in possession of small plots ... generally about two to four statute acres in extent ... In most cases rights ... [to] rough grazing were appurtenant to the holdings, and frequently the tenants possessed the right of cutting and gathering seaweed for manure or kelp burning. The plots were usually planted with potatoes and oats, and the methods of cultivation were extremely primitive; there was no rotation of crops, no adequate supply of manure, and no proper system of drainage, whilst the breeds of livestock were worn out and of little value ... In most cases the people did not really live on the produce of their holdings, but rather on some secondary source of income, such as field labour in England or Scotland; they paid a rent for their holding, generally not because of its agricultural value, but rather because it was necessary to have some home for their family.[2]

The baseline reports prepared by Board officials in the early 1890s supported this depressing picture:[3]

1. W.L. Micks, *An Account of the Constitution, Administration and Dissolution of the Congested Districts Board for Ireland from 1891 to 1923* (Dublin: Eason & Son, 1926), p. 19.
2. Ibid., p. 259.
3. Ibid.

1. Family in comparatively good circumstances

Receipts from farming

Sale of cattle – £6.0.0
Sale of sheep – £2.10.0
Sale of pigs   – £3.0.0
Sale of eggs – £4.0.0
Misc. sales of kelp, butter, fish, fowl etc. – £2.0.0

Total income from all sources – £41.0.0
Total expenditure – £42.15.0

The home produce consumed by the family was valued at £12 to £20.

2. Family in ordinary circumstances

Eggs – £1.3.0
Herding cattle –£4.0.0

Total income from all sources - £8.3.0
Total expenditure - £11.

The following examples show the failure of income from farming to meet the needs of families, even on larger holdings:

3. Family in comparatively good circumstances

Receipts from farming

Sale of cattle – £6.0.0
Sale of sheep – £2.10.0
Sale of pigs   – £3.0.0
Sale of eggs – £4.0.0
Misc. sales of kelp, butter, fish, fowl etc. – £2.0.0

Total income from all sources – £41.0.0
Total expenditure – £42.15.0

The home produce consumed by the family was valued at from £12 to £20.

4. Family in ordinary circumstances

Receipts from farming

Sale of calf – £4.10.0
Sale of five sheep – £3.15.0
Sale of pig – £3.10.0
Sale of eggs – £2.4.4
Sale of corn – £0.15.0

Total income from all sources – £27.4.4
Total expenditure – £30.9.1

The home produce consumed by the family was valued at £5.10.0 to £10.

5. Family in very poor circumstances

Receipts from farming

Sale of calf – £2.0.0
Sale of two sheep – £0.16.0
Sale of pig (profit) – £2.0.0
Sale of eggs – £2.0.0

Total income from all sources – £9.16.0
Total expenditure – £10.19.0

The home produce consumed by the family was valued at £12 to £17.

6. Family in the poorest possible circumstances

Receipts from farming
.9.0

The home produce consumed by the family was valued at about £6.

Eighty four of these reports were produced between 1891 and 1892. The farming system described had clear parallels with the modern developing world: dependence on physical labour, lack of access to capital and a crippling cycle of debt. In all of the examples given, it is clear that income did not match expenditure.

Board officials developed two main strategies to improve these conditions. They worked to increase the size of smallholdings throughout the congested districts, mainly by consolidating holdings to produce larger farms, and they encouraged more commercial farming practices, mainly by persuading farmers to improve livestock management and cultivation techniques on their holdings.[4] CDB officials believed that the work of creating larger, commercially viable holdings had the most potential to improve the condition of farmers in the congested districts, especially in inland areas, 'where agriculture must always be the chief industry.'[5] There was a lot of pressure on the Agricultural Committee and its staff to ensure that best practice was adopted as the Board was limited by statute and could not compete with private enterprise. What it endeavoured to do was purchase unused estates, render them arable, divide the lands and reallocate them to people willing to migrate to new holdings.

In 1902, the CDB's approach was said to be as follows. First of all to arrange with the landlord for the purchase of the estate. Holdings were then consolidated and resold to the tenants. Consolidation often involved 're-striping' the estate, squaring and rearranging the holdings, to make them compact and large enough to be commercially viable. A major obstacle in achieving this was undoing the effects of sub-division. Over several generations, the division of holdings between children meant that a field of one acre might belong to a dozen persons, each of whom owned his own particular plot. Often, also, matters were made more complicated by 'undivided shares' in various fractions of plots, such as three-fourths of one and one-sixteenth of another.[6]

The Board's work on Clare Island in County Mayo was seen as a clear example of successful reorganisation:

> The whole island was held in rundale; no one knew where his land began or ended; he only knew that he had grazing rights over certain parts. There were no fences, and the

4. Anon, 'The Congested Districts Board for Ireland', *Ireland, Industrial and Agricultural* (Dublin: Browne and Nolan, 1902), p. 258.
5. Ibid., p.262.
6. Ibid. p. 263.

cattle strayed practically unrestrained, even over whatever arable patches there were; the holdings were wretchedly small, and over two years' arrears of rent were due.

The first work undertaken was the building ... of a strong stone wall, about five miles long, across the island to separate the pasture from the tillage lands. This was necessary as, owing to the fact that there were no fences, cattle and sheep roamed over the whole island, and when the crops were in the ground the tillage land had to be guarded against the cattle by the members of the tenants' families.

Under the supervision of the Board's Inspector all this has been changed. Cattle sheds have been built, main drains opened, holdings extended, the striping carried out, and over fifty miles of fences constructed. The wages earned by the islanders engaged on these works enabled them to pay their rent, including the arrears[7]

The Board was most effective when carrying out work that could only be done on an estate-wide basis, for example drainage. The organisation of drainage work on the vast Dillon estate in County Mayo during the 1890s was seen as an example of this kind of project at its most successful. On the estate, several thousand acres of low land was made practically useless by constant flooding. Individual tenants could not make the large main or arterial drains, or deepen the beds of the rivers – such work could only be carried out by the owner of the estate. The CDB undertook this large scale work, and at a relatively small cost the production value of hundreds of acres in different parts of the estate was claimed to be doubled.[8]

FARMING METHODS

Officials of the CDB were convinced that the improvement of agricultural techniques could have a major effect on farming output.

7. Ibid
8. Ibid.

> The primitive methods of cultivation of smallholdings [in congested districts] … were capable of such improvement as would nearly double the value of produce, if, with better cultivation, the breeds of livestock and poultry were improved. Such a change was what the Board aimed at in 1892.[9]

Since the eighteenth century, intelligent observers of the Irish rural economy have identified lack of capital as one of the main obstacles to development. Tenants resettled on new holdings had to have access to some working capital in order to establish themselves. The CDB recognised this problem, and responded to it by working along with the newly emergent coperative movement, which established 'agricultural credit societies' to help small farmers. Horace Plunkett, who was a member of the Board, as well as the head of the cooperative movement, organised the introduction of these 'Raffeissen' banks in parts of the congested districts during the 1890s. The CDB cooperated with this. In the early years, this joint initiative was judged to be a great success. It was believed that many seasonal migratory labourers to Great Britain were landholders whose farms would be greatly improved if sufficient capital was made available to allow holders to stay at home and labour to improve their own smallholdings.[10]

Education was also seen as central to achieving the goal of improvement. The Board employed resident agricultural inspectors to advise small holders on the management and improvement of their land and stock, and to organise the distribution of improved farm implements. Inspectors gave out artificial manures and small quantities of seed, in order to encourage smallholders to improve their crop rotations, and try new crops, such as mangolds or new varieties of potatoes.[11] Officials claimed that the most common rotation on small farms was 'a see saw between oats and potatoes until it was thought to require a rest, when it was left to nature'.[12] They aimed to persuade farmers to establish regular rotations, with part of the land being planted annually with grass seed.[13]

Investment in new implements and machinery was also encouraged. For example, the 1903

9. Micks, *The Congested Districts Board*, p. 26
10. *Ireland, Industrial and Agricultural*, p. 264.
11. Ibid, pp. 264–65.
12. Micks, *The Congested Districts Board*, p. 25.
13 Ibid.

report of the Board noted that 'hand and foot' operated threshing machines were being offered to western farmers, as a replacement for the labour-intensive flails that were widely used.[14] In areas where the land was not too rocky for horse ploughing, the Board also supplied small iron ploughs that could be drawn by a team of donkeys.[15]

Instructors were initially sent to Kiltimagh in East Mayo, Achill Island in West Mayo and Clifden in Connemara[16] They entered agreements with about ten farmers in the neighbourhood of each station to work at least part of their holdings in accordance with the advice given.[17] By 1902, the inspectors had charge of nearly forty example holdings, and about five hundred experimental and example plots.[18]

The CDB also intervened directly in livestock management, mainly by improvement of animals through breeding programmes. 'Good bulls' were purchased and then resold to farmers in congested districts at less than half of the original price; the farmer purchasing the bull had to agree to keep it for two to three years. It was recognised that these measures were not entirely successful. Too many of the bulls bought in the first year were 'finely bred, delicately-reared bulls requiring feeding, housing and care that they would not receive in the Western districts. The result was a lesson quickly learnt.'[19] Between 1892 and 1901, 1,026 bulls were supplied by the Board, mainly of dual-purpose breeds. It was claimed that the effects of this initiative were dramatic:

> In the poorest agricultural districts, such as Connemara, the difference made in the ten years from 1892 to 1901 was amazing. In 1891, the cattle were thin, light, raw-boned, degenerate, long-horned specimens of the old worn-out breed, good for neither beef nor milk. In 1901 the majority of cattle were of the polled Galloway breed, … or of the Shorthorn or Aberdeen Angus, where conditions were suitable.[20]

Similar measures were taken to encourage the improvement of sheep and pigs. A total of 321

14. Congested Districts Board Report no. 12 (Dublin: Thom, 1903), p. 13.
15. Pat Bolger, 'The Congested Districts Board', in W. Nolan, L. Ronayne and M. Dunleavy (Eds), *Donegal History and Society: Interdisciplinary Essays on the History of an Irish County* (Dublin Geography Publications, 1995), p. 653.
16. Micks, *The Congested Districts Board*, p. 25.
17. Ibid.
18. *Ireland, Industrial and Agricultural*, p. 264.
19. Micks, *The Congested Districts Board*, p. 29.
20. Ibid., pp. 29–30.

boars were sold in congested districts, mostly of the Large White Yorkshire breed and, between 1891 and 1904, more than 700 rams were sold. The Board also established 32 sheep dipping stations, to combat 'scab'. In some places, including Clifden and Doon in County Galway, and Glenties in County Donegal, portable dipping troughs were supplied.[21] This initiative was generally seen as a success. In the year 1903–04, for example, about 130,000 sheep were brought for dipping.[22]

One problem arising from these initiatives to improve breeding programmes was that farmers often sold off the new improved stock that was produced by the breeding programmes, and held on to their old 'inferior' animals. The CDB's work with horses encountered similar difficulties. 'It was found that most families living near the coast kept a mare, which was used for drawing turf, seaweed and other commodities, while the sale of a foal every other year was an important source of income. The Board bought a number of stallions, which were kept in the congested districts during the breeding season, and then brought back to the Board's stud farm at Shankill, County Dublin.'[23] Spanish jackass donkeys were also introduced. However, as with other livestock, it was found that the best foals were being sold off. The scheme also created controversy with horse breeders elsewhere in Ireland, who feared that the horses (mostly Hackney crosses) produced by the Board's initiative might enter the breeding lines of fine Irish breeds such as hunters, and have a negative effect on the quality of these animals.

Programmes for improving poultry were less problematic. The CDB began by distributing good-quality cockerels. In 1893, 1600 were distributed in the congested districts. However, it was decided that this was too expensive to continue, and fertilised eggs were given out instead.[24] By 1901, almost 230,000 eggs had been distributed. This work was backed up by a poultry expert, who visited small farmers taking part in the scheme, and instructed them in the best ways to manage their fowl.[25] The Board's initiative to encourage beekeeping shows the enthusiasm of many of its members and employees, and their charm. In 1893, the Board supplied swarms of bees to about a dozen cottages, and the scheme was extended in later years, to

21. Bolger, 'The Congested Districts Board', p. 655.
22. *Ireland, Industrial and Agricultural*, p. 265; Micks, *The Congested Districts Board*, p. 29.
23. The following types of stallion were made available by the CDB, mostly between 1892 and 1901: 41 Hackneys, 8 Welsh cobs, 7 Thoroughbreds, 6 Hunters, 4 Arabs, 2 Shire Horses, 1 Cleveland Bay, 1 Barb, 1 Connemara, 1 Norwegian Micks, The Congested Districts Board, p. 28; Bolger, 'The Congested Districts Board', p. 653.
24. Micks, *The Congested Districts Board*, p. 32.
25. Ibid., p.266.

include help with marketing honey. In 1895, eighty hives were sold to smallholders in congested districts. By 1901, this number had risen to 246.[26] The CDB's first Secretary, W.L. Micks, expressed his admiration for the man who was the driving force behind this initiative:

> The Board was fortunate enough to secure the services of Mr. Turlogh B. O'Bryen, who combined the enthusiasm of a missionary with the sagacity and endurance of a commercial traveler. He would take no rebuffs when he found a *likely* family in a good heather or clover district, and he traveled on his push bicycle over all the congested districts from Donegal to Kerry and West Cork. He was frequently to be seen in all kinds of weather on his bicycle, on which he used to carry a great spread of frames etc., for modern bee hives and other requisites, delivering them to beekeepers as he went. He was utterly unofficial, but most businesslike and successful in his work. My association with him is one of the pleasantest memories of my official life.[27]

From the start, the work of the CDB also overlapped with that of other bodies, such as the Irish Agricultural Organization Society. Cardinal O'Donnell of Donegal and other prominent people were active in both organizations. The establishment of cooperative credit societies has already been mentioned, and there were a number of other situations where related projects were run by both institutions. For example, the work of the Board in improving poultry keeping coincided with the establishment of early poultry co-ops in the 1890s.[28]

Most of the agricultural work of the CDB was carried out in the first ten years of the organisation's existence. The overlap between the work of the board and other state bodies was eventually removed:

> For a few years prior to 1891, the Agricultural branch of the Land Commission … had been engaged in the improvement of agriculture and of livestock and poultry throughout

26. Ibid., p. 267.
27. Micks, *The Congested Districts Board*, p.32.
28. Pat Bolger, *The Irish Cooperative Movement* (Dublin: Institute of Public Administration, 1977).

Ireland, including the congested districts ... [so] the Board and the Land Commission agreed that the agricultural work of the Board, exclusive of the amalgamation of holdings, should be carried out in such approved schemes as might be delegated by the Branch to the Board.[29]

A major step in dealing with such overlaps was taken under the Act of Parliament that constituted the Department of Agriculture and Technical Instruction in 1899. Under the Act, the Agricultural Branch of the Land Commission was transferred to the Department, while under the Wyndham Land Act of 1903, the operations of the Board relating to agriculture and livestock were transferred to the Department.[30] The Department took over, for example, the Board's work with the IAOS in providing agricultural credit, and also more specific projects, such as the encouragement of potato spraying.[31]

In the first twenty years of the twentieth century, the biggest impact that the Board had on farming life in the congested districts arose from its role in land reform. In 1910, 'Birrell's Act' established the CDB as a corporate body legally entitled to purchase land, compulsorily if necessary. During its lifetime, the Board purchased 733 estates in Ireland, an area of 1.77 million acres, at a cost of £6.73 million.[32]

DISCUSSION

The CDB was set up with an altruistic mission, and its officials quickly gained the confidence and liking of many smallholders. The Board's willingness to spend money was undoubtedly one reason for its popularity.[33]

However, it clearly did not save farming in the West, where poverty and emigration remained endemic until the late twentieth century. Several reasons can be suggested for this failure.

29. Ibid., p. 24.
30. Ibid., p. 33.
31. Pat Bolger, 'The Congested Districts Board', p. 659–61.
32. Ibid., p. 667.
33. Virginia Crossman, 'Congested Districts Board' in the *Oxford Companion to Irish History*, ed. S.J. Donnelly (Oxford: Oxford University Press, 1999), p. 110.

Figure 10. 1
A well managed infield in
Lissaniska, near
Castlebar, County Mayo,

    The CDB's assessment of Irish farming methods revealed a paternalistic attitude in dismissing farming practices as observed by officials in the congested districts at the time of the Board's inception. Similar attitudes can be seen in the reports of agricultural improvers and government officials from the late eighteenth century onwards. The negativity was often unjustified. The poor practices that were described, such as chronic subdivision of holdings, overcropping, poor crop rotations, and the lack of systematic livestock breeding, were the result of population pressure on land, and the desperate struggle to ensure the survival of farming families from one year to the next. When these pressures were not so overwhelming, the labour intensive methods practised by small farmers in the West of Ireland were remarkable for their refinement and efficiency.[34] An understanding of their potential might have led to more effective development of farming methods.

A clear example of this can be seen in the rundale system of landholding, and its associated farming methods. People living in rundale settlements jointly farmed land associated with a cluster of houses, or *baile*, as a joint tenancy. The houses were surrounded by an *infield* (Figure 10.1), which contained the best arable land on the holding. This was divided into unenclosed strips, which were periodically redistributed among members of the settlement, so that each family could expect to have access to land of different quality. The egalitarian principles underlying the system also extended to the *outfield*, or *talamh bán*, an area used for grazing and occasional cultivation. Control of livestock in uncultivated strips within the infield, or grazing the outfield, was often the responsibility of women, children, or occasionally hired herdsmen. Booleying, or *buailteachas*, the movement of livestock away from arable land during the growing season, was an integral part of the system, and decisions regarding when to move animals to hilly ground were also taken communally.

The refinement of the labour-intensive methods associated with this type of farming can be seen in tillage and harvest techniques. The use of steep-sided cultivation ridges (*iomairí*) was common for growing both oats and potatoes. The size and shape of these ridges might be carefully changed depending on the soil type, aspect, the crop grown, the time of planting and the place of the crop in a rotation.[35]

The most common harvesting tool for cereals was the sickle (*corrán*). Reapers using the sickle held each handful of grain as it was cut. This meant that weeds could be left behind, the grain could be cut very near to the ground, and seed was not lost from the grain heads by shaking.

34. Jonathan Bell, and Mervyn Watson, *Irish Farming 1750–1900* (Edinburgh: John Donald, 1986).

35. Jonathan Bell, 'Aspects of the Use of Cultivation Ridges in Ireland Since the Eighteenth Century', *Journal of the Royal Society of Antiquaries of Ireland* (Dublin, 1983).

36. Jonathan Bell, 'Sickles,
     Hooks and Scythes in
     Ireland', *Folklife*, vol. 18
     (Reading, 1981).

Figure 10.2
Strip farms at
Derrindaffderg, near
Castlebar, County Mayo
(Nat. Lib. No. CDB32)

The skill of Irish migrant workers in reaping grain in this way was said to have held up the introduction of other methods of harvesting in parts of Britain such as Yorkshire.[36]

CDB officials, like most Irish landlords whose attitudes we know of, were almost entirely dismissive of the rundale system of landholding. Landlords and improvers disliked rundale, because they alleged it caused disputes, mainly arising over the allocation of arable strips in the infield, or problems arising from straying animals. Landlords and improvers also claimed that the practice of periodic reallocation of land took away any incentive for farmers to make long- term improvements to their holdings. The response of both landlords and Board officials was to reorganise farms, mostly by 'striping' them, as in the case of Clare Island mentioned above, to create long farm holdings with one dwelling on each farm (Figure10. 2). However, evidence from contemporary writings, folklore archives and oral testimony shows that the rundale system, and its associated farming methods, could operate well where the pressures just listed were not extreme. The possibility that rundale could have been developed as a viable system is strongly suggested by Scottish evidence, where the closely related system of *runrig* still operates in a codified form. People living in the Irish settlements valued the egalitarian aspects of the system, and were also very attached to the communal living associated with the *baile*. The Scottish experience shows that good organisation could have made rundale a viable farming system, and preserved some of the social advantages identified by people in the settlements.

Most of the CDB's initiatives in attempting to improve farming had been recommended or tried by others, including agricultural experts, improving landlords, and cooperators. The recognition that lack of capital was hindering the development of Irish farming had been clearly recognised by the English agriculturalist Arthur Young as early as 1780.[37] Some large-scale projects, such as drainage of estates, had been undertaken by some Irish landlords as early as the 1770s, and the measures taken by landlords in the early nineteenth century to abolish the rundale system on their estates were often the same as those adopted by the Board. Some landlords also gave premiums and grants for the purchase of new implements or livestock, or the improvement of dwellings and outbuildings.[38]

Although many of the measures taken were mistaken, shortsighted, or arose from unexamined prejudices, many of them were beneficial to considerable numbers of people living in congested districts. Unfortunately, the local scale of most initiatives could not overcome the massive problems involved in revitalising the economy of the West of Ireland. Improvers, landlords and Board officials were right to identify the lack of capital as central to achieving this, but it was not the relatively small amount of capital required to set up a horse-breeding pro-

37. Arthur Young, 'General Observations', *A Tour in Ireland*, vol. 2 (Dublin, 1780).

38. Bell and Watson, *Irish Farming*, pp. 2–13.

gramme, or even to drain an estate. The West lacked effective communications and an infra-structure of support services to ensure effective collection, processing and marketing of pro-duce. The level of capital investment required was far beyond anything that the CDB could provide.

Despite its overall lack of success, and allegations that its financial management was poor,[39] most people living in the congested districts saw the Board as a good thing. As Patrick Bolger points out, 'There was a general feeling that the Congested Districts Board had gained the con-fidence of the people. Much of this success could be attributed to the dedication of board members and their understanding of the psyche and condition of the people.'[40] The dedication of Board officials, typified by Turlogh B. O'Bryen, whose work with the development of bee-keeping was mentioned above, was legendary, part of the artistic, economic and political fer-ment that characterised important sections of Dublin's intellectual and cultural elites at the beginning of the twentieth century. If the failure was large-scale, the small-scale successes remain inspirational.

39. Crossman, *Oxford Companion to Irish History*, p. 110.
40. Bolger, 'The Congested Districts Board', p. 656.

CHAPTER ELEVEN

Smallholder housing and people's health, 1890–1915

CIARA BREATHNACH

1. For further information on the Balfour Album see Chapter 3 and Marie Boran, 'The Ireland That We Made: A Galway Tribute to Arthur J. Balfour', in *JGHAS*, 54 (2002), pp. 168–174. See also Tim Collins, 'Praeger in the West: Naturalists and Antiquarians in Connemara and the Islands, 1894–1914, in *JGHAS*, 45 (1993), pp. 125–154.

2. The CDB was founded in 1891 to raise living standards in areas of the western counties of Donegal, Sligo, Leitrim, Roscommon, Mayo, Galway, Cork and Kerry.

3. (369) *Royal Commission on Condition of Poorer Classes in Ireland. First Report, Appendix (A), Supplement; Appendix (B), Medical Relief, Dispensaries, Fever Hospitals, Lunatic Asylums; Supplement*, Parts I. and II. Whately Commission, [HC, 1835] (c. XXXII) p. vi.

This chapter provides an overview of the state of housing for the rural smallholder poor in the West of Ireland during the period of modernisation. Housing standards have always been class sensitive, so the four grades of dwelling identified by census enumerators in the late nineteenth century correspond directly with wealth, in descending order. This work deals exclusively with fourth-class, rural housing under which rubric 'one-roomed cabins' fell. These dwellings were occupied by smallholder families, that is, persons holding, usually on a rental capacity, between one and fifteen acres. Through a number of mechanisms, both public and private, funding was made available in the last quarter of the nineteenth century to build new houses and conduct structural improvements on existing housing with the aim of gradually phasing out the use of one-roomed cabins. To fully appreciate the impact this new housing had on the rural landscape it is necessary to outline and explain the diversity of the lower echelons of the rural class structure and to provide reasons for the poor condition of rural housing stock. A comparative analysis of the 1891–2 album commissioned by James Hack Tuke and the later Robert J. Welch congested district albums,[1] will highlight the effect of improved housing – encouraged and funded by the Congested Districts Board (CDB)[2] and the efforts of benevolent clergy – had on rural life.

A movement to improve the standard of rural housing and abolish the existence of 'cabins' had been afoot since the 1830s when a number of witnesses interviewed by the Royal Commission on the Poorer Classes (Whately Commission) testified to the existence of an overwhelming proportion of sub-standard dwellings in Ireland.[3] But nothing concrete came of these observations and no provisions were incorporated into the 1837 Poor Law to remedy the situation. Many subsequent

4. Ms. Add. 49817 ff.
169–173. Balfour Papers,
BL, William Lawson Micks
to Arthur J. Balfour.
5. For further information
see C. Breathnach, *The
Congested Districts Board
of Ireland 1891–1923:
Poverty and Development
in the West of Ireland*
(Dublin: Four Courts
Press, 2005), pp. 109–13.
6. D.S. Jones, *Graziers, Land
Reform and Conflict in
Ireland* (Washington:
Catholic University of
America Press, 1995)
pp. 31, 35.
7. Caoimhín Ó Danachair,
'The botháin scóir', in E.
Rynne (ed.), *North
Munster Studies: Essays in
Commemoration of
Monsignor Michael
Moloney* (Limerick:
Thomond Archaeological
Society, 1967) p. 493. Ó
Danachair is careful to
note the class lines, or
what he more appropriate-
ly terms 'the very deep and
very real social and eco-
nomic gulf which existed
in the nineteenth century
between these classes of
the rural population of
County Limerick', p. 498.

investigations, from census evaluations to Royal Commissions of varying agendas, identified poor housing as a major obstacle to both urban and rural development. Urban housing had by the mid- to late nineteenth century become subject to more rigorous scrutiny under the public health and sanitation acts, whereas in rural areas these laws were not policed and were more commonly ignored. Rural housing stock remained in a poor condition because people were too poor to conduct independent improvements and, in a barely fluid economy, when money was available it was not habitually spent in that way. It can be argued that smallholders were afraid to conduct improvements because it could cause valuations to increase and this would lead to a rise in rents. Because tenants had no security of tenure people could not see the point in investing in homes of which, in the event of an eviction, the value would be lost – tenants were not compensated for the value of improvements as Ulster tenants were. It was noted by some officials that people simulated poverty in order to increase their chances of obtaining money from outdoor relief sources.[4] However, it was fairly standard, from CDB evidence, that people lived in the dwellings they could afford.

Traditionally, rural Ireland was given special treatment by successive governments but the land legislation of the latter half of the nineteenth century made little distinctions, between the various classes of land occupier. There were varying degrees of landowners and occupiers in the West but the majority population came from the smallholder class; interestingly, such occu-piers would have been classified cottiers in the east.[5] The word 'cottier', which is often used interchangeably with con-acre and denotes persons of the landless labouring class, has many connotations and the definition alters on a regional basis. David Seth Jones defines it as a per-son holding a con-acre of land rented at exorbitant rates from middlemen or graziers.[6] Appreciating that the definition is sensitive to regional differences Caoimhín Ó Danachair is more generous in his definition of Limerick cottiers as 'people who held small portions of land, less than ten plantation acres', whereas Aalen is more rigid in his definition.[7] Using evidence from various British Parliamentary Papers Aalen defines labourers as persons with 'small plots of land, a quarter acre or so'.[8] For those who fell below the level of land occupant there was always Poor Law relief. The rural poor were adept at manipulating the Poor Law system and at times even wielded it to their advantage. Outdoor relief was availed of when opportunities presented and indoor relief was preserved as the last port of call. William Lawson Micks,[9] in his capacity as a local government board inspector, noted the reluctance to engage with formal systems of poor relief in a report to Dublin Castle in April 1889 on the 'Alleged distress in Donegal'. He cites relatively low indoor and outdoor relief statistics, stating that the:

> tenacity with which country people cling to their homes is so well known that nothing short of the most acute suffering and utter despair will compel families to run the risk of abandoning their houses even temporarily and to become inmates of the workhouse.[10]

Until the 1883 Labourers' Housing Act (LHA) very little of a permanent nature was done to ameliorate the plight of the rural poor. The LHA provided capital to construct suitable housing and the architectural plans adopted ensured that the quality of housing stock improved. The provisions of the 1883 Act were quite generous and provided a half-acre site to supplement income. The implications of allocating a half-acre to 'supplement the tenant's income' meant that the government was what Murray terms 'helping to create a quasi-cottier class'.[11] This counteracted the effects of primogeniture, which became more firmly established in the decades after the Famine, whereby the creation and perpetuation of the 'cottier class' through sub-division was halted in favour of consolidating holdings. Despite the favourable conditions the response to the LHA was very poor (see Table 1). The reasons for this are complex and range from political, legal, social and economic to cultural issues but all are embedded in aspects of social class. Crossman argues that political persuasions were more influential in acquiring access to a new labourer's cottage than anything else.[12] She cites how 'In some areas, local branches of the National League incorporated support for the acts into their political programmes …

8. F.H.A. Aalen, 'The rehousing of rural labourers in Ireland under the Labourers (Ireland) Acts 1893–1919', *Journal of Historical Geography* (1986), p. 288.

9. Micks later became Secretary of the CDB.

10. William L. Micks, Balfour papers, Add., 49817. ff. 124–5.

11. M. Fraser, *John Bull's Other Homes: State Housing and British Policy in Ireland, 1883–1922* (1996), p. 28. 47 Vict., Labourers (Ireland) Act, 1883, Amendment.

12. V. Crossman, *Politics, Pauperism and Power in Late Nineteenth-Century Ireland* (Manchester: Manchester University Press, 2006), p. 168–9.

Progress under the acts became a measure of achievement for nationalist guardians in areas where there were concentrations of labourers'.[13] Among the lower classes LHA and parallel land legislation served to augment existing divides between those who could raise the capital necessary to purchase lands under the various schemes and those who could qualify for social housing.

TABLE 1
NUMBER OF LABOURERS' HOUSES BUILT, 1883–94

Province	Number of cottages authorised	Estimated cost of cottages authorised	Number of cottages built	Actual cost of cottages built
Ulster	246	£30,769 3s. 8d.	201	£20,553 0s. 8d.
Munster	7,528	£821,653 10s. 6d.	6,192	£707,492 10s. 2d.
Leinster	4,596	£536,399 2s. 8d.	3,675	£464,863 13s. 5d.
Connaught	95	£9,666 12s. 10d.	74	£7,919 11s 3d.
Totals	12,465	£1,398,488 9s. 8d.	10,142	£1,205,829 1s. 5d.

Source: Return, by Counties, Unions and Electoral Divisions in Ireland, of Number of Cottages built and authorised under Labourers Acts [HC, 1893–94], LXXV,

Unlike landless labourers, the majority of congested district inhabitants held occupancy of a four to six acre plot of land.[14] In the West landless labourers were fewer than in the East and the extent to which the LHAs were implemented there was reflected in the low numbers who chose to categorise themselves as such. In 1893, ten years after the Act was applied, a mere seventy-four houses had been built in Connaught compared with 6,192 in Munster.

A further county by county breakdown highlights that in the congested counties few took advantage of the generosity of the scheme, with no takers in Donegal or Mayo (where housing was poorest), a mere 7 cottages built in Sligo, 37 in Leitrim, 17 in Galway, 13 in Roscommon, rising to 391 in Kerry and a return of 2,444 being built in Cork –the largest Irish county.[15] Poor participation in the congested districts is not surprising given that most agricultural work was

13. Ibid., p. 166.
14. CDB, First Annual Report, p. 8.
15. For electoral reasons Cork was divided into east and west ridings and only six areas in West Cork were congested.

conducted communally in a *meitheal* system with no monetary exchange, so the extent to which a landless labouring class could survive in the congested districts was negligible.[16] David Fitzpatrick warns that it is 'inadmissible, to divide the agricultural workforce into distinct classes of wage-labourers and of farmers with their unpaid assisting relatives', stating that the census returns and their organisation precludes such evaluations (census categories were rigid and often enumerators only returned the head of household as employed, assisting relatives were not counted).[17] While the poor response to the LHA is not enough to suggest that agricultural labourers did not exist in the West, it does imply reluctance. Literacy and political issues might have precluded further participation but it is more likely that it reflects the obstinacy of a class that refused to degrade itself by participating in the scheme. Rather, the labouring class in the congested areas comprised a population of temporarily assisting siblings or relatives, who were not prepared to commit long term to life on the land; trends in the West favoured migration, emigration or alternative employment for surplus children. Until the inheriting son married surplus siblings were permitted to remain in the family home: they contributed to the family budget with cash earnings from hiring out, seasonal migration or outwork. They conducted household chores, primarily in exchange for lodgings in the family home but mainly in the hope that family finances would eventually afford opportunities for marriage or emigration.

It was well recognised – primarily through the work of philanthropists like James Hack Tuke – that the West was significantly poorer than the East and the CDB was founded in 1891 to ameliorate circumstances. When the baseline inspectors of the CDB[18] conducted their survey in 1891–2 they found a number of different dwellings in the West, varying from mud huts to crudely constructed stone houses of between one and three compartments.[19] Major Ruttledge-Fair, a baseline inspector, who was commissioned by James Hack Tuke to photograph his baseline study, found that in Sligo most houses were constructed out of loose stones with no mortar binding or plastering. In some houses there were 'no chimneys, the only exit for the smoke being the doorway, or a small hole made in the roof directly over the fireplace' (see Figures 11.1 and 11.2

16. For further information see: Anne O'Dowd, *Meitheal: A Study of Co-operative Labour in Rural Ireland* (Dublin: Comhairle Bhéaloideas Éireann, 1981).

17. David Fitzpatrick, 'The disappearance of the Irish Agricultural Labourer, 1841–1914', *Irish Economic and Social History*, 7 (1980), p. 69.

18. Six temporary inspectors were employed for a period of six months between 1891 and 1892 to survey all aspects of life in the 84 congested areas.

19. Fraser, *John Bull's Other Homes: State Housing and British Policy in Ireland, 1883–1922* (1996), pp. 30–3; Aalen, 'The rehousing of rural labourers in Ireland' Aalen notes that census enumerators liberally applied the term 'mud cabin' and argues that large, tastefully-built farmhouses tempered with clay were unjustly categorized as mud cabins in the returns.

for examples).[20] Most of these poorer classes of house had no windows and were poorly ventilated. Unmortared loose stone houses like Mick McQuaid's Castle (Fig 11.1) were commonplace in the congested districts. There were other slightly better houses containing two rooms,
one being a living area and the other for sleeping. Anywhere between one and twenty people
slept in these one- and two-roomed cabins, which was a matter of grave moral and medical concern. Officials noted that very often children of both sexes occupied the same sleeping space.
Evidence to the Royal Commission on Congestion for Ireland showed that 'In Dingle there
were twelve houses of one room, with seven in the room; in Kenmare there were ten such houses with seven in the room; in Tralee Union there were twenty-nine with eight, and twenty-three
with nine in the room; in the Killarney Union there were forty-eight with eight in the room'.
It was advised that 'these houses should all be swept away'.[21]

Baseline reports attest to the fact that the floors were literally the earth beneath the house.
Such dwellings were inhabited by humans and their animals. Cattle, pigs and poultry roamed
freely in and out of the dwelling during the day and were kept inside by night. People had no
idea of the health risks associated with living in such close proximity to animals. There were
no chimneys. Roofs were made of thatch and were ideal incubators for bacterial spores. A
cesspool for waste matter was located outside the door. Communicable diseases were spread
both directly and indirectly in these environs. For example, exposure to faecal matter caused
gastro-intestinal disease. The cesspool attracted rodents and insects, which acted as vectors or
modems for the transmission and spread of diseases like typhus and cholera. The most preva-
lent diseases in the 1890s were infectious and included fever, a generic term used to describe
symptoms of everything from typhus and cholera to respiratory tract infections. The spread of
droplet diseases such as TB was endemic when cohabitation with animals was commonplace.
The only effort made by local authorities to stop the spread of disease was to give out free lime
in times of rampant 'fever'.[22]

Baseline inspector Gahan noted that the peasantry was slow to improve their circumstances

Figure 11.1
Mick McQuaid's Castle
W14-05-48. This image is a per-
sonification of the left side of
Fig. 3.3.

20. Major Ruttledge-Fair, Joyce
Country baseline report, pp.
443–5. These 84 reports
were compiled between
1891 and 1892 by six tem-
porary inspectors. There are
two copies of the baseline
reports in the Early Printed
Books Department, Trinity
College, Dublin.
21. RCCI, Appendix to the
Eighth report, minutes of evidence taken in Kerry and
Cork, 3–19 July, 1907, [HC,
1907], Cd. 3839, p. xx.
22. Gahan, *Teelin baseline
report*, p. 15.

Figure 11.2
View of unsanitary house in Monivea, County
Galway, CDB9

23. Henry Gahan, *Grange* baseline report, p. 292.
24. Ciaran Walsh, Siamsa Tire,
Tralee, pointed out that these
planks look very like those
used in nearby light railway
construction. A. Gailey,
*Rural Houses of the North of
Ireland* (Edinburgh, 1984), p.
94; Desmond McCourt and
E. Estyn Evans, 'A Late Seventeenth-Century Farmhouse
at Shantallow, near
Londonderry, in *Ulster
Folklife*, 14 (1968),
pp 14–22.

because they resigned themselves to the 'same old groove' and were 'keenly sensitive to ridicule'.[23] An overview of the average expenditure budgets in the baseline reports shows that cash incomes were not used to conduct household repairs (see Table 2, which shows a fairly detailed household budget). Ready-made building materials were in short supply, of course a reflection of the demand. With the exception of Mick McQuaid's humble abode having a few planks of timber helping to batten down the thatch, nearly all forms of housing were built out of freely available materials, such as stones, wood, clay and thatch for the roof.[24]

If paucity of materials determined the physical construction and exteriors of cabins in the congested areas it had an equal effect on the contents of smallholder dwellings. The extent of furniture, or what can be described as such, was very limited. Furniture making in the congested districts was

TABLE 2
RECEIPTS AND EXPENDITURE OF A FAMILY IN ORDINARY CIRCUMSTANCES, THE RECEIPTS BEING DERIVED FROM
AGRICULTURE, FISHING, AND HOME INDUSTRIES

Receipts	£	s.	d.	Expenditure	£	s.	d.
Sale of heifer	4	10	0	Rent	2	0	0
Sale of 5 sheep	3	15	0	County cess	0	5	8
Sale of pig	3	10	0	Tea	5	17	0
Sale of eggs	2	4	4	Sugar	1	19	0
Sale of flannel or tweed	3	10	0	Meal	7	14	0
Sale of corn	0	15	0	Flour	1	17	6
Sale of fish	8	0	0	Clothing	6	8	6
Sale of knitting etc	1	0	0	Tobacco	2	7	8
				One young pig	0	15	0
				Implements	1	4	9
Total	27	4	4		30	9	1

Home produce consumed by the family is valued at from £5 10s to £10.
Source CDB, First Annual Report, p. 33

crude to say the least and lacked the artisan sophistication of contemporary pieces produced by the 'Killarney' craftsmen. In the late nineteenth century distinguished artisans were manufacturing elaborate pieces out of birch and oak bogwood.[25] The lack of forested areas in the congested districts limited the range of furniture but, given that most of these areas contained extensive bogland it is a wonder why bogwood, which was used as an item of barter in Desertegney, County Donegal, was not used for furniture making. Welch's equipment, as described in Chapters 5 and 7, was cumbersome and relied heavily on natural light so, with the exception of larger dwellings, for example the interior image of a Kerry farm kitchen, near Kenmare (Figure 11.3), rural interiors were not captured by Welch or Ruttledge-Fair. But we do have baseline inspector accounts that described interiors as 'unhealthy, mean and comfortless'.[26] That furniture was primitive is obvious from the baseline accounts but we have some idea of its appearance from pieces Welch placed outside the dwellings, such as those captured in Figure 13.1. Sometimes dual-function furniture

25. John Teahan, *Irish Furniture and Woodcraft* (Dublin: Country House, 1994). pp. 37–8.
26. CDB, First Annual Report, pp. 8–9.

Figure 11.3
A Kerry Farm Kitchen, Loo,
Kenmare, W40/03/14.

was used to create partitions but this was not a common practice.[27] According to Gailey, the divisions of the traditional brye-dwelling were of recent origin and were usually of a 'flimsy construction'.[28]

In keeping with the predominantly poor housing, it was found that the range of social classes resident in the West was not as diverse as in the East of the country.[29] Census breakdowns highlight that in the West there were few resident landlords, few members of commercial classes or industrialists. However, where there were some resident and caring landlords their civilising influence was indisputable. For example, in the district of Grange, County Sligo, a baseline report notes that Lord Palmerston offered prizes for the best-kept homes and as a result of this competition homes were comfortable.[30] Where Catholic clergy took an interest in improvements homes were notably cleaner and better ventilated.[31] Fr McFadden was parish priest in Gweedore and he encouraged the people to maintain clean homes and to whitewash the walls both inside and out.[32] In congested areas where the LHA's had made an impact close to where Crossman notes 'concentrations of labourers',[33] there was a natural trend of smallholders – who regarded themselves as socially superior – conducting household improvements to maintain their position as visibly higher than landless labourers. For example, a better class of house could be found in Kerry (areas of neighbouring North Cork had responded well to the LHAs) where baseline inspector Redmond Roche noted that of a total number of 1,074 dwellings in Brosna, 374 were slated – slate was a required material in houses constructed with LHA funds.[34] It is also likely that because the LHA set architectural precedents local merchants began to stock building supplies; an example was McCowen's of Tralee town.[35]

Initially the CDB was strictly limited by statute and it did not have a specific budget for rehousing or improving existing stock; in fact, it was not empowered to conduct new house building except on new holdings.[36] Under its initial structure the Board had a Treasury-approved budget of £50,000 for what it termed 'works' but this was pre-allocated to infrastructural development (construction of marine works such as piers, boat slips, causeways, roads and bridges),

27. Mohill, p. 277. H. Doran, Ballaghdereen baseline report, p. 309, Second Annual Report, [HC, 1893] C. 7266, p. 9

28. Alan, Gailey, 'Kitchen furniture', *Ulster Folklife* 12, (1966), p. 18.

29. *Royal Commission on Condition of Poorer Classes in Ireland. First Report.* [HC, 1835] (369), also known as the Whately Commission reports, p. vi. The Whateley Commission reported in 1835 that few 'substantial capitalist farmers' could be found in Ireland, that the trading class was much smaller than in England and that the resident gentry class was almost negligible.

30. Gahan, Grange, p. 10.

31. J. Mac Laughlin, *Ireland the Emigrant Nursery and the World Economy* (Cork: Cork University Press, 1994), p. 10.

32. Father MacFadden was a strict disciplinarian and moral guardian to his parishioners. For further information on his notoriety see B. MacSuibhne, 'Saggart aroon and gombeen-priest: Cannon James MacFadden, 1842–1917', in G.P. Moran (ed.), *Radical Irish Priests 1660–1970* (Dublin: Four Courts Press, 1998), p. 155.

Cont.

cont.
33. Crossman, *Politics, Pau-perism and Power*, p. 166.
34. R. Roche, Brosna baseline report.
35. CDB, Nineteenth Annual Report, 1911, p. 38.
36. CDB, Eighteenth Annual Report, p. 12.
37. CDB, First Annual Report, [HC, 1893], C. 6908, p. 5: 'probably works may be undertaken by the Board at a time when destitution exists in a locality, but the object will be not of the providing of "relief works", but the making of an effort to permanently and materially improve the trade and resources of such a district in connec-tion with agriculture and industries'. See also CDB, Second Annual Report, p. 29.
38. Doran, general report, p. 424.
39. Doran, Ballaghdereen, p. 310.
40. CDB, Fourth Annual Report [HC, 1895], C. 7791, p. 7.
41. CDB, Fifth Annual Report [HC, 1896], C. 8191, p. 7. CDB, Sixth Annual Report, [HC, 1897], C.8622 p. 26.

as it was anxious to incorporate careful planning to disassociate its endeavours from 'relief works'.[37] There were, however, ways and means of manipulating the Act to allow for house-hold improvements and, given that most industry was cottage based the Board could justify such a budgetary allocation. Henry Doran, an engineer who had won a gold medal in recogni-tion of a large-scale drainage project he had conducted on his own land, was appointed as base-line inspector to the CDB in 1891 and was subsequently re-employed as an agricultural inspec-tor to provide the holdings with better quality housing. Doran emerged as a crusader for the cause of improving rural housing: he felt so strongly about improving the condition of the peo-ple that, apart from the ordinary baseline reports, he issued a separate aggregate report on gen-eral trends and conditions of the areas he surveyed, also adding a list of recommendations. In this general report he advised that

> No person should be allowed to keep cattle, pigs, or fowl in their dwellings; a manure heap should not be kept within 20 yards of a dwelling, the houses should be whitewashed inside and out at least once a year; it should be illegal to keep milk or butter in a sleeping apartment.[38]

Doran, in his recommendations for improvements in Ballaghdereen district, advocated the amendment and proper enforcement of the sanitary laws by the police force and medical offi-cers for health.[39] He decreed from the outset that money should be set aside to improve homes in the very poor district of Kiltimagh, convincing Board members to allocate a temporary fund in 1894 to pilot a scheme in Kiltimagh to improve dwellings and construct out-offices for ani-mals.[40] It was continued until 1896, when Doran approached the Board to formalise the Kiltimagh scheme into general Parish Committee Schemes (PCS).[41] The fact that sanitation laws were in abeyance for many years was a crucial component in the argument for the board to cre-ate and allocate funds to PCS. By 1896 Doran's Kiltimagh scheme was ratified by the board and extended to other counties. The primary purpose of these schemes was to allocate grants to incentivise the removal of animals from the home and the relocation of the cesspool to a safe distance.[42] Like the LHA this scheme was aimed at elevating a particular class in this case, it was land occupiers whose valuation (land and house inclusive) did not exceed £7.[43] As distinct from general improvements made to CDB lands prior to resale, the parish schemes were allocated from a different fund. A system of grant-in-aid was initiated to encourage a self-help mentality among the people. Prizes were given for clean and neat houses. In tandem with the improvements to existing structures, the Board carried out new house building as part of its estate improvement schemes. For example, when the Board purchased the Ffrench estate in 1894 it was careful, under the supervision of Doran, to spend £370 on the building of four new houses and £134 on repairing existing ones. Tenants provided labour free of charge; and the new houses (like that in Figure 11.5) were built to high specifications and all the walls were concrete.[44]

Voluntarism on the part of the people was of course intrinsic to the success of the Parish Committee Schemes. It was difficult to dissipate old fears that if a tenant conducted improvements it would raise the valuation and thus the rent. Eight years after the induction of PSC, when the Dudley nurses arrived in their respective districts they conducted a preliminary count of the prevalence of one-roomed cabins.[45] In Aranmore, County Donegal, the resident Nurse MacMahon noted that seventy-four one-roomed cabins were occupied by between one and twelve people (two of which were occupied by twelve and upwards), in Geesala, County Mayo, Nurse McCoy noted eighty-seven one-roomed cabins housing between one and nine persons.[46] According to this report, of a total population of 1,841, 305 lived in one-roomed cabins,[47] while in Aranmore the figures were 361 of a total population of 1,396. A similar image to that Figure 11.4 was used in the report to give an idea of 'this wild and desolate stretch of country which extends from Spiddal to Costello, covered by a network of straggling stone walls enclosing small patches of barren land – land which produces little beyond the countless stones of which these walls and cabins of the people are built'.[48] Such conditions, where extended families lived in

42. CDB, Third Annual Report [HC, 1894], C. 7522, p. 6.
43. CDB, Eighteenth Annual Report, p. 23.
44. CDB, Fifth Annual Report, p. 13. When the board purchased Clare Island in 1895 it immediately set about improvements, it built a 5 mile wall of 6 feet high with the help of local labour at a cost of £1,600 to separate tillage from pasture land. New houses were built to accommodate tenants on reorganised plots 'it is hoped that nearly all, if not all, the dwelling-houses will be improved before the island is sold to the tenants'.
45. See Chapter 12.
46. Lady Dudley's scheme, First Annual Report (1904), p. 19 NLI, IR 614L3.
47. Ibid., pp.1 8 and 19.
48. Lady Dudley's scheme, Second Annual Report (1905), p. 5.

clachan's or clusters, were of grave medical concern and contributed to the spread of disease.

Figure 11.4
Ballyhoorisky, Fanad, County
Donegal, W04/37/01

Through its household improvements and new house building the CDB inadvertently found itself conducting work that should rightfully have been carried out by local authorities. In tandem with the Dudley scheme (see Chapter 12) it also worked to improve public health and sanitation.[49] Both entities found that the ignorance of the people was the primary obstacle to improvement. Because of this the function of the Dudley nurses was extended to beyond that of medical healthcare practitioners to that of sanitary officers as they helped to establish basic sanitary education. The nurses were required to keep good records and from their accounts the links between the nature of disease and poor housing were further highlighted. One nurse noted how she had

... been very busy this month with chest cases, pneumonia and bronchitis among 13 children. All these patients' homes were in the bogs (no roads to any of them). Am glad to say the children are all quite recovered ... [but] they appeared quite hopeless in their miserable homes, with damp mud floors. In several of these rooms the cows were also kept.[50]

Called at 2pm to attend a case of pneumonia. I found the patient, a woman aged about 35, in bed in a very small room, which, besides lacking ventilation, was in a very dirty condition. After attending to the patient I cleaned the room, and succeeded in opening the window, which she informed me had never been opened before. I spoke to her on the subject of fresh air, and explained its beneficial effects. I was greatly pleased to find that every time I visited subsequently the window was open and the room very clean and tidy.[51]

Despite the fact that progress was slow under the Parish Committee Schemes, by 1909, when the Royal Commission on Congestion for Ireland had concluded, a number of witnesses gave evidence on how much positive work had been conducted by the PCS.[52] Thousands of previously unsanitary dwelling houses were made comfortable, animals were removed, concrete floors were

49. CDB, Thirteenth Annual Report [HC, 1904], Cd. 2275, p. 42.
50. Lady Dudley's scheme, Sixth Annual Report (1908), p. 10.
51. Ibid., p. 12.
52. The CDB's request for additional funding resulted in the appointment of the RCCI, also known as the Dudley Commission, in 1906 to investigate the efficiency of the CDB. It reported in 1909 and concluded that the CDB be continued, expanded and given more funds.

TABLE 3
RETURNS PER COUNTY DETAILING MONEY SPENT ON HOUSING UP TO 31 MARCH 1915.

County	New houses built by CDB	Total amount Spent on new houses	No. of new houses built by tenants	No. of new houses built by tenants with CDB assistance	Total spent on new houses or on improvements to existing houses by tenants	Total columns 2 annd5
Donegal	76	£6,059	129	198	£7,102	£13,161
Leitrim	5	£713	16	15	£1,288	£2,001
Sligo	99	£16,459	42	87	£3,056	£19,515
Mayo	946	£143,919	773	845	£40,487	£184,406
Roscommon	523	£110,231	320	780	£17,502	£127,733
Galway	673	£126,952	267	220	£16,194	£143,146
Clare	25	£4,239	8	39	£1,025	£5,264
Kerry	72	£11,452	319	785	£29,671	£41,123
Cork	29	£3,441	74	106	£3,853	£7,294
Totals	2,448	£423,465	1,948	3,075	£120,178	£543,643

Source: CDB, Twenty-third
annual report, [HC,
1915], Appendix XVI,
p. 88.

put in kitchens, bedrooms floors were
boarded and easy-to-open double sash windows replaced fixed ones.[53] It is hard to
gauge the full impact the PCS money made
on communities but it was estimated that it
represented eight to twelve times the original amount.[54] More importantly, the habit
of spending money on new housing and
household improvements was established,
and it was noted in 1909 that a 'more
hopeful and energetic spirit has been

Figure 11.5
*New house of John Commons,
farmer and tailor, Ryehill,
Monivea, County Galway* (fig.3
CDB10).

infused into the minds of thousands of the poorest class'. Quite apart from improvements to
family dwellings some 10,476 cattle sheds were built or improved.[55] CDB figures on housing
expediture are provided in Table 3.

With improved housing respiratory tract infection and fever cases reduced considerably and
the nature of the Dudley nursing reports altered accordingly. Instead, documentation focused
more on general lumps and bumps, midwifery and orthopaedic cases.[56] Aesthetically, the *Irish
Builder* described CDB houses as a blot on the landscape but the marked improvement is indisputable.[57] The houses were bigger, constructed out of durable materials and separate accommodation was built for animals at a safe distance from the family home. These new dwellings allowed
for separate compartments for food storage and proper bedrooms (see Figure 11.5).

General observations by government agencies and visitors alike make it clear that sanitation
laws were not policed in rural Ireland in the late nineteenth and early twentieth centuries.
Unsanitary conditions and poor housing were common as a result. Home improvements were
simply not a priority among a population that suffered hunger periodically. Throughout the
nineteenth century the Irish were regularly accused of exaggerating conditions to increase the

53. CDB, Eighteenth Annual
    Report [HC, 1909], Cd.
    4927, p. 11.
54. CDB, Sixteenth Annual
    Report [HC, 1907], Cd.
    3767., p. 33.
55. CDB, Eighteenth Annual
    Report, p. 23.
56. Lady Dudley's scheme,
    Ninth Annual Report
    (1911), p. 18.
57. *Irish Builder,* 22 April, 1916;
    p. 177, 4 January, 1913, p.
    19, cited in Murray.

chances of monetary assistance – photographic evidence changed this perception. Ironically, Welch's photographs were not used to show the true extent of Irish poverty; they served a different agenda of highlighting improvement. Documentary evidence shows that the poor people of the West were slow to avail themselves of relief and reluctant to engage with officialdom in general. The pro-active approach of the CDB and Lady Dudley's scheme were key aspects to encouraging change in a political climate that economised in the provision of basic healthcare and sanitation. Both the Dudley nurses and CDB officials acted as *de facto* sanitary officers and because they lived among the people they led by example and inspired confidence. It is important to note that these Welch images were commissioned by the CDB and cannot be employed as certain proof of its success; however, the statistics show that under its auspices much improvements occurred. The success of the CDB schemes over the efforts of other agencies such as the Department of Agriculture and Technical Instruction may be ascribed to the popular response. Without the intervention of the Congested Districts Board it is unlikely that the people would have prioritised spending on improving housing standards until a much later period when cash incomes increased.

CHAPTER TWELVE

Nurses and Teachers in the West of Ireland in the Late-Nineteenth and Early-Twentieth Centuries[1]

MARGARET Ó HÓGARTAIGH

1. This article is dedicated to the memory of Lawrence McBride, who made an enormous contribution to Irish history. My thanks to Ciara Breathnach for all her advice and encouragement.
2. See, for example, the various essays in Bernadette Whelan (ed.), *Women and Paid Work in Ireland, 1500–1930* (Dublin and Portland: Four Courts Press, 2000); Margaret Ó hÓgartaigh, 'Archival Sources for the History of Professional Women', in *Irish Archives*, vol. 6, 1999, pp. 23–5; idem, '"Am I a Lady or an Engineer?" Early Irish Female Engineers' in the *Irish Engineers' Journal*, December 2002, 48–9; idem, 'Councillor Tully's Views on Women and Paid Work', in *Ríocht na Midhe. Records of the Meath Archaeological and Historical Society*, vol. xv, 2004, pp. 173–9; idem, 'Women in Pharmacy in the Early Twentieth Century', in *The Irish Pharmacy Journal*, vol. 82, no 6, June 2004, pp. 273–8; idem, 'Books
Cont.

Any discussion of women working in professional occupations in the late-nineteenth and early-twentieth centuries must begin with the admission that we know so little and much remains to be revealed.[2] However, the photographs from the Congested Districts Board (CDB) albums from the West of Ireland discussed in this article reveal hidden aspects of the lives of teachers and nurses and, more importantly, their students and patients.

NURSING

Nursing, it has been argued, 'demonstrated the limitations of a separate female world that lacked an effective power base within its own domain.'[3] A distinct hierarchy was most obvious in the medical world, with nurses (female) invariably subordinate to doctors (usually male): in the hospital setting, nurses were directly controlled by a female matron. However, district nursing managed to surmount these limitations by providing women with much professional autonomy while simultaneously bestowing on them great responsibility for the health and welfare of their patients.

The attraction of a respectable profession, and its association with traditional female virtues, encouraged many of those who could afford it to opt for a career in nursing. Nurse training was expensive, sometimes as high as 100 guineas per annum, so nurses tended to be drawn from those who had disposable income. Social connections could also play a role in selecting

Cont.

and Baths and Run all the Way: the Cultural and Educational Formation of Female Primary Teachers in the Early Twentieth-Century', in *Irish Educational Studies Journal*, vol. 23, no. 2, Autumn 2004, pp. 55–65; idem, 'Female Teachers and Professional Trade Unions in the Early Twentieth Century', in *Saothar*, vol. 29, 2004, pp. 33–41; idem, 'Women in Irish Dentistry', in *Journal of the Irish Dental Association*, vol. 51, no. 4, Winter, 2005, pp. 185–6; idem, 'Female Veterinary Surgeons in Ireland, 1900–30', in *Irish Veterinary Journal*, 2006 pp. 388–9. The work of workhouse nurses is discussed by Siobhan Langan-Ryan in Margaret Preston and Margaret Ó hÓgartaigh (eds), *Medicine, Gender and the State in Ireland and the United States 1700–1950* (New York, 2007).

3. Martha Vicinus, *Independent Women: Work and Community for Single Women, 1850–1920* (London, Virago press, 1985) p. 120.

4. See the first report of the Jubilee Institute, 1898, Dublin; Lady Dudley's husband, Lord Dudley, the

Cont.

candidates for training. District nurses were always midwives, and were vital public health workers. Jubilee nurses (that is, district nurses) were established in 1887, on the silver jubilee of Queen Victoria. The Dudley nursing scheme was established in 1903, by Lady Dudley (the Viceroy's wife) to provide district nurses in the congested districts of Ireland. These Dudley nurses were prominent in Donegal, Sligo, Galway, Kerry, Cork and Mayo. The aim of the Jubilee Institute, which trained district nurses, was to create an interest in home nursing, supply home nurses and organise a 'central or county nursing association in every county in Ireland'.[4]

Dudley nurses' work was similar to that of the Women's National Health Association (WNHA): the latter employed district nurses to work towards eliminating tuberculosis.[5] In order to qualify as a Jubilee nurse, one had to be state registered, hold the certificate of the Central Midwives' Board and have three years' general experience.[6] The Dudley nurses' badge featured the motto 'By Love Serve One Another' and they were known affectionately, as late as the 1970s (when the scheme was disbanded) as 'Dudleys'. It was believed that Dudleys were particularly valuable, because it was difficult to entice nurses of Jubilee calibre to the West, where social conditions were appalling. As a rule, nurses were not well paid: such was the voluntarism expected of the profession that salaries were supposed to sustain nurses but not necessarily compensate them for long hours. For example, in 1928, the Local Appointments Commission advertised for a trained nurse. She was to be paid £75 a year, with 'rations, fuel, light and accommodation'.[7] The rations may not have been that impressive given that some nurses sought money instead.[8] The one advantage of state employment was the promise of a pension, which could be transferred if one moved from one local authority to another.[9] Given these benefits-in-kind, some nurses were better off financially than teachers. But their salaries did not increase significantly with service. Public health nurses were better paid than most: in 1923, two public health nurses in Louth received between £150 and £200 per annum. Meanwhile, in County Cork, they were paid between £140 and £150. Many of these nurses would also have had midwifery qualifications, as well as being registered.[10]

Midwives needed to be medically meticulous in their work. They could be struck off for failing to keep proper medical records.[11] The profession thought their reputation had to be safeguarded, partly because they had to contend with 'handy women', who worked as midwives but did not have any qualifications. Maternity cases accounted for about 70 per cent of Dudley work and 'handy women' were a big problem as some of them brought midwifery into disrepute by their methods. The *Irish Nurses' Union Gazette*, in 1925, vowed to keep agitating against 'quacks'.[12] In 1928, the Department of Local Government and Public Health pointed out that 'while there had been substantial progress in the elimination of the activities of handy women, it had not been easy, in rural areas, to break through the tradition of using untrained persons.'[13] Eventually, legislation was introduced, in the 1930s, to eliminate the unqualified. An examination was introduced for those who did not have the state certificate and, as an indication of the need to encourage all to sit the examination, Annie Smithson (who was a qualified midwife) assured her readers that it was, 'a simple qualifying one, and need not frighten anyone.'[14] Yet so many, especially in rural Ireland, relied on 'handy women' in the absence of trained medical practitioners.

Where nurses were established their work was usually greatly appreciated by the local population. The need for district nurses was clear. Bishop Fogarty of Killaloe requested a nurse for the district of Kilbaha, in County Clare. 'The local priests tell me that a district nurse would be a great boon to the poor people and be much appreciated by them.'[15] Both patients and nurses endured grim conditions: one nurse on a maternity case spent the night in a freezing room without a fire.[16] But they were appreciated. Fr McHugh, the parish priest at Carna, in County Galway, commented on Nurse Wills. 'She is an excellent person, fond of her work, kind and nice to the poor. She is an ideal nurse.'[17] Nightingale suggested that district nurses should be 'Health Missionaries'.[18] This phrase further emphasising the link between medicine and an

Cont.
  Lord Lieutenant, headed the commission on the Congested Districts; for the history of the Congested Districts Board see, Ciara Breathnach, *The Congested Districts Board of Ireland, 1891–1923* (Dublin, 2005).

5. *WNHA Golden Jubilee 1907-1957*, p. 5. The 1909 WNHA report referred to the link between the WNHA and the Jubilee Institute, in relation to the employment of district nurses, p. 20. On the WNHA, see Greta Jones, *'Captain of All these Men of Death': The History of Tuberculosis in Nineteenth and Twentieth Century Ireland* (Amsterdam and New York, 2001), pp. 101-126 and Margaret Ó hOgartaigh, 'The Babies' Clubs in Ireland and the Children's Bureau in the US', in Chester Burns, Ynez Violé O'Neill, Philippe Albou and José Gabriel Rigau-Pérez (eds.) *Proceedings of the 37th International Congress on the History of Medicine* (Galveston, 2001), pp. 99–103.

6. *Queen Victoria Jubilee Institute Irish Branch, Fourth Report*, 1927, pp. 4, 18, 21 and 22.

7. *Irish Nursing News* [hereafter, INN], Nov. 1928, p. 15.
                              Cont.

Cont.
8. INN, Jan. 1929 p. 46.
9. *Irish Nursing Union Gazette* [hereafter, INUG], May 1925, p. 7.
10. For example, Nurse Richardson was appointed, in 1923, at £150 per annum as a health visitor and school nurse, Dept. of Health files, NAI SM28/41.
11. One midwife was struck off the roll for failing to keep a record of the pulse of a patient, and not notifying the 'local supervising authority that medical aid was required', INN, Mar. 1928, p. 71.
12. INUG, May 1925, p. 2. Later that year, the INUG reported on a deputation to the Coombe Hospital 'whereby the students from the hospital would discourage the presence of "handy women"'. The difficulties facing midwives, given that many people could only afford a handy woman, were made clear. The Board of the hospital pointed out that, 'in the case of poor people,' they accepted help wherever they could obtain it, INUG, Oct. 1925, p. 5.
13. Joseph Robbins, 'Public Policy and the Maternity Services', in Alan Browne (ed.) *Master's Midwives and*
                                        Cont.

evangelical desire to help others. As Fox remarked, the district nurse is 'supposed to exert a generally uplifting influence on her community.'[19] Sometimes this was quite a challenge. For example, in Carna, County Galway, the Dudley nurse reported the following incident:

> At 9 p.m. four men and a boy called to my cottage, all were under the influence of drink. The boy's hand was badly injured by becoming entangled in the spokes of a moving cart. After attending to his wounds I had much difficulty in getting rid of the escort, as they were scarcely able to maintain their balance, and I feared they would fall asleep in my kitchen, where they waited while I dressed the boy's hand.[20]

Communication with patients in the congested districts, many of which were in the Gaeltacht (Irish-speaking areas), must have been severely strained given that some of the district nurses could not speak Irish. A classic example of this is Nurse B.M. Hedderman, whose memoir of her time spent nursing on the Aran Islands has been carefully assessed by Nellie Ó Clérigh. Nurse Herderman arrived on the Aran Islands in 1903, just as these photographs were being taken, and remarkably, 'found it hard to be accepted'. Perhaps her inability to speak the language of the islanders was a factor. She admitted that her patients would be 'her silent instructors', her 'teachers'. However, Herderman admits that she 'could not grasp much of what they were saying'. One of the locals offered to take her 'ashore in all the "Bearla" (English language) he could command'. She admitted that Irish was a 'beautiful and expressive language'. Her appearance, especially her coiled hair, intrigued the young girls on the island. Cultural conflict was inevitable between Hederman and the local ('handy') women who traditionally tended to childbearing women. She wrote, 'I had promised to visit a newly-made mother, because lactation had not been established, and well-meaning neighbours have a habit of giving babies many fearful abominations. I dreaded interference, and had some doubts as to the treatment the baby would receive if entrusted to these ignorant women.' Despite her disdainful attitude, she

Figure 12.1 'Waiting to Guide Nurse' (photo taken by W.J.D. Walker)

Cont.
Ladies in Waiting: The Rotunda Hospital 1745–1995 (Dublin: A & SA Farmar, 1995), p. 283.
14. INHW, Sept. 1931, p. 20.
15. *Lady Dudley's Scheme. Second Report*, 1905, p. 15.
16. *Lady Dudley's Scheme. Seventh Report*, 1910, p. 10.
17. *Lady Dudley's Scheme. First Annual Report*, 1904, pp. 5 and 10.
18. N.M. Falkiner, 'The Nurse and the State' in *Journal of the Statistical and Social Inquiry Society of Ireland*, October, 1920, pp. 29–60, p.38. My thanks to Mary E. Daly, who alerted me to this revealing article.
19. Enid Fox, 'Universal Helath Care and Self-help: Paying for District Nursing before the National Health Service', in *Twentieth-Century British History*, vol.7, no.1, 1996, pp. 83–109, p. 87.
20. *Lady Dudley's Scheme for the Establishment of District Nurses in the Poorest Parts of Ireland. Eighth Annual Report*, 1910, p. 13.
21. Nellie Ó Clerigh, *Hardship & High Living, Irish Women's Lives 1808–1923* (Dublin, 2003), pp. 125, 127, 128, 129, 131, 136, 138, 141, 144, 146.

praised the islanders since they were 'inured to every conceivable hardship, with the result that their power of endurance is greater, strengthened perhaps by the compelling influence of having to earn a livelihood under almost the worst conceivable conditions of soil and climate'. Given their hardiness and the almost complete absence of formal medical care, it is hardly surprising that the local dispensary was seen as 'a kind of guillotine or death trap – a tribunal from which, if they entered, they were never to emerge.' Hederman's 'dissertations' on infections and temperance were not appreciated by these islanders, who had few avenues for entertainment. She realised that the 'responsibility of a district nurse in such a spot is truly great, and more exhausting than the heaviest hospital work'.[21]

Figure 12.2
Nurse's Cottage (photo taken by Miss Bradshaw)

22. *Lady Dudley's Scheme for the Establishment of District Nurses in the Poorest Parts of Ireland. Eighth Annual Report* 1910, p. 9.
23. Ibid., p. 15. This is almost certainly Myrrha Bradshaw who edited, in 1907, *Open Doors for Irish Women: Irish Central Bureau for the Employment of Women.* This book was published in Dublin. The Bureau was first opened in 1904, when there were 3,160 requests for information. It was an advice centre with correspondents from all over the country. The Bureau was still in existence in 1930. See *Thom's Directory*, 1930, p. 935
24. Daly, M.E. 'Essay in Review. Women and Labour: Margins to Mainstream?' in *Saothar*, no.19, 1994, pp. 70–4, p.71.

The photograph by W.J.D. Walker, a CDB inspector, which indicates a young man 'Waiting to Guide Nurse' suggests that the locals were intent that the nurse would be guided around the area and that she was valued.[22] Another photograph which displays, in all its frugality, the nurse's cottage in Annagry, County Donegal, was taken by 'Miss Bradshaw', of 30 Molesworth Street, Dublin.[23]

While jobs were scarce for Irish women, status was still sought. Clothing was one indicator of status. It has been argued that uniforms 'indicate social distance', and the nurse's uniform was not dissimilar to a maid's uniform.[24] This was to ensure 'that nursemaids and untrained women [could] ... no longer usurp the nurses' uniform.' To nurses' horror, 'chemists would sometimes readily supply drugs to women in a nurse's uniform'.

Meanwhile, registered nurses, and midwives, would be refused in the chemist's shop, if they

Figure 12.3
Nurse visiting a family in the congests, CDB 55

were not in uniform.[25] Uniforms, then, had a double role; they conferred a certain authority, yet, simultaneously they suggested an inferior position. Uniforms summed up the dual nature of nursing, with its ambivalent mixture of respectability and subordination. Another important symbol of the profession was the wearing of a badge, which was bestowed upon nurses on the completion of their studies and was considered an important acknowledgment to be worn as part of the daily attire.

This focus on uniforms is particularly relevant when assessing the photographs provided in

25. INUG, Oct. 1925, p. 3.

the annual reports of the Lady Dudley scheme. When the nurse arrived at her patient's home, her uniform was an immediate symbol of middle-class authority and respectability, hence she stood out from her patients, some of whom were shoeless. The Dudley's authority was hidden but evident in subtle ways. Nurses were on a par with teachers and priests in that they wielded considerable authority in small communities, the result of a cooperative venture on the part of both nurse and priest: clergymen sought nurses for their areas; when repairs were performed to the nurse's cottage in Carna, Rev. Father O'Hara, (a CDB board member) was thanked.[26] In the photograph (Figure 12.3), where the nurse is smiling at the camera while the Arranmore family in County Donegal look at the ground, her respectable clothing ensures that she stands out. The fact that she is the only one looking directly at the camera suggests that this photograph was more for her benefit than for the family's sake. They do not make any eye contact with the camera: the two barefoot children have their heads turned away, while their mother is laden with a baby and a basket. She too is barefoot and focused on her youngest child. The man is beside the small pile of turf and he is staring at the ground, perhaps an unwilling participant. What did they think of this nurse? We may never know.

TEACHERS

The other female professionals who feature in these photographs are teachers. The mode of entry to that profession varied from region to region.   There were several routes: monitorship, pupil-teachership or by competitive entry to one of the training colleges. But many aspiring teachers received their initial training as teenagers (at about fifteen or sixteen) in a local primary school. It was not unusual for a fully trained teacher, after two years at college, to begin his or her (usually the latter) professional career at nineteen. As early as 1911, 63 per cent of teachers were female.[27] Students were selected by their teachers or inspectors to become candidate monitors. After extra study, and an examination, they could then be appointed as mon-

26. *Lady Dudley's Scheme. Eighth Annual Report*, 1910, p. 21.
27. Mary E. Daly, *Women and Work in Ireland* (Dundalk, 1997), p. 39.

itors. The 'model schools' (there were twenty in Ireland) were used as training institutions for future teachers. As Marshall has noted, the effectiveness of the training received in these institutions 'depended greatly on the efficiency, interest and enthusiasm of the staff of the school, in particular of its headmaster: the size of the school and its location might also be influential.'[28] Healy suggested that the 'higher prestige which was attached to the pupil-teacherships (they would have attended secondary school) was reflected in their salary'. Monitors received £5 per annum, while female pupil-teachers, in their first year, received £14; males were paid £18.[29] The pupil-teacher system was also dependent on links between primary and secondary schools. Starkie argued that poor links between the two militated against the development of the system. Students in urban areas were at an advantage. Religious orders, such as the Christian Brothers, and the Mercy and Presentation Sisters, managed primary and secondary schools (which frequently did not charge expensive fees), so pupil-teacherships were available for students from modest backgrounds.

Monitors, in a sense, were like apprentices in the education system. It was not unknown for teachers to be 'apprenticed' to certain schools. Teachers were instructed to serve their masters and 'their secrets keep, their lawful commands every where gladly do'.[30] The most common entry route for most teachers remained the monitorship system,[31] which suggests that most primary teachers came directly from primary school to the training colleges. As Clear has noted, the 'girl who attended the free school could, if she was encouraged at home, become a paid monitress and eventually a teacher'.[32]

The introduction of the Queen's scholarship (later known as the King's scholarship, and then the Easter scholarship) examinations in 1885 provided monitors with the opportunity to qualify for a training college place. Pupil-teachers also sat this examination. These candidates usually went to an intermediate (second-level) school. If they had done sufficiently well at the intermediate examinations, they could be selected to practice teaching in a model, or in an ordinary, school. They would then proceed to a training college. In 1919–20, there were 1,400

28. Ronald Marshall, *Stranmillis College Belfast* (Belfast, 1972), p. 2. I am grateful to the librarian of Stranmillis College, Wesley McCann, for alerting me to this work.
29. James Healy, 'Teacher Education Policy in Ireland 1920–1975 with Comparative Reference to International Trends' (M.Ed., U.C.C., 1981). p. 70.
30. Indenture of Sarah Potts, Public Record Office of Northern Ireland, T.1848/2.
31. See, for example, *Student Registers* for Baggot Street/Carysfort College in Mercy Archives, Booterstown, Dublin. This material has now been transferred to Mercy Archives, Baggot Street, Dublin. These list: 'Registration number, College number, Date of Entry, Name of Candidate, Address, Age on Jan next, Married or not, Roll number [of school they attended], District number, Diocese of birth, Diocese of present residence, Parish of birth, Parish of residence, Position in school (whether Principal, Assistant Monitress or Pupil), If monitress date of appointment, Date and Result of last examination, If teachers when appointedto present school, when appointed under board,   Cont.

Cont.

to present school, when appointed under board, Class and Division and when obtained, Name and address of manager, Examination results during training, first year, final year, Date of leaving, Classification when leaving, special subjects: (French, Drawing, Vocal Music, Instrumental Music, Hygiene, Botany, Physics, Domestic Economy, Practical Cookery), Doctrine and Scripture History, Training Diploma, and Remarks'. The latter were usually of a financial nature, for example, 'Diploma awarded and grant of bonus awarded'. This grant of £7 was not given to the college until the student had passed her two years of probationary teaching. Students who had been monitors were the most numerous candidates in the Carysfort registers.

32. Caitriona Clear, *Nuns in Nineteenth-Century Ireland* (Dublin, 1987) p. 27.

Figure 12.4
Young girls outside the school, Connemara, Tuke38

Figure 12.5
Older boys outside the school, Connemara, Tuke 37

monitors and 500 pupil-teachers.[33]   It was also possible to enter the training college without any previous experience, once one passed the King's scholarship examination.

Teachers, like the 'Dudleys', were supposed to set an example by their scholarliness and standards of hygiene in the classrooms. Inspectors did not only note academic faults: They also commented on the cleanliness and 'moral tone' of the classroom.[34] This emphasis can be seen in the photographs of the students. In Figure 12.4, where the students are lined up outside the school, many are wearing smocks or over-garments to protect their clothes and give a semblance of cleanliness. These young girls in Connemara, County Galway in the early twentieth century, would almost certainly have been familiar with lice. Students from a much later period, the 1940s, have distinct memories of head lice falling from student's hair onto copies,[35] though teachers were supposed to present clean students to the all-seeing eye of the inspector. It is revealing, as in one of the nursing photographs, that most of the children in the picture are studiously avoiding the camera. A few confident, smiling children, four out of a total of twenty-nine, are actually looking at it. These children were not used to being the centre of attention and, like their Donegal contemporaries, are barefoot.

The young boys outside a school, possibly the same school, are also barefoot, but seem more cheerful (Figure 12.5). One child, fourth from the right, is positively beaming at the camera. Others are gazing skywards: perhaps they were told to 'look up' and interpreted this literally. All of these young boys are in dresses. Local folklore suggested that young males were seen as more valuable than young females and it was hoped that if they were 'disguised as girls' they would not be abducted by fairies or other supernatural beings. The photograph of the older boys outside a school suggests that they too wore dresses, though as least two students were in trousers. Again, all bar one are barefoot but several seem happy to smile for the camera. Unusually, most of the boys are actually looking in its direction. Perhaps they anticipated a day off for good behaviour!   What their school experience was like is difficult to surmise. After the 'adoption of a compulsory attendance policy in 1892 [just before these photographs were

33. Marshall, *Stranmillis College* p.2.
34. See ED8/4 in NAI for inspectors' reports.
35. Information courtesy of Jim Whelan, a student in a one-teacher rural school in East Clare in the 1940s.

Figure 12.6
School Children outside the school,
Connemara, Tuke35

36. Lawrence W. McBride
'Young Readers and the
Learning and Teaching of
Irish History, 1870–1922',
in Lawrence W. McBride
(ed.) *Reading Irish Histories.
Texts, Contexts and Memory
in Modern Ireland* (Dublin
and Portland, 2003),
pp. 80–117, pp. 82–3.
37. Camilus O'Keefe, *Our Lady
of Mercy College* (Dublin,
1977), p. 24. I am grateful
to Sr. Frances Lowe of the
National Library of Ireland
for giving me a copy of this
booklet.

taken] only 50 per cent of the children attended the required seventy-five times in each half-year – schools were open a minimum of 200 days – and attendance was dreadful in depressed urban areas and in the western counties.'[36] Further changes in the early twentieth century made an impact on their learning environment.

By 1910, the Irish language movement was making an impact on the curriculum, with Irish examinations being introduced for the first time for students who wished to teach in a bilingual school.[37] It is also likely that fewer and fewer local teachers were employed in the congested districts given the gradual professionalisation of primary teaching. Two of the photographs show a teacher in action. In one, a young woman, possibly a teenager and almost certainly a monitor, is watching a semi-circle of children who are possibly playing an instrument (see Figure 14.1). The monitor is, relatively speaking, well dressed with a shawl on her shoulders and a full skirt. She also appears to be wearing shoes. The above photograph obviously shows a teacher demonstrating conkers to younger children. Was this a game they played or was there a more serious peda-gogical intent? We can see the children clearly in this photograph. Most, whether male or female, has short hair, perhaps to prevent head lice. Yet again, while the teacher is quite well dressed with an apron over her full-length dress, shoes or boots on her feet, the children are bare footed. Was she a local woman? We cannot tell, but there were serious concerns about nepotism in education, particularly at primary level. Given that most of the teachers were probably elevated locals, they would not have been as respected as the nurses, who were invari-ably, at this stage, better-trained outsiders. Even in the twenty-first century the triumph of prox-imity over performance is still an issue.

The local dimensions of the teaching profession are all too evident in the correspondence between the Roman Catholic Archbishop, William Walsh, and Sr Evangelist Forde (Principal of Baggot St. Training College for Catholic women from 1883 to 1888). She 'implored' him to 'use his influence' to ensure that her graduates were employed. Forde told Walsh that parish priests (managers of local national schools) were filling vacancies with untrained teachers instead of trained teachers. Dr Walsh 'promptly contacted the Bishops asking them to point out to parish priests the unacceptability of their behaviour.'[38] He noted, 'apart from this injus-tice to the young teachers, there was also an injury done to her college as payment for the stu-dents' board and lodging was not made till evidence of efficiency as teachers – after a proba-tionary number of years – was supplied to the Commissioners by Inspectors.' Walsh wrote a letter to one bishop who, it seems, attended retreats and was able to influence the clergy. He explained that sixty-one Baggot St. students had yet to find employment.

In a comment that reflects the local nature of school appointments, Sr Evangelist Forde wrote:

> in many cases local circumstances and influence prevent Parish Priests (who are usually the managers) from appointing a stranger; and they are often obliged, even against their own judgement and inclination, to get an untrained teacher (because a parishioner) appointed.

38. Papers Regarding Education Box xxvii in Mercy Archives, Booterstown.

It strikes me that what a P.P. [Parish Priest] cannot do, without, perhaps, giving offence to his parishioners, the Bishop of the Diocese could effect, without any such inconvenience, by expressing his wish that in making appointments to their schools, the Managers should, as far as possible, give the preference to those candidates who have regularly trained in a Catholic Training College.

Forde further argued that having trained teachers was a 'great advantage' to the school. She wanted Walsh to be aware of the danger of 'bankruptcy to the College'.[39] As the capitation grant per student was lower for females, the all-female college would have been under more financial pressure if their students did not obtain jobs after qualifying. The correspondence between Forde and Walsh suggests that Catholic networks were used in order to guarantee the survival of Catholic institutions. Given the minimum fees at the training colleges, this profession was attractive for those who could not afford a university education.

Ironically, the sectarian nature of Irish society benefited teachers in some respects. Just like the Roman Catholic Church, the Church of Ireland thought it was 'of the utmost importance that the children committed to the spiritual care of our church should be early and earnestly taught in schools whose managers and teachers belong to one communion'.[40] This policy ensured the proliferation of small Protestant schools and, consequently, more jobs for teachers. The Board recognised schools with as few as fifteen students.[41] Many of the schools in the congested districts would have been small, one-teacher institutions and by 1909, 70.7 per cent of students were being educated in mono-denominational schools.[42] In rural areas, this would have affected Protestants more than Catholics, as they were scattered throughout the country. For example, only forty-three protestant schools had an average attendance of over seventy pupils, while 171 had an average attendance of less than fifty pupils.[43]

The link between female teachers and kindergarten education was further reinforced in 1905 by the Commissioners of Education, Rule 127(b). This decreed that 'boys under eight

39. Walsh to 'My Dear Lord', 4 July 1885, also enclosed is Forde's letter of 28 June 1885 to Walsh, P/L/11 in Mercy Archives, Booterstown. Forde's letter is yet another example of locals gaining preference in the allocation of jobs which were supposed to be allocated on the basis of professional merit.

40. Quoted in Susan Parkes, *Church of Ireland Training College* (Dublin, 1983), p. 93.

41. Parkes, *Church of Ireland Training College*, p. 92.

42. Parkes, *Church of Ireland Training College*, p. 94.

43. Parkes, *Church of Ireland Training College*, p. 112.

are ineligible for enrolment in a boys' school where there is not an assistant mistress, unless there is not a suitable school under a mistress in the locality'.'⁴⁴ This meant that small one-teacher schools were under threat, and females would teach the younger students in a larger school. This rule was changed after criticism from the Roman Catholic Church who thought that it would lead to co-education. It was also felt that males were less likely to opt for a teaching career, so needed every encouragement. Not surprisingly, all the teachers in the photographs are female.⁴⁵ They were teaching both young males and young females.

The inspector greatly affected one's progress in the profession. Utilitarian educational philosophies, so wonderfully exposed by Charles Dickens in his portrait of Mr Gradgrind, the facts-obsessed teacher in *Hard Times*, would have been a familiar picture for many in the Irish educational system. Concentration on rote work, and memorisation without comprehension, were the direct results of the inspection system. Prior to 1900, primary teachers were paid according to the performance of their students. This approach won particular support from Patrick Keenan, one of the Commissioners of the National Board of Education, and the only Catholic on the Board.⁴⁶ His influence was so far-reaching that his sister, Mother Ligouri Keenan, used his connections in establishing the college in Baggot St. for training Catholic females.⁴⁷ However, payment by results had come under a sustained attack an in 1900 the system was changed. From then, primary teachers were to be inspected, and their schools examined. One of the Head Inspectors complained, in 1896, that 'one of the defects of the results system, as carried out, is that it makes no provision for directly rewarding a teacher whose school, by its good organisation, order, discipline and cleanliness merits such an award'.⁴⁸

The visit of the inspector spelled an important day. Perhaps women would have preferred the more objective examination system, rather than the assessment of male inspectors. Very little escaped the inspector's gaze. If he gave a poor report, then the teacher would not be promoted; in fact, she could even be demoted. He (they were invariably male, though women were recruited as junior inspectors in the 1920s) commented on the cleanliness of the room. It was

44. Quoted in Parkes, *Church of Ireland Training College*, p. 120.

45. For an excellent discussion of the impact of JAMs, that is junior assistant mistresses, on the teaching profession, see Úna Ní Bhroiméil ' "Sending gossoons to be made oul' mollies of'": Rule 127 (b) and the feminisation of teaching in Ireland', in *Irish Educational Studies*, vol. 25, no. 1, March 2006, pp 35–51.

46. Coolahan, John 'The Origins of the Payment by Results Policy in Education and the Experience of it in the National and Intermediate Schools of Ireland' (T.C.D., M.Ed, Minor thesis, 1975), pp. 4 and 8.

47. I am grateful to Sr Magdalena Frisby, Archivist at Booterstown, for pointing out the connection between Mother Ligouri Keenan and Patrick Keenan. Mother Ligouri Keenan was an important figure in the training college. She was principal of the college from 1877 to 1882, from 1888 to 1894 and from 1900 to 1908. See Angela Bolster, 'Catherine Mc Auley, Her Educational Thought and Its Influence

Cont.

Cont.

on the Origin and Development of an Irish Training College', in Education Box xxvii, Mercy Archives, Booterstown. Keenan was described as 'queenly'. Her initiative and energy during the early years of the training college helped to sustain it. However, the many petty regulations at the training colleges were attributed to the 'semi-aristocratic' views of Mother Ligouri. See Education files Pres/H/6-9 (miscellaneous, untitled documents) in Mercy Archives, Booterstown.

48. Quoted in Coolahan, 'Payment by Results', p. 106.
49. See ED8/4, NAI for inspectors' reports.
50. Coolahan, 'Payment by Results' p.136.
51. Janet Nolan, *Servants of the Poor. Teachers and Mobility in Ireland and Irish America* (South Bend, 2004), pp. 25–42.
52. John Musson, 'The Training of Teachers in Ireland, from 1811 to the Present Day' (QUB, 1955, Ph.D.), p. 208.
53. For a selection of some of these activities see Virginia Davis, 'Curious Goings-On in the National Schools

Cont.

not unknown for teachers to be criticised for having 'cheerless' rooms. The number and variety of maps, as well as the type of seating, were also noted. However, the most important comments were reserved for the performance of the pupils and their teacher.[49] Inspectors were frequently seen as unhelpful: they were employed as the result of a competitive examination and no prior teaching experience was required.[50] The arrogance displayed by some inspectors was not conducive to good relations with the teaching profession.[51]

From 31 March 1900, with the abolition of payment by results, teachers were allocated to various categories, depending on the report of the inspector: grade three, grade two and grade one. All grades were divided into class two and class one.[52] Only a certain number were admitted into each grade, so it was not a strictly meritocratic system. This introduction of categories meant that the inspector made pivotal decisions regarding the future prospects of primary teachers.

It is difficult to ascertain whether or not inspectors were harsher towards female teachers. Judging from their comments, it is clear that many had no concept of diplomacy. Students were, on occasion, described as 'extremely dull'; we are not told if any students were bright. None the less, some teachers indulged in highly unusual behaviour, if the inspectors' reports are to be believed.[53]

The Killanin Committee,[54] in 1918, noted that 'three-fourths of the schools are rural ones, scattered over a country of sparse but general inhabitancy; and a teacher, as a factor in social life, fills a very prominent and influential position in such surroundings.'[55] The photographs suggest that the school buildings were quite basic in structure, but clearly the teacher had a position of authority in that environment. The difficulty for teachers was that poor pay paradoxically coincided with social status. A 'respectable' lifestyle was assumed, if not always financially possible. The Committee was critical of the 'lowness of the salary'.[56] but the report also suggested that, of the 'large supply of women candidates ... many ... [were] not up to standard'.[57] 'Special qualifications' could be 'recognised financially'. A Higher Certificate should have been awarded if a primary teacher had passed a university examination. However, the Committee did not believe that male and female teachers should be rewarded equally. 'We have made a man's salary somewhat higher than a woman's, because his expenses are greater; and in fixing all remunerations we have taken into account the degree of security of income and tenure which a teacher enjoys.'[58]

Teachers' pay was dependent on attendance, and poor attendance was attributed to poor teaching, regardless of social circumstances. 'The good school is nearly always well-attended, and it is quite appropriate that the principal teacher in it should benefit accordingly.'[59] Arguments regarding local illness or social disadvantage were brushed aside. Attendance on a particular day was often dependent on the state of the roads. The radical conclusion of the report was that 'no difference in salary should be made between rural and urban schools, or between schools for boys and girls and those for one sex only',[60] It did however, favour females in recommending that a normal salary scale be introduced in schools with an average attendance of thirty for males, and twenty for females, recognition that girls' schools tended to be smaller. The maximum salary maintained sex differentials, with £200 for men, as compared to £170 for women. Male teachers, 'with an average attendance of 20 to 29 pupils, should receive the scale of salaries assigned to women teachers,' the report suggested.[61]

The concentration of small schools in female hands was encouraged. Most of these would have been in the West of Ireland. 'Trained teachers of schools under twenty average, should always be women, and should receive remuneration at the normal commencing rate for women teachers, £90 per annum, and should be eligible to rise by ten annual increments of £4 to a maximum of £130 per annum,' the Killanin Committee suggested. Furthermore, it recommended that 'teachers of mixed schools of 35 pupils or under should, as a general rule, be women'. This policy meant that female teachers would receive less pay, but they enjoyed better job prospects. However, 'untrained women teachers appointed in future should leave the service on marriage, or on attaining the age of 30 years'.[62] This encouraged teachers to see their job as a 'filler' prior to marriage. In the event of non-marriage, they would be replaced by a fresh supply of poorly paid young females. These women are the focus of pupil's attention in the photographs.

1870–95', in *Retrospect, Journal of the Irish History Students' Association*, 1980, pp. 24–32; see also the inspectors' reports, ED8/4, NAI.

54. This major report, on a profession dominated by women, had only one female on its committee, Margaret Doyle, M.A. Women's Assistants' Representative, Irish National Teachers' Organisation. The Committee was to 'inquire and report as to possible improvements in the position, conditions of service, promotion and remuneration of the teachers in Irish National Schools, and the distribution of grants from public funds for Primary Education in Ireland with a view to recommending suitable scales of salaries and pensions for different classes of teachers, having regard to the character and length of training necessary, special qualifications obtained, the nature of the duties which have to be performed, and other relevant considerations.'

55. Killanin general report, p. 4.

56. Ibid., p. 7.
Cont.

CONCLUSION

The one advantage of state employment was the promise of a pension, which could be transferred if one moved from one local authority to another.[63] Given these benefits-in-kind, some nurses were better off financially than teachers, but their salaries did not increase significantly with service. Public health nurses were better paid than most. Many of these would also have had midwifery qualifications, as well as being registered nurses. While they were recognised in the community, these nurses frequently lived alone. A circulating library was established to ward off loneliness. This is hardly surprising given that there would have been very few professional women in the congested districts and language difficulties would only have exacerbated the isolation. While teachers and nurses were both working professionally in depressed parts of Ireland, there were differences in their social status. The nurses were invariably outsiders, therefore they were likely to be considered of higher status in small communities than the teachers who were usually locals, so their status was lower.

The photographs considered here and the lives of nurses and teachers in the congested districts do not always intertwine. A photograph captures a moment in time. Professional lives were lived over a period of many years, if not decades. However, while much is revealed in state and professional sources regarding the opportunities and impediments faced by professional females, we know so little about the lives of those they served. Here photographs can tell us a little about the attitudes and even socio-economic environment of the families who endured harsh lives in the congested districts of the West of Ireland in the late-nineteenth and early-twentieth centuries.

57. Killanin General Report, p. 8.
58. Ibid., p. 9.
59. Ibid., p.11.
60. Ibid., p. 12.
61. Ibid., p. 12.
62. Ibid., p. 14.
63. INUG, May 1925 p. 7.

CHAPTER THIRTEEN

Occupied and Earning:
Child, Girl and Women Workers in County Donegal

MARY CLANCY

The photographs under review in this chapter were selected for their value as sources of personal information about child, girl and young women labourers. For the historian interested in working-class or poor women and men, who cannot easily claim private archives, the formal photograph is a promising source in any attempt to reconstitute the narratives of lives led in congested areas of Ireland, like Donegal. Public collections, such as those of R.J. Welch, are valuable, for, whatever his personal or professional purpose, he has created visual public histories of certain sympathy and detail, interestingly so, considering the differences of religion, social class, language and gender that these encounters entailed. The intention in this chapter is to use the images as a way of understanding the lives of these workers. In so doing, the chapter also explores how issues of relief led interested voluntary and official visitors to congested districts. Mostly, it is hoped that this investigation will help to complicate rural histories for, as is evident in too many commentaries, the identity of the rural working woman is rarely offered the status of nuance. She is a 'surplus' commodity; she is there in 'abundance'; worse, she is a 'peasant'; later, she is a *cailín*. None of these terms project any notion that she might be intellectual, artistic, political, interested in fashion – or, like middle-class girls – in going to theatre or taking holidays. She was to be trained, not educated; she is talked about, not talking. It is hoped, therefore, that something of what the girls and women were trying to communicate in these images will help to re-assert the historical value of their stories.

1. M. Luddy, *Women and Philanthropy in Nineteenth-Century Ireland* (Cambridge: Cambridge University Press, 1995).
2. Personal research relating to Galway.
3. For discussions, see, for example, H. Blackburn, *A Handy Book of Reference for Irishwomen* (London, 1888).
4. For an overview of key developments and debates, see, in particular, P. Larmour, *The Arts and Crafts Movement in Ireland* (Belfast: Friar's Bush Press, 1992); D.M.Smith, "'I thought I was Landed!": The Congested Districts Board and the Women of Western Ireland', *Eire-Ireland*, 31, 3&4, (1996), pp. 209–27; N. Gordon Bowe and E. Cumming, *The Arts and Crafts Movements in Dublin and Edinburgh, 1885–1925* (Dublin: Irish Academic Press, 1998); J. Bourke, *Husbandry to Housewifery: Women, Economic change and Housework in Ireland, 1890–1914* (Oxford: Clarendon Press, 1993); C. Breathnach, *The Congested Districts Board of Ireland, 1891–1923* (Dublin: Four Courts Press, 2005).
5. In 1898, when the exhibition was held in Landowne House, Berkeley Square, an
Cont

THE PHILANTHROPISTS

As is fairly well known by now, women worked in home-based industries like sewing, knitting, embroidery and lace-making to ensure family survival during the recurrent famines of the nineteenth century. Also involved was the important, if also complex and controversial, effort of philanthropists intent on working with those regarded as marginal, disinherited or outcast.[1] Local newspapers readily admit to relief efforts by women of the resident landlord class, religious women, Protestant clerical families and businesswomen working separately or together or with parish priests.[2] Such research has the potential to tell of the realities of power, work and survival within labouring communities. By the 1880s, increasing attention to problematic issues like sales and markets, design, quality, standards, training and general coordination of localised effort led to the home industries sphere becoming more noticeably formal and organised.[3] There were associations, shops in Dublin and London, publications, participation in international exhibitions and, later, state funding, instruction and support through the Congested Districts Board (CDB) and the Department of Agriculture and Technical Instruction.[4] In London, exhibitions of Irish industrial work were especially prominent on St Patrick's Day, when aristocratic patrons gathered in prominent, fashionable venues to sell Irish produce.[5] With the prominent exception of Ishbel Aberdeen, who instigated the Irish Home Industries Association during her first vice-regal stay in Ireland in 1886, such women seem to have been Tory and anti-Home Rule.[7] Middle-class reformers, influenced by social science and feminism, also considered the question of women's industries in Ireland. The Valentia-born campaigner, Helen Blackburn, who was typical of this strand, advertised Irish home industries in publications on women's rights[8]. The changing context of women's social, economic and political rights, then, added a new dimension to the politics of philanthropy, though reformer and aristocrat did have contact. The assured progress of agrarian and nationalist Irish politics made matters more testing for this generation since the best cottage industry could not, in the end, stall Home Rule and even the landed woman was among those now seeking relief.[9]

Of the women associated with reviving and developing cottage industries in Donegal, Mrs Alice Rowland Hart is possibly the best known.[10] In the early 1880s, she travelled to Donegal to train workers, introduce new embroidery designs and encourage the use of local natural dyes while drawing upon illuminated Irish sources – notably the *Book of Kells* – for inspiration. Work[11] was sold through the Donegal Industrial Fund shop in Wigmore Street, known as Donegal House[12]. By 1887, *The Times* reported that Hart was providing work for more than 800 people, mostly in homespun woollens, with an estimated 3,500 spinners and 140 weavers applying for work.[13] Women were also trained at Donegal House, producing ecclesiastical garments and embroidered materials for royals and international exhibitions,[14] where workers won prizes. Some attended the prestigious Chicago Exhibition of 1893[15]. This was not charity,[16] as its adherents invariably hastened to explain: the girls and women trained, worked and were paid; they had the status of a wage, not the demoralising handout. Alice Hart, who had trained in medicine and later turned her attention to Japan[17], was more typical of the reformer than the upper-class provider, though she came into contact with the latter through her work in London.[18]

Another visitor, Dorothea Roberts, who set up a knitting industry in the Rosses in 1882 with the support of a 'liberal Catholic priest' and a 'conservative Protestant land-agent'[19], seems to have been closer to London's philanthropic elite.[20] A letter of October 1890 details her ideas on agricultural matters, at a moment when land legislation was about 'to convert the poor Irish-speaking labourer of the West into a landed proprietor'.[21] She advised instruction in farming methods. This approach, where the knowledgeable outside observer easily distributes advice and comment, is found time and again in letters to the press about conditions in the West of Ireland. Her sharp rebuke of the 'little farmers', whose alleged 'absolute indifference' she decides to write into public print, shows something, too, of the tactless freedom of the philanthropists in their public discussion of the Irish poor. Also, local merchants who had sold woollen produce internationally for decades may have resented the operation, and views, of

Cont.
estimated £20,000 was sent 'to poor peasants' in Ireland. *The Times*, 18 Mar. 1898.

6. A Scottish woman, Ishbel Aberdeen was possibly the most prominent of the vice-regal women of the closing decades of empire, associated with public health as well as industries, though her politics, as liberal Home-Ruler, situated her oddly, especially during her second period in Ireland.

7. For excellent insight into one of the families who hosted such meetings, in Londonderry House in Park Lane, see D. Urquhart, 'Peeresses, Patronage and Power: The Politics of Ladies Frances Anne, Theresa and Edith Londonderry, 1800–1959', in A. Hayes and D. Urquhart, eds., *Irish Women's History* (Dublin: Irish Academic Press, 2004), pp. 43–59

8. Helen Blackburn, ed., *A Handbook for Women Engaged in Social and Political Work* (1881); see supplement advertising Irish women's industries in *A Woman's Suffrage Calendar* (1889).

9. This latter category, mostly widows and single women, was the focus of philan

Cont.

Cont

thropic attention in post-
1880s Ireland and the Irish
Distressed Ladies' Fund
(1886) was the key organisation.

10. Further details in P.
Larmour, N. Gordon Bowe
and E. Cumming; see also J.
Helland, 'Rural Women and
Urban Extravagance in Late
Nineteenth-Century
Britain', *Rural History*, 13,
2 (2002), pp. 179–197.
Hart also promoted music
in working-class London,
for example, *The Times*, 14
Mar. and 17 Apr. 1883.

11. Among these workers were
'about 80 impoverished
Irish ladies', *The Times*, 25
May 1887.

12. For details of work made
and sold, see, for example,
The Times, 6 Dec.1886;
Blackburn, *A Handy Book
of Reference*,
pp. 21–2.

13. *The Times*, 25 May, 1887.
For a letter critical of Mrs
Hart, see *The Times*, 28
Dec. 1887.

14. See, for example, 5 Mar.
1889.

15. The Chicago Exhibition, a
highlight of the end of the
century, saw Mrs Hart and
Ishbel Aberdeen each organise a model Irish village.

Cont.

IRISH HOMESPUNS. CARDING WOOL AND SPINNING, DONEGAL HIGHLANDS. R.WELCH. 1372.

Figure 13.1 Irish Homespuns. Carding wool and spinning, Donegal Highlands, W04/99/02

philanthropists like Miss Roberts, especially on questions of fair pay.[22]

There were others, too, such as Mrs Young, in Culdaff, [23] and the wealthy American, Mrs Cornelia Adair, of Glenveagh. By the time of her death in 1923, the latter's properties included the Glenveagh estate, another estate in County Laois, a house in Bath, another in London, as well as extensive property in Texas.[24] What was in it for Cornelia Adair? Another philanthropist who mixed in Tory and royal circles in London,[25] perhaps she was trying to fit in; whatever the motivation, she is but one more example of those briefly relevant figures whose actions affected sections of the rural and urban labouring poor.

SKILLS AND VALUES

In training girls to work at industries like knitting, lace, crochet or embroidery, organisers[26] invariably also sought to impart skills and values. The young girl now occupying the role of family breadwinner was also expected to change her personal habits, behaviour and dress. Advocates like Mary Power Lalor and Augusta Goold rarely wrote about women's industries without reminding the audience of moral and personal advantage. This story is only half available, though. It is the writings of the philanthropists that inform of what they tried to do, and to inculcate, in the rural and congested workplace. It is important, therefore, not to focus on the more outrageous of such sentiments. Perhaps what the girls said about the philanthropists was equally spectacular; just because we do not have such evidence does not mean that it was not said.

THE PHOTOGRAPHS – WHAT WE SEE

Figure 13.1, showing older girls and women, projects a somewhat assured picture of women working in a relaxed manner, interacting with each other, even in the formality or artificiality

Cont.

16. 'One of the curses of Ireland' according to Mary Power Lalor, leading organiser. See Blackburn Preface, *A Handy Book of Reference*, p. v.
17. By 1900, Hart was exhibiting Japanese art, *The Times*, 7 May 1900.
18. See, for example, *The Times*, 24 July 1884; 18 May 1886; 25 May 1887.
19. H. Blackburn, *A Handy Book of Reference*, pp. 22–3.
20. She may have been a relative of Lord Roberts, lauded for his military role in India and South Africa and, likely, the same Dorothea presented at Buckingham Palace by Lady Roberts of Kandahar, lauded for nursing philanthropy in India. They also supported Irish industries. See, in particular, *The Times*, 5 May 1897; 20 Mar. 1901; 16 Nov. 1914.
21. *The Times*, 22 Oct., 1890.
22. See, for example, Blackburn, *A Handy Book of Reference*, p. 23.
23. References in, for example,, Blackburn, *A Handy Book of Reference*.
24. *The Times*, 26 Jan. 1922; 9 June, 1923. She left legacies to various servants.

Cont.

Cont.
25. Titled visitors came to kill stags and to fish on the Glenveagh estate, *The Times*, 29 Sept., 1903.
26. Convents, too, were important lace-making centres, especially in southern counties.

Figure 13.2
Reeling the yarn for Irish Homespuns, Donegal Highlands near Ardara, W04/01/07

of the setting. One girl appears redundant, though offered a role as interested onlooker, directing attention to the more mature woman spinner, tightly tied-up hair and shawl further confirming her status. The carding work of the girl on the far left enables Welch to show another of the tasks involved in producing the final product. The setting is real, though perhaps not authentic; this is Donegal, though not necessarily the household of the women in the image. It is also similar to – and perhaps influenced by – the exhibited worker that philanthropists, like Aberdeen and Hart, liked to place in the various international exhibitions. The staged tableau as a method of transmitting knowledge about women workers was, as here, misleadingly serene. The worker is dislodged from the surroundings and tasks of the household; the placing of the worker out of door – in winter time – distorts the nature of an indoor work practice. It is also about showing the homespun worker as content, tidy, industrious, the public ideal of the reforming activist. The dress, and the type of spinning-wheel, suggests enhanced status in the context of a congested community. There was, perhaps, CDB funding for new equipment and contact with a training instructor. The confidence and clothing of this group seems somewhat ill-matched to a stone cabin lacking whitewash, thus raising an interesting doubt about photographic authenticity.[27] These women appear as modern, young women who might have civil service, teaching or nursing jobs[28] rather than sitting out of doors with spinning-wheels. What place or status did confident-looking women like these enjoy within their localities? Were these the women who stayed – with good prospects for marriage – or was this a cluster of friends with plans of America?

The image of the solitary woman, with shawl, despite the shared setting of a cabin background, is quite different (Figure 13.2). It is more forcibly about poverty. The woman seems more suited to the stone cabin, somehow; the shawl is a basic, working design and the spinning wheel is of an older variety, worked with the hands rather than the foot and hand, as did users of the more modern wheel. The picture appears less contrived, the hair is loose and there is a slight hint of movement as she sits in place for the taking of the photograph. How did she feel,

27. For detailed discussion on housing, however, see Chapter 11.
28. These were growing areas of professional employment for women.

the singular sitter, facing the photographer without the company of friends? Who was calling out to her, arranging and re-arranging this public performance resulting in a lasting image of a working identity?

The image of the woman as spinner tells only a partial aspect of her working life. The migration of men to England and Scotland that marked out labouring history, especially in Donegal, meant that women had to undertake agricultural work to an inordinate degree. Nonetheless, the ideology underlying cottage industrial work allowed for it to be arranged around other work. Cottage industries were not meant to occupy the whole time of women and girls; rather, such work was to be carried out when women were not hay-making or harvesting, carrying seaweed or turf, or setting potatoes. As Helen Blackburn elaborated with philanthropic eloquence, these industries 'are done in hours that otherwise would not be used at all.'[29] Winter, therefore, as Blackburn also advised, was the best time to contract the work. Yet, though aware of the agricultural tasks, none seemed to fully appreciate the housework that the women had to do.[30] When reformers did consider domestic work, it was mostly as an ideal to train the young woman in skills or manners. Clues were not even fully hidden from view. As this photograph reveals, for instance, there is a cooking pot visible through the spinning wheel, evidence not only of household tasks but also of the time and lifting of weights that such work involved: carrying water, finding fuel for fires, preparing and attending to cooking on open fires. It can be imagined that the taking of the photographs interrupted the work of the household, or caused additional work to be carried out if the women felt that they had to clean up and prepare for the arrival of the visitors.

The young carpet workers in Figure 13.3 offer up a different set of information about rural working lives. This is the world of the formal industrial setting, leading workers into contact with structure, time-keeping, interaction with outsiders, regulations, wages and management. Outside of the Morton enterprise in Donegal,[31] for instance, the Foxford Woollen Mills in County Mayo was a rare enough example of relief effort that assumed anything like factory

29. Blackburn, *A Handy Book of Reference*.
30. See Bourke, *Husbandry to Housewifery*, for discussion on rural work. For pioneering research on the important and still contested question of housework, see C. Clear, *Women of the House: Women's Household Work in Ireland, 1922–1961* (Dublin: Irish Academic Press, 2000).
31. Alexander Morton, of Ayrshire, established factories in Donegal in conjunction with the support of the Congested Districts Board, initially in Killybegs, later in Kilcar, and, after 1904, at Anagry and Crolly. The factories were to provide for 150–200 workers. W.L. Micks *An Account of the Constitution, Administration and Dissolution of the Congested Districts Board for Ireland from 1891 to 1923* (Dublin: 1925), pp. 71–2; E.J. Riordan, *Modern Irish Trade and Industry* (London: 1920).

Figure 13.3
Hand-tufted carpet weavers, Crolly, Donegal. W0/23/14

proportions.[32] The conditions that helped to define the Foxford enterprise – existing infrastructure though the Sisters of Charity, advice and training through the northern businessman, private and public funding – indicate something of what was required to ensure success. The individual philanthropist, even of the calibre of Mrs Hart or, perhaps, the campaigning priest, was operating in quite a different context though one practical result of their effort was to ensure skilled labour. The businessman, therefore, who knew to look in areas of high unemployment for workers, also found workers with existing skills. In business enterprises like the carpet factory, the worker, in an important sense, has moved beyond the sphere of philanthropy and relief. The photograph conveys the business ethic wonderfully through the presence of the young man on the left of the group: shoulders back, hands in pockets, wearing a somewhat worried or weighty expression on his face and, importantly, a pocket watch in good view. The young man to the far right represents, almost, what the alternative could have been for the young manager: standing at ease, hands hanging down, no white shirt, no pocket watch. It is the girls who fill the picture, though one woman decides to hide: workers who inter-link or rest their arms in a casual show of solidarity,[33] the exceptions pointing perhaps to shyness (like the young girl on the far left) or to some falling out, maybe, like the girl sitting third from the left in the front row, who keeps her hands determinedly entwined on her own knees.

THE PLACE

The link between image and place is also of interest. The photographs place the workers in specific, geographical and physical spaces, in the important and familiar industrial centres of Ardara and the Rosses.[34] Such detail is almost unnecessary in a series of images that see the workers fill the frame or set against an ill-defined background. In the case of the factory workers, the background is almost unknowable – the plain contour of the Rosses allowing the focus to stay on the workers in the foreground who fill the frame. And so, though from the Rosses,

32. T.A.Finlay, 'A Miracle of the Wilderness: How a Nun Transformed a Congested Distrcit', W.G. Fitzgerald, *The Voice of Ireland* (1923), pp. 344–6; Micks, *Congested Districts Board*, pp. 67–8; *Agnes Morrogh-Bernard, 1842–1923: Foundress of Foxford Woollen Mills* (pamphlet, Foxford, c. 1992).

33. There may have been groups of sisters in the group too.

34. These place names are found regularly in newspaper accounts. Ardara was an important commercial centre, something that its architecture, and its weaving and knitting industries, continue to convey to the visitor today.

Figure 13.4
Donegal spriggers at work,
Ardara. The Queen's Order.
W04/1/03

DONEGAL SPRIGGERS AT WORK, ARDARA.   (THE QUEEN'S ORDER)   R.W. 1378.

these young workers are able to reach out to others of their age and situation wherever the location. The trees, walls, houses and distant buildings, viewed in the photograph of the 'Donegal spriggers at work' (Figure 13.4) may, certainly, situate the scene in Ardara – but just about. It, too, despite these local markers, could be anywhere. The bare trees, strewn turf, all point to a wintry period between autumn and early spring, the contract period. Yet some of the girls are barefoot and even sitting on the ground. In contrast, the overseeing woman, already heavily clothed, also has a scarf around her neck; the man, also in heavy overcoat, likewise protects his head. Welch, in selecting a sparse or natural setting for the out-of-door shots – rather than, for instance, the factory or workshop buildings – is actually divesting the workers of the formal, material aspect of their waged day. This was, perhaps, the bias of the naturalist over the man interested in showing conditions of labour.[35]

The photographs, then, while they give information about women's work, have a far more valuable function. The girls and women who stare out are subjects of historical enquiry; they dare us to ignore them any longer. But if their legacy is to prompt questions, then these rural working-class girls and teenagers are already showing their strength. The photograph of the spriggers, a traditional skill of the area, working outside is especially complex and disturbing. The standing couple are looking on in the manner of the outside observer – gentry, religious, business, philanthropic – who ever gazed at, or interfered in, the lives of the rural poor.[36] They pose as passive bystanders, misleadingly so given their power to affect the material well-being not only of the workers, but also of the families who depended on their paid labour. This image of the serious faces, sewing in public, with no coats, jackets or shawls, has the power to disturb. The young, barefoot girl to the far left, hunched over her piece of fabric, looks like a six-year -old; four others seem to be under the age of ten. These, then, are the faces of the children whose time is not ordained for schooling or play, but for occupation as helpers, or apprentices, to the skilled, older girls who operate the intricate stitches of the large centrepiece. Reformers like Blackburn shied away from rules and regulations, and failed to noticeably consider the con-

35. For details on Welch, see, for example, E. Estyn Evans and B.S. Turner, *Ireland's Eye: The Photographs of Robert John Welch* (Belfast: 1977).
36. This is tentative, though of interest. Some photographs of Ishbel Aberdeen, for instance, place her in the centre, rather than to the side, when visiting groups.

ditions of children who worked in congested areas.[37] The tendency to see such work as filling time, even when tending cattle[38], divested it of the harsh, ill-paid tedium of what was otherwise generally referred to as sweated labour. Mostly, it was the corrupt agent, who paid in inferior kind rather than cash, who drew inspectors such as Rose Squire, Lucy Deane and May Abraham to areas like Donegal.[39] As is clear, such investigation was fraught at a number of levels: the government official asking questions, the stigma of informing, the power of the agent-shopkeeper in local communities and the terrible need to endure poor working conditions and pay in the absence of anything else.[40] Yet, as Margaret Irwin's inquiry into home work in Belfast and the north of Ireland revealed in 1909,[41] much of the work undertaken in cabins and workshops of rural areas by women, children and the elderly veers towards the sweated effort that she charts. Even for the child and young women spriggers, who paused to accommodate the taking of the photograph, the Queen's order still had to be filled, and the working day in question likely lengthened.

What else can the photographs tell us? What other work did these women do? Lace-workers, or so is claimed, were exempted from rough farm work. Hands toughened through contact with clay, turf, weeds, stones, were not the tools of the worker in fine needlework. As can be imagined, such reasoning on the part of girls was a useful way out of doing tedious, dirty, cold work. Did this privilege set them apart from older family and friends? In some cases, the lace scholar was as young as thirteen and, in contrast to older family members and parents, she was able to read, write and speak English.[42] Some observers thought that the lace girl was inclined to be anaemic or pale looking, that she liked to spend money on dress. Officials of the CDB regretted the more contentious decision of lace-makers to emigrate 'after receiving a good training'.[43] Further study is required before such important insights can be evaluated in any meaningful way but it does seem that lace, like spinning and textiles more generally, did indeed introduce economic and social possibility into congested areas.[44] As well as trying to understand, then, conditions and motivations, the photographs urge us to ask what next? Were, indeed, later formal photographs produced

37. Vynne and Blackburn, *Women Under the Factory Act*; letter on the Factories Bill, *The Times*, 4 May, 1900.
38. *The Times*, October 1890.
39. For details of these pioneering professionals, see M.D. McFeely, *Lady Inspectors: The Campaign for a Better Workplace, 1893–1921* (Oxford: Basil Blackwell, 1988).
40. See McFeely, *Lady Inspectors*. Lucy Deane, a member of the 1901 committee to investigate the Boer War concentration camps, also comes across as formidable in her work as inspector of factories in London, regularly – and successfully – taking employers to court. See, for example, *The Times*, 10 Aug. 1898; 24 Jan. 1903; 22 Feb. 1905.
41. M.H. Irwin, *Home Work in Ireland. Report of an Inquiry* (Glasgow: Scottish Council for Women's Trades and Union for the Abolition of Sweating, 1909, 1913).
42. Based on research in relation to Co. Galway.
43. H. Doran, 'Self-Help Among the Western "Congests".' p. 335. Doran reported that in one district thirty of 'the best workers'
Cont.

Cont.

emigrated, withdrawing sums of money from the local savings bank.

44. For details and praise, see Micks, *Congested Districts Board*, 68–71.45.

45. This may, too, have been a lace-instructress, though more likely the Hamiltons (see below).

46. I have been unable to locate anything of substance on the Hamiltons. Some brief details about the White House, Portrush, suggests a story of certain promise. See bbc.co.uk.

47. For this and other details, see Theresa Moriarty, *Work in Progress: Episodes from the History of Irish Women's Trade Unionism* (Irish Labour History Society and Unison, n.d.)

Figure 13.5
CDB Lace Class, Ardara.
W04/01/5

in the studios of Boston or New York? And, if so, and as the emigrant women arranged their city hats and clothing and jewellery, did they talk about the day that R.J. Welch arrived in Ardara or the Rosses to capture an image of their younger selves?

The girls in the lace class image appear well-dressed, wearing boots, their youth again reminding of how the 'nimble-fingers', so beloved of philanthropists and capitalists now as then, were highly valued tools. The sheets of paper hanging on the far wall could suggest that the employer was displaying workshop regulations. Here, too, the lace curtains – maybe made by the workers during a dreaded idle moment – suggest a more discreet scenario, as well as a tidy, well-lit workplace, with an eye to standards, reputation and profit. With its numerous windows and slated roof, this space was quite different to the housing typical of the congested districts. The workboxes on the table are intriguing artefacts of the teenage lace-worker, prompting questions as to what, in addition to work materials, she might have kept in the box and what this possession meant to her.

The figures at the end of the room,[45] standing, are most likely Henry Hamilton and his wife, the former Miss Allen; he was owner of the White House in Portrush, a businessman influenced, as the name of his store explains, by an earlier sojourn in America.[46] Yet, despite the good-looking conditions of the factory and the quality of their dress, it is the seeming discomfiture of the workers that stands out. The faces are baleful, restrained, subdued. What can this mean? What are they communicating? They look indeed, at least the three girls on the far right, as though they had been rebuked. Were they giddy or chatting when they shouldn't have been, growing bored during the lengthy process of setting up and taking the photograph? Someone in the room may have said something to produce such unhappy and almost cowed looks on the faces to the far right. In nearby Derry, investigators found evidence of shirt-factory owners imposing fines for lateness, as well as for laughing and looking out of windows.[47] The Welch photograph cannot impart that information but it can lead us to ask questions of how these young pre-teen and teenage workers were treated.

In the outside shot, where the same couple also appears, the information that the girls are

working on the Queen's order is of interest.[48] The association between the royals and cottage or Irish industries was a staple of philanthropic practice, as noted; they opened exhibitions in England, for instance, and came to gaze at stalls selling Irish produce. Irish lace-work featured regularly among the gifts sent over on royal events. One detail, relating to a court train of Irish needlepoint lace, made a decade later, gives a useful indication of the work that was involved, as well as the ecumenical nature of such working networks. This gift, paid for by the women of Belfast and made at the Convent of Mercy, Youghal, was a train made up of five and a quarter million stitches and an estimated twelve miles of fine thread, employing sixty needlewomen full-time for six months.[49] Here, it is of interest to see the link between these young workers and the royal contract made visible. This is how it was done when children and teenagers were used – their young fingers making stitches for a garment that hung on the shoulders, arms or head of a distant royal wearer or, in the case of the Welch image, sitting, barefoot, on a patch of ground in Donegal to make up a public photograph – as proof or propaganda for Hamilton's business achievement or loyalty.

CONCLUSION

These images are important testimony of perceptions of Ireland, as of women's work. The worker in question – the rural labouring girl – was well known in illustration and in print; she was even familiar in person through appearances at the various exhibitions. As a leading philanthropist estimated in the late 1880s, there were about 70,000 such girls and women[50] – the raw material that made Ireland so suited to feminine industries and able to compete with continental workers in established industrial areas like Germany and Switzerland. This point was reiterated in commentaries on Irish industrial exhibitions in England and internationally. Such commentary created a space, in the formal, public domain – including parliament and *The Times* of London – where philanthropic opinion about Irish girl workers was shared with an

48. Website information about the White House states that their 'most distinguished customer was Queen Victoria, who put in an order for linens in the late 1890s.' Victoria's final visit to Ireland, in 1900, may also have resulted in some work.
49. *The Freeman's Journal*, 6 Nov. 1911.
50. Mary Power Lalor, Preface, *A Handy Book of Reference*, pp. iii–v.

elite public. It was, for the most part, a comforting or pleasing stereotype: the worker was nimble-fingered and quick – thus likely to reward the philanthropist and funding agency – yet also recalcitrant and so open to remoulding, a pleasing prospect for the reformer. Such soft discourse removed these rural workers from the difficult world of the urban factory, sweated labour or union organising. One of the strengths of the photograph is its power to hint, if not proclaim, that the child, girl or woman in rural Ireland was not simply an icon formulated to fit philanthropic enterprise but that she was also a worker required to meet the needs of the enterprise. For no matter how authentic or contrived the 'tableau' that we view, R.J. Welch has led us to consider the circumstances, the surroundings and the stories of the working rural woman.

CHAPTER FOURTEEN **Well Wear and Soon Tear: The Clothes We Once Wore**

ANNE O'DOWD

1. P.J. Corish, 'Women and Religious Practice', in Margaret MacCurtain and Mary O Dowd (eds) *Women in Early Modern Ireland* (Dublin: Wolfhound Press, 1991), p. 219.
2. A. T. Lucas, 'Local Traditions. Folk Life' in James Meenan and David A. Webb (eds), *A View Of Ireland: Twelve Essays of Different Aspects of Irish Life and the Irish Countryside* (Dublin: Published for the British Association for the advancement of Science by the Local Executive Committee, 1957), pp. 196–205.
3. We are a growing band of workers including museum curators, archivists and college lecturers whose teachers included Kevin Danaher and Bo Almqvist of the Department of Irish Folklore at University College Dublin – now the UCD Delargy Centre for Irish Folklore.

'Poorer people are harder to track precisely because they are not vocal. When they do surface it is as observed rather than observers'.[1]

The words are not mine but those of the historian Patrick J. Corish. The comment may have some merit on the topic which Corish is talking about, namely women and religious practice in early modern Ireland. Echoes of the opinion are found elsewhere.[2] However, it has to be said that the concept applies to many areas of historical study and not solely to the lives of those whom we might describe as poor. Where I diverge from the writer is that as a folklorist and ethnologist I know the value of the spoken word as a tool in allowing us to make sense of and document the everyday lives of those who did not 'make history' in their time. This is not new: to many of my contemporary colleagues, and to many more who have worked before us, the value of the spoken word has been and is the key to our researches.[3] As a museum curator in a national museum for many years, the value of every individual object acquired is only as good as the information pertaining to it – the object's spoken word. It is that information which gives the object life and meaning.

As an example is an area of interest particular to me, the immense collection of straw objects used around the house and yard, including horse harness, tethers, spancels, mats, mattresses, hens' nests, chairs, stools, baskets and festival and ceremonial costume. This collection would of course be important in its own right not only because the objects are aesthetically beautiful and display the ingenuity of their makers in the chosen medium, which was readily available literally

outside their back doors, but also because their manufacture points to the strength of traditional methods of craftwork and simple design. 'If it's not broken, don't fix it' is a simple way of
describing the meaning of tradition: if the basket made from rods, or the noggin made from
sycamore, or the houses made from local stone, were those that were proven to work over time
in an economy where money was a scarce resource, the materials that were used to make them
and the form that was used to create them were those that continued to be used. Introduced
methods were tried and adopted if they were at least as good as that which had pertained before.

In the area of research that deals with the whole abundance of clothing and what people
wore in their everyday lives, we are fortunate to have an immensely rich and informative body
of documentation in a questionnaire that was circulated by the Department of Irish Folklore in
1940.[4] It is an area of study where several examples of the tenacity and endurance of tradition
are to be seen: from the untanned footwear of the late Christian period and the untanned *bróga
úrleathair* of the Aran Islands still worn as everyday wear by some in the middle of the twentieth century, to the red petticoats and tight-fitting bodices worn by women from the eighteenth
to the twentieth centuries, and the outer coats, knee breeches and tail coats worn by men from
at least the late 1700s to the 1930s.[5]

The questionnaire was simply called 'Dress' and was circulated to several hundred informants throughout the country. It has rarely been referred to by researchers as a body of information, I suspect because the replies are, for the most part, so detailed and so descriptive that
sorting out the specific and the regional variations from the generality would prove to be
daunting and a lifetime's task.[6] It is far wiser to break replies down into constituent parts and
for this present chapter, with reference to the Tuke and Welch photographs included in these
pages, I will refer only to the clothing of women and children from the West of Ireland and the
County of Mayo in particular.

The questionnaire runs to four pages and the format was borrowed from Seán Ó
Súilleabháin's seminal work, *Handbook of Irish Folklore* and guide for folklore collectors.[7]

4. The questionnaire is called
'Dress'. It is bound in man-
uscript volumes 745–51 and
1137 in the Delargy Centre.

5. A.T. Lucas, 'Footwear in
Ireland', *Journal of the
County Louth
Archaeological Society*, vol.
X111, no. 4 (1956), pp.
309–94; A.T. Lucas, 'The
Hooded Cloak in Ireland',
*Journal of the Cork
Historical and
Archaeological Society*, vol.
56 (1951), pp. 104–19;
Mairead Dunlevy, *Dress in
Ireland* (London: Batsford,
1989).

6. See Brid Mahon, *Irish Dress*,
vol. 10 of the Irish
Environmental Library
Series, Folens, n.d.; Anne
O'Dowd, *Common Clothes
and Clothing* (Dublin:
National Museum of
Ireland, 1990).

This is a volume of some seven hundred pages consisting of multiple questions and suggestions that could only have been conceived and written by someone whose life emanated from the tradition, and was steeped in it, with a consequent personal, in-depth knowledge of the totality of Irish folklore. The dress questionnaire begins with general questions pertaining to, for example, a prejudice against wearing certain colours, the traditions associated with new clothes and second-hand clothes, materials used, dyeing methods and the wearing of ornaments including badges and emblems. Infants' dress, children's dress and girls' dress are brief sections designed to elicit details and memories of the customs connected with the clothing of newborn babies, the blessings given to new clothing, and the rite of passage in girls' lives when they adopted both the clothing and the hairstyles of an adult. The questionnaire's section on women's dress asks for all available information on every detail of clothing from the skin out: the names which each individual garment was called, the makers of each, the materials and where they came from, nightwear, clothes for 'special' occasions – going to mass, festivals, wakes etc. and bridal clothes – to the bright red petticoats and the full-bodied hooded cloaks that were so commented upon by the visitor and observer of the nineteenth and early twentieth centuries. The last section of the questionnaire asks equivalent questions about the clothing of boys and men.

Although it was not asked as a specific question, most of those who replied to the questionnaire give an indication of the time period to which the collected information pertained. As a general rule, the questionnaire's function was to ask the respondent to fill it out based on their personal memories or a combination of their own memories and those of the informants they visited. As such, the body of information refers to the clothing worn around the turn of the nineteenth and twentieth centuries (with an indication of the time period if it differed from this). Essentially the questionnaire information describes the clothing worn by the 'previous' generation to the one that held the memories and wrote down the replies. One of the most complete questionnaire replies was received from Michael Corduff of Rossport, Erris

7. Seán Ó Súilleabháin, *A Handbook of Irish Folklore* (Dublin: Educational Company of Ireland, 1970).
8. IFC MS 754, p. 248.
9. *Línteog*, i.e. *léinteog*, a little shirt or shift; cowell, i.e. *cabhail*, the body of a shirt, coat. Rev. Patrick S. Dinneen, *Foclóir Gaeilge agus Béarla*, (Dublin, 1927).

– a seasoned folklore collector and as such a respondent who not only gathered the details but who also commented on the content. Among his opening remarks, for example, he tells us:

> Having restricted resources in the production of cloth, (there was) hardly any variety of cloth patterns. Clothing material was practically uniform and beyond black, white and magenta there was very little others used except for some fancy articles like scarves, stockings and mufflers.[8]

The implication in the sentence at the outset might lead one to expect the rest of the reply to be equally bland, but thankfully the opposite is the case and he proceeds to write several pages of immense observation.

According to Corduff's account, the first garment for babies and infants was a little shirt or waistcoat known as a *línteog*. It was made of linen and was left open at the front. Over this there was a red flannel garment that he called a 'cowell', which was similar to the *línteog* and differed only in that it was secured, presumably by buttons or cloth ties, at the front. The suc-

ceeding layer was a long flannel robe – a 'walla *cóta*/barrow' – folded in such a way that it fitted very tightly across the baby's body.[9] A little cap of white linen was placed on the infant's head and we are emphatically told that a needle, and not a pin, was concealed in the cap on the way to the church when the child was ready for baptism. The cap, by the way, was never removed until it eventually became too small for the child's head – a custom undoubtedly connect-

10. Additional detail that ought not to be ignored in this context is included in a questionnaire reply from Lanach Mór, Ballycastle, County Mayo, IFC MS 754, p. 370. The first garment which went on a newborn baby was a 'wally coat', that was like a little jacket and made of white linen. It opened down the front and was not provided with buttons. A piece of flannel was pinned with a big pin around the body and the lower end of this was tied around the feet with a band. This latter garment was the *plúideog*. Some women kept their children's feet thus for three months. After a fortnight or three weeks a little dress was put on the infant. A very good description of the dressing of an infant is included in the questionnaire reply from Swinford, IFC MS 754, pp. 186–7. A petticoat went over the *plúdog* and 'people insisted on the baby's body being very tightly squeezed in to the *plúdog* and petticoat because it kept his back straight and protected the spine.' See also the reply from Ballycroy, IFC MS 754, p. 222.

Figure 14.1
School children outside their school, Connemara (Tuke34)

ed with protection from malevolence.[10] Boys and girls, as is well documented, were dressed the same until the age of ten or twelve years: a flannel petticoat to which was sewn a 'body' of linen or calico. The 'body' was back buttoned and over it was worn a 'coat' of red flannel, also back buttoned. If underwear was worn it consisted solely of a linen or calico 'shirt'.[11] (see Figure 12.5, 'Schoolchildren outside the school, Connemara', and Figure 14.1.) As the girls grew in size and years they were supplied with little white bibs and at school-going age they were dressed with a cotton pinafore over their flannel petticoat (see Figure 14.1). The colours of the outer garments were of various colours once the girls 'had passed the red stage' in Corduff's phrase.[12] With regard to girls' hair, they wore it long and plaited, except for Good Friday when 'in imitation of the Blessed Virgin it was let hang loose'.[13]

The women always wore two 'petticoats' along with an outside skirt. These, along with the upper jacket, which was dyed red, were all of flannel and the outer skirt was dyed either red or black. The petticoats and skirt were secured at the waist at the back, and the jacket was buttoned in the front. It was the petticoat and outer skirt that were the most versatile of women's items of clothing in that they were not only worn for the purpose for which they were made – a covering for the lower part of the body – but they also provided head covering and a handy carrying sack. When going on a short errand, for example to visit a neighbour's home, women, instead of a shawl, wore a white undyed flannel petticoat suspended loosely from the top of the head or the shoulders. As in the image captured by Major Ruttledge-Fair (Figure 14.5) the waist of the petticoat rested on the shoulders with the waistband being gathered close to the neck. When returning from a trip to the town for shopping, the outer skirt was turned up at the back and the lower end of the skirt was pulled around the shoulders, thus forming a convenient vessel for carrying the purchases and indeed also for carrying two or three young children.[14] The outer skirt was the one that had the most use and abuse and in fact served to protect the under-petticoats if an apron was not worn.

Corduff's account is fairly well attested to in other parts of the county of Mayo, including:

11. IFC MS 754, pp.255–6. Throughout the Mayo questionnaires we learn that underwear or 'knickers' were rarely if ever worn by either women or children.
12. The importance of red as a colour is included, among other colours, in Ó Súilleabháin's *Handbook*, pp. 426--7.
13. IFC MS 754, p. 257.
14. IFC MS 754, pp. 259–60.

Rosturk, Westport; Brackloon, Westport; Cushlecka, Mulranny; Ballintober, Claremorris; Parke, Castlebar; Aghamore, Ballyhaunis; Swinford; Ballycroy; Kilbride; Murrisk and Lanach Mór, Ballycastle. The exceptions, of course, are in the detail – calico jackets or 'bodices' that might have been trimmed with crochet were worn during the warm months of the summer as a cooler version of the heavier flannel kind;[15] the bodices, instead of being buttoned down the front, were laced with black velvet in a criss-cross fashion and tied in a bow at the waist; some bodices had sleeves that were gathered into a band or cuff at the wrist and fastened with a button. Others were left loose 'like a nun's sleeve'.[16] For everyday wear the outer skirt over the two petticoats might have been dispensed with in favour of a checked cotton apron and, in circumstances where the household budget did not extend to buying a length of cotton, a sack was utilised and became known as a *práisig*.[17] Striped drugget (a material with a linen warp and a woollen weft) in colours of purple, yellow, black and red – instead of red or black flannel – was the material used for the outer skirt in north Mayo, where the 'mant' (that is, the upper part of the dress) had a tight-fitting, front-closing bodice with long sleeves and a very low neckline. Sewn in gathers to the lower edge of the 'mant' was a skirt with a cutaway front.[18]

The correspondent from Lanach Mór, Ballycastle in north Mayo adds some interesting information about the making of the garments and the materials used. She describes the four main garments – the shift, the bodice, the petticoat and the gown or dress. The first two were made of white calico, which was shop bought in the town of Ballycastle; the petticoat's red flannel was manufactured from locally available materials; and the gown or dress, in colours of black, navy, blue or red, was made from shop-bought cashmere. The women made all these garments themselves.[19] They wore various other pieces of clothing: the 'headkerchiefs', the 'neckerchiefs' and 'kerchiefs' were large and small versions of shawls and scarves and were mostly shop bought; the 'crossovers' or 'hug me tights'[20] were knitted from home spun and dyed woollen yarn, as were the socks and stockings. Known variously as *bionnoga* and *binneoga*,[21] the headscarves were almost universally of red or blue and white cotton and white calico.[22] The

15. IFC MS 754, p. 126, Parke, Castlebar, County Mayo.
16. IFC MS 754, p. 177, Swinford, County Mayo.
17. IFC MS 754, p.171, Swinford, County Mayo. *Práiscín*, an apron, esp. a coarse apron with many pockets, Dinneen, *Foclóir Gaeilge*.
18. IFC MS 754, p. 355. Kilbride, Ballycastle, County Mayo.
19. IFC MS 754, p. 374, Lanach Mór, Ballycastle, County Mayo.
20. I have described these elsewhere: O'Dowd, *Common Clothes*, p. 8.
21. *binneog*, a cloth tied around the head. Dinneen, *Foclóir Gaeilge*.
22. IFC MS 754, p. 68, Ballintober, Claremorris; IFC MS 754, p. 127, Parke, Castlebar, IFC MS 754, p. 92, Murrisk.
23. Lucas, 'The Hooded Cloak'.

pride of place in women's clothing was given to the warm outer garment. For most of the nineteenth century this was a full-length and usually hooded shawl.[23] By the end of the century it had, to a large extent throughout the country, been replaced by woollen shawls, some of which were knitted at home in various colours while others were shop bought.

The variety of outerwear and headgear worn by women is seen particularly clearly in Welch's 'Market Day at Clonbur' (Figure 14.4). In the right foreground we see the plaid shawl – probably in colours of salmon, white and blue – worn as a headscarf or headkerchief as it was undoubtedly known.[24] The woman wearing the shawl has a lightweight and fringed shoulder shawl, which she is wearing at waist length with the ends draped over each arm. A second plaid shawl is being worn over the shoulders by the woman in the centre of the view; she also wears a headscarf secured by tying it under the chin. The front of the headscarf protrudes out over the woman's face almost like a visor on a contemporary baseball cap. A probable explanation of how this was not only achieved but, more importantly, maintained is provided by an observation made by Michael Corduff and included in his questionnaire reply:

> When worn (i.e. the headkerchief) it was sometimes customary to reinforce the edge of the front with a nice little straw rope in the fold. This enabled the headkerchief to be extended outwards so as to cover the sides of the face for protection against cold wind or strong sun. In this position the kerchief was called a pokogue.[25]

The woman immediately to the pokogue-wearer's left is wearing a heavy woollen shawl that covers most of her body. Both her outer skirt, and that of the woman to the left of the fish barrel, are pinned or tucked up at the side and the back, revealing the – probably red – petticoat underneath. The shoulder shawl of the woman by the fish barrel is possibly a home knitted or crocheted garment. By far the most 'modern' and most expensively dressed person at the mar-

Figure 14.2
Children spinning and reeling wool for homespuns, Donegal highlands W04/99/03

24. Kerchief, a square piece of cloth worn to cover the head, neck etc. *Chambers Twentieth Century Dictionary*, Edinburgh, 1981.
25. IFC MS 754, p. 264. The word that Corduff wrote as 'pokogue' is from the Irish *púcóg*, a covering for the eyes. Dinneen, *Foclóir Gaeilge*.

ket is the woman wearing the so-called 'Paisley' shawl, the second woman from the left of the image. Both her shawl and her richly flounced skirt were up to the minute fashions when Welch took the photograph and she announced herself at the market as a married woman by wearing her white frilled or 'lace' cap. In a previous generation the frilled caps were worn by married women along with the fine black or navy blue hooded cloak. The caps were usually made at home of fine white cotton, linen or muslin. Some were what was known as 'piped' at the outer edge, i.e. provided with a waved edge with a special iron known as a tally or tallon iron,[26] while others had an edge of fine lace. White caps in the National Folklife collection include examples made from linen, muslin and cotton; those that are most like the one worn in the image are from Galway and Tyrone. The Galway example was owned by a woman who died in 1915; it is made from two panels of muslin sewn together. One of these is 8 cm wide and forms the front of the cap, running over the head from side to side; the other panel forms the back of the cap. Both are decorated with sprigging of dots and leaves. Three frills of lace about 1.5 cm wide are sewn to the front edge of the cap and two similar frills decorate the bottom edge. Such caps were secured to the wearer's head by means of ribbons attached to each of the front corners and tied in a bow under the chin.[27]

It is the shawl, however, that requires some detailed comment as the wearing of it, more than any other garment worn by women in the late nineteenth century, announced to neighbours and the larger community that the woman of the house who could afford to buy such an expensive piece of apparel was from a well-to-do and improving household. Its history as an everyday garment in Ireland is contemporary with the time of the taking of the photograph. Its history as a fashion garment, however, is much older. Comparable to the mini skirt of the 1960s, the platform shoes of the 1970s and the fad for large and expensive handbags in the 2000s, the eighteenth century saw a fashion for oriental shawls spreading from Asia through India, Persia and Turkey into Europe. It was the century that also saw the diffusion of a second familiar household item – the willow-pattern plate. As with the earthenware

26. See for example, Pamela Sambrook, *Laundry Bygones* (Buckinghamshire: Shire Publications, no. 107, 1983), pp. 24–6.

27. The registration number of the Galway cap is F1954:58 and its provenance is Lissarula, Clareglway, Dunkellin, Co. Galway. The Tyrone examples of white cotton have registration numbers F1961:12 and 13.

Figure 14.3
Women
washing clothes (Tuke 3)

delph, the shawls were also locally imitated once the fashion became universal and the potential for a thriving business was recognised.

The manufacture of the shawls became especially associated with Paisley in the South-West of Scotland and the garment in time became known as the 'Paisley shawl'. Among the weavers themselves the early shawls made from silk and cashmere were known as the 'harness pattern' shawls after the loom on which they were woven. The business began in the late eighteenth century and was at its height 1820–70. Despite a decline at the beginning of the 1870s, there were still an estimated 700 weavers of silk and cashmere shawls in Paisley in 1874 and 622 so-called plain weavers who specialised in tartan, plain and check shawls. The business received a very welcome reprieve when a new type of shawl was introduced and apparently became instantly popular as a warm and colourful garment among the women of the west of Ireland in particular. In its place of manufacture – Paisley – the shawls were known as 'velvet and fur' shawls and from the evidence especially of numerous photographs dating from the late nineteenth and early

Figure 14.4 *Market day in Clonbur* W14/05/18

28. 'Traditional Finery', *Connacht Tribune*, 10 September 1971. The late Lillias Mitchell, the weaver and textile historian, produced a two page leaflet in 1978 in which she describes seeing the women wearing the shawl and red petticoat at the Saturday morning markets in Galway City 'until fairly recently'. Her publication is accompanied by Thomas Mason's wonderful photograph of a group of people at a market in Oughterard. Four of the women in the group are wearing the heavy Paisley or Galway shawl. A copy of the leaflet, which is dated 30 May 1978, is held in Information File F48, in the Irish Folklife Division archive, National Museum–Museum of Country Life, Turlough Park, Castlebar, Co. Mayo. See also two articles by A. Morrison Stewart, F.E.S, 'The History and Romance of the Paisley Shawl and the Men who Produced it,' and 'Paisley Shawls: The End of the Chapter', in *Scottish Home and Country*, Apr. 1932, pp. 130–3 and Aug. 1932, pp. 270–1.

29. Lucas, 'The Hooded Cloak'.

twentieth centuries, the women of Galway took to wearing the shawls with gusto. They were woven from a wool fabric, the finishing process of which left the material with a texture of soft velvet or fur, hence their name. The wearing of the shawls was still being remarked upon as recently as the 1970s and a wonderful article in the *Connacht Tribune* in September 1971 includes a photograph of three women – Mrs Bridget King, 81 years; Mrs Mary O'Donnell, 76 years; and Nora Flynn, 70 years – wearing their, what are now termed, 'Claddagh' shawls after the village in Galway where they were last to be seen on a regular basis. The shawls were given names depending on the border pattern and the cotton fringing that was incorporated into the weave and design of the shawl. The three women in the photograph each wears a different pattern (the Brown Castle, the Housekeeper's and the White Castle); further names mentioned in the article included the Brown diamond, the Brown ring and the Brown '98. The shawls were woven in double weave, and fawn and 'turf' brown were the predominant colours with touches of green, red and crimson included in the border pattern. They were traditionally worn over the shoulders (Robert Welch, 2194) and were folded not in a triangle, as were the headkerchief and the neckerchief, but lengthways with one side longer than the other. According to the unnamed writer of the article in the *Connacht Tribune*, 'This was to show off the fringe against the background of the shawl, and the folds falling over each arm was a good cover for a basket held under it'.[28]

Earlier in the century the predominant outer garment worn by women had been the full-length hooded cloak, which A.T. Lucas has described in some detail.[29] Apart from it being a very warm garment it covered a multitude of sins for with the poverty of the early decades of the nineteenth century especially, the donning of the cloak quite often covered the nakedness or near nakedness of the wearers. A variety of woollen weaves and colours were used to make the hooded cloak – frieze, flannel and broadcloth or pilot cloth in red, blue, navy and black. For reasons of style and cost the hooded cloak began its decline in popularity in the closing years of the nineteenth century, helped no doubt by the introduction of the brighter Paisley shawl. And, as with all introduc-

tions not all observers were uncritical and accepting of the change. Sir Arthur Grant, who visited Galway City in 1891, described the clothing of the women very curtly when he wrote:

> they mostly wear a short red petticoat of very coarse home-spun wool, a blue shirt (sic)[30] or apron, and a blue or black shawl. However many of the hideous Paisley brown shawls now appear on the Square in the centre of the town.[31]

Of course, the tradition of women wearing the full-length hooded cloak remained in some areas, most notably several areas in County Cork. Elsewhere, and among those who could not afford the expense of the material, which was shop bought, and the tailor's expertise, the cloak was never adopted and the unique custom of wearing a petticoat in place of a cloak became a tradition, which we know from the literature happened in several places from at least the early 1800s. The Reverend James Hall gave vent to his romantic side when he saw a young woman so dressed in Longford in 1813 for he wrote his memory of the scene with the following eloquence:

> Here the prevailing colour for the women's cloaks is red; however, a young woman, when she goes to public places, if she have no cloak, generally ties a petticoat double about her shoulders, be it green, white, or any other colour. According to their notions, this not only served to keep them warm, but, by hanging loosely, flows about gracefully, when dancing, and appears as pleasing in the eyes of the young men, their acquaintance, as the feathers and finery of a modern belle in the eyes of her lover at a Lord-Mayor's ball.[32]

Later in the century the custom was still adhered to and it is pertinent that Mrs Houston, a visitor to Connaught in 1879, was able to describe the scene that she saw at her home in the vicinity of Glenumra, near Killery, when the, what we might call 'hoodless' cloak was combined with the petticoat as protection:

30. This should of course read *skirt*.
31. Sir Arthur Grant, *Eight Hundred Miles on an Outside Irish Car*, Aberdeen, 1891, p. 43.
32. Rev. James Hall, *Tour in Ireland*, vol. 2 (London, 1813), pp. 26–7.

The third stranger within our gates was to outward appearance childless. She was also to a degree better clad than her companions, her figure being enveloped in one of the ample dark blue cloaks, almost habitually worn by the better-to-do amongst the Connaught peasant women … (and the petticoat hanging around her neck) had whilom [formerly] performed the duty of protecting its owner's unkempt head from the assaults of the weather."[33]

The one thing about looking at clothing of the ordinary people of the late nineteenth and early twentieth centuries is that there is an abundance of information. I once wrote on the subject in a very general way in a publication that accompanied the travelling National Museum exhibition *Common Clothes and Clothing*. While the findings in this publication are still pertinent, this study of the Mayo questionnaire replies, and the in-depth investigation of a selection of late nineteenth-century black and white photographs allows us to see the detail. The picture of the women washing clothes (Figure 14.3) is a very good candidate for detailed comment. It is possible to look at a photograph and not only see the detail of the captured image, but also the story behind the image and most importantly its contextual detail – some of which the photographer might have seen with his eye if he did not capture with his lens. The story of this photograph is important in two respects: while the image of a woman washing clothes by a stream or a water hole is one that has captured the observant traveller's imagination throughout the centuries, none of the observers give us the contextual details, that is, they did not tell us in the words of the washerwomen the detail of the task at hand. The clothing worn at the time, as described above, was of linen and woollen materials primarily. The layers of clothing – two or three woollen petticoats, a woollen skirt, a linen shift, a woollen bodice, heavy woollen shawls and cloaks, etc. – were of some weight compared to the lightness of our clothing nowadays. Not only would the clothes have become soiled during the course of the day's work in the yard, in the fields and in smoky kitchens, but it would also have required quite extensive soaking and scrubbing to remove stains and get it clean to wear once again. The

33. Mrs Houston, *Twenty Years in the Wild West; or Life in Connaught*, London, 1879, p. 24. Frank Stephens, the photographer, captured the image on a few occasions on the Aran Islands in the early decades of the twentieth century where the custom was slightly different in that the women wore the petticoat more decoratively over the head and adorned it with a colourful woven belt, the *crios*. Phrases to describe the fashion included *cóta ar mo bhráid* and *cóta ar mo mhuinéal*. See also O'Dowd, *Common Clothes*, p. 35 for a photograph by Stephens; Charles R. Browne, 'The Ethnography of Garumna and Lettermullen, Co. Galway', *1898–1900*, *Proceedings of the Royal Irish Academy*, 3rd Series, Vol. 5, (Vol. 21 cont.) pp. 223–68; Rev. James Hall, *Tour Through Ireland*, vol. 2 (London, 1813), p. 52 and Sir Charles Coote, *Statistical Survey of the County of Monaghan*, Dublin, 1801, p. 133.

laundry process was an arduous one and in many households a day a week or a fortnight was set aside for the task.

The story behind this photograph is told in a nice cameo recorded from Peig Sayers by Seosamh Ó Dálaigh in 1951 when she was 79 years old. She was living in Baile Bhíochaire, Dún Chaoin, County Kerry, at the time, but her memories refer to her married life on the Great Blasket some thirty or forty years previously:

> Whenever it was necessary clothes were washed … Monday was generally washday because they changed their clothes every Sunday. They put them soaking in cold water overnight. Then the following morning when the woman of the house had time she would wring the water from them and she would rub soap into them and she would put them in water until the following morning. Then she would get very hot water which had pieces of soap dissolved in it and she would agitate the clothes in the water and she would wring them and put them in a basket. If there were white shirts in the wash, and sheets, she would take them from the wooden tub in which they were soaking and she would put them down into a large pot filled with water and pieces of soap and put it on the fire and boil it. She would take them and throw water and all into a tub and when the water was cold enough, she agitated them well and squeezed the water from them and carried them on the basket to the river and she threw them in a hole of water and rinsed the suds from them. Then she beetled them with a beetle [beating implement] and wrung them again and put them on the basket. They were taken then and spread on the fence or hedge … Each townland had a washing flag by the river.[34]

34. IFC MS 1201, p. 504–31.
See O'Dowd, *Common
Clothes*.

The celebrated John O'Donovan was a very important nineteenth-century observer and, as an intelligent and erudite antiquarian, he was no doubt aware of the antiquity of the custom which women had of beetling clothes at a ford by a stream. On 12 August 1837 he noted the following at the ford that he referred to as Ath Skuseab near Elphin in County Longford:

> ... a celebrated ford which is on the very boundary of MOY NAOI and CORCHLANN rendered passable by a good bridge of four arches, and viewed the sluggish course of the river CIAISE UAIR ... women are still in the habit of beetling clothes in this ford.[35]

The wording of O'Donovan's written observation is important not only for the use of the word 'still', implying a continuity he viewed as important to note, but also because the ford at which he saw the women beetling is in fact the ford more accurately known in Irish as Áth Slisean, i.e. the ford of the beetles, otherwise called Béal Átha Sliseann and in English Ballaslishen, a place about a mile south of Elphin in County Roscommon on the river Uar, that is the river Ciaise Uair, and in English the Owenure.[36]

As with so many traditional customs and ways, the washing of clothes by women at fords and by streams has great antiquity. An early tenth century reference occurs in the life of St Maedoc of Ferns, in which we read of that holy man's seeming disregard for the work of women, a perhaps not uncommon occurrence among such men in times gone by, but leaving one wondering if afterwards he ever washed his clothes or was able to find a woman to do so. It is reported in the *Vita sancti Maedoc episcopi de ferna* that as he was building his monastery at Ferns his disciples complained that there was no water. He told them to cut down a particular tree and when they followed his instructions a well sprang from the tree's roots.

> The stream which flowed from the well ran beside the field of a man named Becc. The women of Becc's household used come to the stream to wash clothes. This displeased the saint who ordered them away. The women refused saying that the place and the water belonged to them ...[37]

35. *Ordnance Survey Letters*, County Roscommon, vol. 11, 1837–8, p. 76.
36. Professor Dáithí Ó hÓgáin, UCD, Delargy Centre for Irish Folklore, kindly replied to a request for assistance with the location of the ford visited by O'Donovan. A beetle is an all-purpose implement used for washing clothes and mashing food for animals and humans. An example in the National Folklife collection by great coincidence was collected from a house at Ballyslish (i.e. Béal Atha Sliseann/Ballaslisheen, the townland of the beetle), near Elphin, Co. Roscommon. It is made from a single piece of wood 37 cm long and it is shaped with a handle at one end and a head for pounding at the other. A very good sketch of women washing and beetling clothes by a stream is printed in Mr. and Mrs S.C. Hall, *Ireland: Its Scenery and Character*, vol. 1. (London, 1840), p. 130.
37. Carolus Plummer, *Vita sancti Maedoc episcopi de Ferna. Vitae Sanctorum Hiberniae.* Tomus Secundus (Oxford: Oxford University Press, 1910), p. 151, xxvi.

Cont.

Cont.

38. *Life of Maedoc of Ferns (11).*
Lives of Irish Saints. Charles
Plummer. (Oxford: Oxford
University Press, 1922), vol.
2, pp. 211, 218, (101–2).

39. A selection of examples of
these from Connaught alone
includes references to obser-
vations of the custom from
the early to the late decades
of the 1800s. Hely Dutton, *A*
Statistical Survey of the
County of Galway (Dublin:
printed at the University
Press, by R. Graisberry 1824),
pp. 9–10 and p. 358;
Anonymous, *Letters from the*
Irish Highlands of
Cunnemara, by a Family
Party (London: printed for
Longman, Hurst, Rees,
Orme, Brown and Green,
1825), p. 344; J.D., *Irish*
Penny Magazine, vol. 1, no. 2,
Jan. 12 (1833), p. 9; Caesar
Otway, *A Tour in Connaught:*
Comprising Sketches of
Clonmacnoise, Joyce Country,
and Achill (Dublin, W. Curry,
Jun. and Co., 1839), p. 205;
William M. Thackeray, *The*
Irish Sketch Book, vol. 2
(London, 1843), pp. 4, 98;
Sir William Wilde, *Lough*
Corrib, Its Shore and Islands,
3rd ed. (Dublin, 1938), p.
201; John Hervey Ashworth,
The Saxon in Ireland

Cont.

Afterwards a fair and comely daughter of Becc son of Eogan was washing clothes with her feet on the stones. Her feet clave to the clothes, and the clothes to the stones, and the stones to the earth; and thus she stood there like a statue or any human image ...[38] The poor woman was fortunately freed from her unenviable state on her father's intercession by prayer to St Maedoc.

There is no shortage of references in the literature from around the country to adduce that the custom of women washing clothes by a stream was commonplace.[39] In the Tuke view (Figure 14.5) a young woman looks on while an older woman bends over a stave built tub in which she has probably soaked the garment being cleaned in detergent before bringing it to the water to beetle it on the large flat stone to the left of the view.

Peig tells us she used soap for her washday, presumably something she bought for the task. Not only was the washing of the clothes the woman's work, but so also was the task of pro-viding the scouring emollient – the pre-soap product if you will. Hely Dutton writing from County Clare at the beginning of the nineteenth century, like so many of his contemporary observers of Irish work habits, described the men of the areas in the county that he had visited for his survey as 'the most slovenly farmers, and none of them ever think of mowing thistles, nettles, ferns, or even briars'. Their wives, however, do not appear to have left such a bad impression as he tells us that they did cut the offensive vegetation, not from any wish to keep the land clean as to burn for its valuable ash, which was subsequently used for the household laundry.[40] The work was well worth the effort as it was subsequently brought to the market and sold either in a powdered ash state or in hard cakes that measured about 8 inches in diam-eter and weighed about 3 pounds. These fetched 4d. each.[41] In 1953, Richard Denihan, an 88-year-old labourer from Athea in County Limerick, was able to answer the obvious questions arising from Dutton's observation:

Before soap came into being the people used to make homemade soap. They used to cut the ferns and save them like hay and then burn them and make paste from the ashes. Sometimes they used to mix the goose grease through it and make little cakes of it and it used to be as good as any soap you'd see nowadays.[42]

The astringent quality of the soap was very strong for it could take the raddle or tar (used to mark sheep) from the hands and remove tar from wool. The raw material in this latter case was the male fern or bracken and the process involved stripping the outer skin from the fern and leaving it to boil in a pot of water over the fire until it turned into a paste-like mass.[43]

Cont.
(London, 1851), p. 75; Charles R. Browne, 'The Ethnography of Inishbofin and Inishshark, Co. Galway', *Proceedings of the Royal Irish Academy*, 3rd Series, vol. 3 (1893–96), p. 363.

40. *Statistical Survey of the County of Clare* (Dublin: Dublin Society, 1801), p. 76–7.
41. Ibid., p. 266.
42. IFC MS 1357, p. 144.
43. The account was recorded from Micheál Ó Siochfhradha a 79-years-old farmer who was born and reared in Mill a' Goilín, but who was living, at the time of the recording in 1948, in Clochán na nUagha, in the parish of Prior, Co. Kerry. IFC MS 1146, pp. 570–1.

Figure 14.5
Woman wearing shawl standing outside house (Tuke 6)

44. William Tighe, *Statistical Observations Relative to the County of Kilkenny made in the years 1800 and 1801* (Dublin: printed by Graisberry and Campbell, 1802), p. 49; *Calendar of Christ Church Deeds*, Appendix to Twenty Third Report of the Deputy Keeper of the Public Records in Ireland, N. 493, p. 80, dated c. 1249; John T. Gilbert (ed.), *Chartularies of St Mary's Abbey, Dublin*, vol. 1 (London, 1884), p. 351; Arthur Wollaston Hutton (ed), *Arthur Young's Tour in Ireland*, vol. 1, (London: George Bell & Sons, 1892), p. 233. See also, *Calendar State Papers Ireland 1608–1610* (London and Dublin: Longman, 1874), p. 317 with reference to the Survey of Derry Plantation in October; Hall, *Tour through Ireland* p. 61 and p. 68 with reference to Balnafad, Co. Sligo and Sligo town in 1813.

45. Other than the accounts quoted in notes 43 and 44 above, memories of ashes of various forms of vegetation being used to make soap

                                                              Cont.

William Tighe noted the custom in Galmoy, County Kilkenny, in 1800. Arthur Young had seen 'heaps of weeds' burning throughout the countryside around Ballymote in Sligo fourteen years earlier. We may assume that the same method was being utilised by Adam Saponarius, or Adam the Soapmaker, in Dublin City in the thirteenth century and also the soapmaker who is referred to in the seventeenth-century Calendar of State Papers. The latter decried the importation of soap from Holland and Flanders and undertook to give the privilege of making soap from the materials available in Ireland.[44] It was undoubtedly this economic support that saw the custom alive and well in several parts of the country in the later years of the nineteenth century and the early decades of the twentieth.[45]

The use of detergent or soap *per se* was undoubtedly known at the time the photograph was taken but, of course, branded products were utilised only if the household economy could afford to spend hard-earned and often, scarce cash on such luxuries. Quite often there was no spare money even to pay the weaver for producing the fabric to make the clothing and there is no doubt that clothes were patched and recycled for many years. Welch's 'View of Connemara natives' (Figure 14.6) and the three Tuke views of schoolchildren outside the school' (Figures 12.4, 12.5 and 12.6) show a good deal of evidence of this – the father's clothing being 'cut down' to fit his sons and his own clothes being repatched several times. The views contrast sharply with observations by James Mc Parlan at the beginning of the nineteenth century when he was travelling around Mayo researching for his statistical survey of the county. In the barony of Tyrawley the women on Sundays 'wore cottons and stamped linen gowns, stuff petticoats, with cloaks made of finer stuff than frieze and bought in the shops'. In the extreme western barony of Erris the clothing of friezes and linens was deemed by him to be better than anything he had seen being worn further inland. In the baronies of Costello, Carra and Clanmorris the clothing also passed his scrutiny and, in describing the clothes of frieze, linen, flannel and drugget being worn, in addition to the recently introduced cotton, his words almost paint the country with an air of prosperity.[46] Of

Figure 14.6
Connemara natives (W14/05/79

Cont.
were recorded well into the
twentieth century: ashes of
cabbage stumps were used to
make soap in Garra Dubh,
Monagay, Co. Limerick, IFC
MS 629, 483, 1939; brack-
en ashes were used in
Iveragh, Co. Kerry, IFC MS
1005, 436–7, 1947; clothes
were whitened with fowl
droppings in the parish of
Prior, Co. Kerry, IFC MS
1003, pp. 142–50; soap sub-
stitutes in Kilmocomogue,
Bantry, Co. Kerry were
made from briars and thistles and also ash leaves
mixed with buttermilk, IFC
MS 789, pp. 327–8 and
clothes were cleaned in
potato water in Beltany,
Kilmacrenan, Co. Donegal
and Clochar, Kilmore, Erris,
Co. Mayo, IFC MS 799, pp.
54–5 and IFC MS 590, pp.
57–8.

46. *Statistical Survey of the
County of Mayo* (Dublin:
Graisberry and Campbell,
1802), pp. 86–7, 89, 90,
164.

course, he was writing during the opening days of the nineteenth century before the awfulness of the 1820s, 1830s and 1840s was to destroy so much. The aftermath of these decades and the further famines in the 1870s and the 1880s is what we see in Welch's and the Tuke photographs. Prosperity and a very definite move away from subsistence had happened for many – but not for all.

Bibliography

Aalen, F.H.A., 'The Rehousing of Rural Labourers in Ireland Under the Labourers (Ireland) Acts 1893–1919', *Journal of Historical Geography* (1986), pp. 287–306.

Andrews, J. H., *A Paper Landscape: The Ordnance Survey in Nineteenth-Century Ireland* (Dublin: Four Courts Press, 2002).

Anglesea, Martyn, 'The Art of Nature Illustration', in Foster, John Wilson (ed.) *Nature in Ireland: A Scientific and Cultural History* (Dublin: The Lilliput Press, 1997), pp. 497–523.

Barthes, Roland, *The Eiffel Tower,* translated by Richard Howard, (New York: Hill and Wang, 1979).

Breathnach, Ciara, *The Congested Districts Board for Ireland, 1891–1923: Poverty and Development in the West of Ireland* (Dublin: Four Courts Press, 2005).

Boran, Marie, 'The Ireland That We Made: A Galway Tribute to Arthur J. Balfour', *Journal of the Galway Archaeological and Historical Society,* 54, (2002), pp. 168–74.

Browne, C.R., 'The Ethnography of Garumna and Lettermullen', *Proceedings of the Royal Irish Academy.,* 3rd series, no. 3, (1897) pp. 317–70.

Burke, Peter, *Eyewitnessing: The Uses of Images as Historical Evidence* (Ithaca: Cornell University Press, 2001).

Carville, Justin, 'Photography, Tourism and Natural History: Cultural Identity and the Visualisation of the Natural World', in Cronin, Michael and Barbara O'Connor (eds), *Irish Tourism: Image, Culture and Identity* (Clevedon: Channel View Publications, 2003), pp. 215–38.

Collins, Tim, 'Praeger in the West: Naturalists and Antiquarians in Connemara and the Islands, 1894–1914', in *JGHAS,* 45 (1993), pp. 125–54.

Crossman, V., *Politics, Pauperism and Power in Late Nineteenth-Century Ireland* (Manchester: Manchester University Press, 2006).

Cullen, L.M., and T.C Smout (eds), *Comparative Aspects of Scottish and Irish Economic and Social History 1600–1900,* (Edinburgh: Donald, 1977).

Curtis, Edmund, *A History of Medieval Ireland, 1110–1513* (Dublin: Macmillan, 1923).

Dutton, Hely, *A Statistical and Agricultural Survey of the County of Galway* (Dublin, 1824).

Evans, E. Estyn, *The Personality of Ireland: Habitat, Heritage and History,* (rev. ed., Belfast: Blackstaff Press with Cambridge University Press, 1981).

Evans, E. Estyn with Brian S. Turner, *Ireland's Eye: The Photographs of Robert John Welch* (Belfast: Blackstaff Press, 1977).

Fitzpatrick, Thomas, *The King of Claddagh: A Story of the Cromwellian Occupation of Galway* (London: Sands, 1899).

Foster, John Wilson, *Fictions of the Irish Literary Revival: A Changeling Art,* (Syracuse: Syracuse University Press, 1987, 1993).

——, 'Nature and Nation in the Nineteenth Century', in Foster, John Wilson (ed.), *Nature in Ireland: A Scientific and Cultural History* (Dublin: Lilliput Press, 1997), pp. 409–39.

——, 'Natural History in Modern Irish Culture', in Bowler, Peter J. and Nicholas Whyte (eds), *Science and Society in Ireland: The Social Context of Science and Technology in Ireland* (Belfast: The Institute of Irish Studies, 1997), pp.119–33.

Foucault, Michel, *The Order of Things* (London: Tavistock Publications, 1970).

——, *The Archaeology of Knowledge,* translated by A.M. Sheridan Smith (London: Tavistock Press, 1974).

Fraser, Murray, *John Bull's other Homes: State Housing and British Policy in Ireland, 1883–1922* (Liverpool: Liverpool University Press, 1996).

Gailey, Alan, *Rural Houses of the North of Ireland* (Edinburgh, 1984).

Gibbons, Luke, *Transformations in Irish Culture* (Cork: Cork University Press in association with Field Day, 1996).

Greene, Miranda J., *Dictionary of Celtic Myth and Legend* (London: Thames and Hudson, 1992).

Hill, Myrtle and Pollock, Vivienne, *Women of Ireland: Image and Experience c.1880–1920* (Belfast: Blackstaff Press, 1993).

Ireland, John de Courcey, *Ireland's Sea Fisheries: A History* (Dublin: Glendale Press, 1981).

Hardiman, James, *History of the Town and County of Galway* (London: W. Folds, 1820).

Kibberd, Declan, *Inventing Ireland* (London: Jonathan Cape, 1995).

Kinmouth, Claudia, *Irish Rural Interiors in Art* (Yale University Press: New Haven & London, 2006).

Lysaght, Sean, 'Contrasting Natures: The Issue of Names', in Foster, John Wilson (ed.), *Nature in Ireland: A Scientific and Cultural History* (Dublin: The Lilliput Press, 1997), pp. 440–60.

Lysaght, Sean, 'Science and the Cultural Revival: 1863–1916', in Bowler, P.J. and Nicholas Whyte (eds), *Science and Society in Ireland: The Social Context of Science and Technology in Ireland* (Belfast: The Institute of Irish Studies, 1997), pp. 153-165.

——, *Robert Lloyd Praeger: The Life of a Naturalist,* (Dublin: Four Courts Press, 1998).

Mac Laughlin, Jim, *Ireland the Emigrant Nursery and the World Economy* (Cork: Cork University Press, 1994).

MacMonagle, Paddy, *Paddy Mac's Collection of Vintage Postcards* (Killarney: Mac Publications, 2006).

Maguire, W. A., *A Century In Focus; Photography and Photographs in the North of Ireland 1839–1939* (Belfast: Blackstaff Press, 2000).

Marien, Mary Warner, *Photography: A Cultural History* (London: Laurence King, 2002).

Micks, W. L., *An Account of the History of the Congested Districts Board of Ireland* (Dublin: Eason and Son, 1925).

Moran, G.P. (ed.), *Radical Irish Priests 1660–1970* (Dublin: Four Courts Press, 1998).

Nolan, William, Liam Ronayne, and Mairead Dunleavy (eds.), *Donegal History and Society. Interdisciplinary Essays on the History of an Irish County* (Dublin: Geography Publications, 1995).

Ó Danachair, Caoimhín, 'The Botháin Scóir', in E. Rynne (ed.), *North Munster Studies: Essays in Commemoration of Monsignor Michael Moloney* (Limerick:Thomond Archaeological Society, 1967).

O'Dowd, Anne, *Meitheal: A Study of Co-operative Labour in Rural Ireland* (Dublin: Comhairle Bhéaloideas Éireann, 1981).

O'Heidain, Eustas, 'The Blessing of Galway Bay', in *Spirituality* (Galway: Dominicans Publication, Jan. 1996).

Outram, Dorinda, 'The History of Natural History: Grand Narrative or Local Lore?', in Foster, John Wilson (ed.), *Nature in Ireland: A Scientific and Cultural History,* Dublin: The Lilliput Press, 1997), pp. 461–71.

Rosenblum, Naomi, *A World History of Photography* (New York: Abbeville Press, 1984).

Rouse, Sarah, *Into the Light: An Illustrated Guide to the Photographic Collections of the National Library of Ireland* (Dublin: National Library of Ireland, 1998).

Sheehy, Jeanne, *The Rediscovery of Ireland's Past: The Celtic Revival, 1830–1930* (London: Thames and Hudson, 1980).

Sontag, Susan, *Regarding the Pain of Others* (London: Penguin, 2004).

Synge, John M., *The Aran Islands, Illustrated by Jack B. Yeats* (New York: Dover Publications, 1998, in an unabridged republication of the work by John W. Luce and Company in 1911).

Tagg, John, *The Burden of Representation: Essays on Photographies and Histories* (London: Macmillan, 1988).

——, 'Totalled Machines: Criticism, Photography and Technological Change', *New Formations,* no. 7, (1989), pp. 21–34.

Teahan, John, *Irish Furniture and Woodcraft* (Dublin: Country House, in association with the National Museum of Ireland, 1994)·

Thompson, Spurgeon, 'The Politics of Photography: Travel Writing and the Irish Countryside, 1900–14', in Laurence W. McBride, *Images, Icons and the Irish Nationalist Imagination,* (Dublin: Four Courts Press, 1999), pp. 113–29.

Valpy, Richard, 'The Resources of the Irish Sea Fisheries' in the *Journal of the Statistical Society of London*, 11 (1848) pp. 55–72.

Villiers-Tuthill, Kathleen, *Alexander Nimmo: The Western District,* (Clifden: Connemara Girl Publications, 2006).

Wakefield, Edward, *An Account of Ireland, Statistical and Political*, vol 1 (London: Longman, Hurst, Rees, Orme, and Brown, Paternoster-Row, 1812).

Walker, Brian M. and Hugh Dixon, *No Mean City: Belfast 1880–1914 in the Photographs of Robert French* (Belfast: Lagan Books, 1983, 2003).

Welch, Robert J. (n.d.), *Notebooks*, MSS, Ulster Museum (The Welch Collection).

——, *Excursions Diary*, MSS, Ulster Museum (The Welch Collection).

Woodham-Smith, Cecil, *The Great Hunger, Ireland 1845–1849* (New York: Harper & Row, 1962).

Index